GOLDEN DOOR

COOKS AT HOME

Favorite Recipes from the Celebrated Spa

DEAN RUCKER *with Marah Stets* | PHOTOGRAPHS *by Quentin Bacon*

Clarkson Potter/Publishers
New York

Copyright © 2009 by Golden Door Owner L.L.C.

Published in the United States by Clarkson Potter/Publishers,
an imprint of the Crown Publishing Group,
a division of Random House, Inc., New York.
www.crownpublishing.com
www.clarksonpotter.com

CLARKSON POTTER is a trademark and POTTER with colophon is
a registered trademark of Random House, Inc.

Library of Congress Cataloging-in-Publication Data
Rucker, Dean.
Golden Door cooks at home / Dean Rucker with Marah Stets. — 1st ed.
p.   cm.
Includes index.
1. Cookery (Natural foods)   2. Golden Door.   I. Stets, Marah.   II. Title.
TX741.R8185   2009
641.5'636—dc22   2008038884

ISBN 978-0-307-45079-1

Printed in China

Recipe photographs by Quentin Bacon
Location photographs by Thomas Hart Shelby
Design by Level, Calistoga, CA

10 9 8 7 6 5 4 3 2 1

First Edition

contents

introduction

On almost every Sunday of the year, the stunning, embossed, golden doors that have been opening wide to guests for all of the Golden Door's five decades open once again to welcome forty new souls. They come for myriad reasons, and what each of them finds is a sanctuary where the mind, body, and spirit can be revived and healed; in the process, an essential awareness of how each element is connected to the other is born. Many experts provide vital guidance along the way, helped in their work by our surroundings: walking the labyrinth, some guests discover meditation for the first time in their lives; hiking the miles of trails that weave through the mountains, some learn of stamina they didn't realize they had; and exploring the rows of our expansive organic garden, many ascertain how crucial the earth's bounty is to our sustenance. At the Golden Door, nature and nurturing merge; nowhere is this more apparent than in our kitchen and dining room, where every day the harvest from the garden and groves is transformed into nourishing dishes that feed body and soul.

It used to be that the term "spa food" evoked images of unadorned dishes without flavor or flair, created to contain as few calories and as little fat as possible without regard for how enjoyable it was to actually eat them. Long ago, people almost always came to a spa to lose weight and they expected that—to be successful—they would be deprived. Certainly there was success; anyone eating 700 to 800 calories a day for a week is going to lose weight. But can one live that way in the real world for any length of time? Of course, the "real world" was not terribly grounded in reality, either, for the persistent message was to strip your diet of fat and calories at all costs. There was little emphasis on creating something new within these confines. The focus was on creating low-calorie, low-fat versions of regular food by any means possible. This led to the pervasive use of food substitutes such as imitation whipped cream, nonfat mayonnaise, chocolate replacements, and artificial sweeteners. In short, anything that took calories and fat out of food was, by definition, good, no matter how it tasted or made you feel. Missing from all of this was anything about being strong or good to your body.

Thankfully, all of this has changed. Our mission at the Golden Door has nothing to do with a virtue diet; it's about feeling sated, nurtured, and above all, healthy. As the recipes in this book show, the dishes we serve at the Door make full and glorious use of the huge array of delicious foods that you *can* eat; there's no need to dwell on what you are missing. Lean proteins, whole grains, and fresh vegetables are the building blocks in our kitchen; this is the very opposite of a diet of deprivation.

Although we use many low-fat and low-sodium ingredients, in general I prefer to judiciously use ingredients

with more calories and fat that invariably have much more flavor. For example, I never use nonfat cheese because ½ ounce of real Parmesan is a far tastier and more natural option than ½ cup of nonfat cheese that is full of stabilizers and additives and lacks flavor. Similarly, instead of using artificially flavored oil sprays, a small amount of herb oil (see page 272) drizzled over a finished dish adds beautiful color and a delicious, fresh, herb flavor. The fact is that the distance between real food and these replacements is enormous. Rather than mimicking with pale imitations of the originals, I prefer to pursue the best new possibilities using fresh and natural whole foods.

A key component to a healthy diet is portion control, and this is made far easier when the food is both delicious and filling. When you're satisfied by the big, bold flavors of what you're eating, you don't need to consume a huge amount of it to feel satisfied. I like to think of good food as a celebration of ingredients, with the focus on taste, not quantity. We do employ a few special techniques and practices in the kitchen and beyond, and these are well worth replicating in your home. Many are explored in more detail on page 13 and in the sidebars in this book, but the most obvious one from my point of view is the sensible use of the starter course. We serve a first course for both lunch and dinner almost every day at the Golden Door, and it's for a very specific reason: a flavorful and fiber-rich first course allows you to eat a smaller main course than you normally would, when most of the calories and fat of a meal are usually consumed. Note that complete nutritional information for the recipes in this book is on page 276.

Of course, all of this talk of serving whole foods and maintaining portion control is frankly not very useful to many of us in the rush and tumble of our daily lives if it remains only talk. This is why my favorite part of every

anniversary. While most of the recipes on these pages are new, there are a few that have been on our regular menu for decades because they are just as wholesome and delicious today as they were when the first Golden Door chefs made them generations ago. These classics are marked with an asterisk (*). Make any one of them and you will see why they have stood the test of time.

Like our guests, I am nourished and sustained by the beauty and serenity of the Golden Door, where, as I make my way in each day, the scent that wafts from the orange groves commingles with the aromas pouring out of our kitchen. This particular melding of sensations may be unique to this place, but the dishes it has inspired can be savored no matter where in the world you are. Whether or not you have ever passed through these golden doors, I heartily hope that through the food and advice in this book, you, too, will be nourished and sustained as you pass through all the doors of your life.

week is the cooking class, when I finally get to actually teach our guests how they can create my dishes in their own kitchens. I confess that sometimes I think I get more out of those classes than my eager students do; their many questions challenge me to see what I do in the kitchen through their eyes, compelling me to really ponder what is possible in a home kitchen. I am grateful to our wonderful guests for their curiosity and enthusiasm; they have made me a better teacher and that has led inexorably to this book. Cook from my recipes and you will learn how to create tasty, flavorful, healthy food, and through these dishes, bring a little of the Door into your home.

This book is being published to commemorate the Golden Door's fiftieth

from my kitchen to yours
ingredients and techniques

No fancy or exquisitely expensive ingredients are regular occupants of my pantry, and I don't practice any unattainable techniques, but a few basics are central to my dishes. For best results, when preparing the recipes in this book or whenever you're cooking wholesome, healthy food, I hope you'll adopt them, too.

- **Oils:** Use cold- or expeller-pressed unrefined oil. Common vegetable oils are extracted using a petroleum-based solvent. I believe that there is no place in our diet for even a trace of petroleum. To apply oil to pans and, occasionally, directly to ingredients, use a pump spray bottle available at salon supply and hardware stores (make sure it is food safe) and fill it yourself with cold- or expeller-pressed unrefined oil. I have a few of them in my kitchen filled with olive, grapeseed, canola, and other oils. Whenever a recipe calls for an oil spray, this is what is meant. Spray the bottle three times to grease most pans for sautéing. When using these bottles, pull on the pump handle firmly and quickly so that the oil is forced from the bottle in a misting spray. If you pull too slowly the oil will come out in a single stream that will not effectively cover the bottom of the pan. (Where "vegetable oil cooking spray" or "baking spray" is called for, use store-bought, pre-filled, pressurized bottles.)

- **Salt:** Any salt that is completely white is likely to have undergone refining processes that can strip it of trace minerals that are important to our health. These refining processes can also contribute undesirable additives. I use natural, unrefined sea salt that has not been processed. Redmond Real Salt comes in several grinds, including my favorite, kosher, and has superior taste and quality to any common table salt, kosher salt, or refined sea salt (see Resources, page 283).

- **Sugar:** I use cane sugar, which comes from sugarcane, instead of regular granulated sugar, which is extracted from beets. Cane sugar is believed to contain more trace minerals than regular white sugar and I prefer its deeper flavor for cooking and baking.

- **Parmesan cheese:** Wherever I call for the democratic "Parmesan cheese" in this book, I use authentic Italian Parmigiano-Reggiano. Rather than buying it pre-grated, buy a chunk and grate it yourself; not only does it taste fresher but this way you know you're getting the real thing, for the rind is stamped with the words "Parmigiano Reggiano." I grate Parmesan on the fine side of a microplane grater, which results in very fluffy grated cheese. If you use a different type of grater or buy pre-grated Parmesan, it is likely to be more compact and ¼ cup of it will weigh more than ¼ cup of microplane-grated Parmesan. To avoid using more than is intended, measure by weight instead of by volume if you do not grate the Parmesan yourself with a microplane grater. (I grate other types of hard or semi-hard cheeses on the large holes of a box grater.)

- **A word about chopping:** Whenever an ingredient is to be cut into dice, I mean ½-inch cubes unless otherwise noted. For matchsticks, aim for pieces ⅛ x ⅛ x 2 inches long.

Crudité Platter **16** • *Beer-Steamed Shrimp with Avocado-Citrus Vinaigrette and Mixed Greens* **19** •

Spiny Lobster and Mango Gazpacho Shooters **22** • *Baked Artichoke Spinach Dip with Corn Crisps* **24** •

Coriander-Crusted Tuna on Wonton Crisps with Sesame Slaw and Wasabi Cream **26** • *Corn and*

Scallion Pancakes with Oven-Roasted Chipotle Salsa **29** • *Chicken and Scallion Potstickers with*

Chile Lime Sauce **32** • *Mango-Avocado Summer Rolls with Sweet and Sour Dipping Sauce* **34**

appetizers

Crudité Platter

A raw vegetable platter, even when enhanced by the more elegant name crudités, *as it is known in France, is a party classic that more often than not is passed over, even by the most health-conscious guest. The vegetable platter we serve daily at the Golden Door, however, is always devoured. This is thanks not only to the super-flavorful dips with which we serve the vegetables but also because we very lightly cook the vegetables. I confess that raw broccoli has never been my favorite snack, either. Quickly blanching the vegetables in boiling water gives them a much more pleasing texture and makes them easier to digest.*

Romanesco (see photograph, opposite) is an unusual and really beautiful vegetable that we grow here in the Golden Door garden. It is a member of the Brassica *family, along with cabbage, broccoli, and cauliflower, to which it is most similar in taste and texture, although it has a pleasing nutty flavor all its own. The florets can be carefully broken apart—leave some stem attached—for a dramatic presentation.*

The vegetables can be prepared up to a day in advance and covered and refrigerated until ready to serve. **SERVES 12**

4 ounces green beans, trimmed

4 ounces sugar snap peas, trimmed

5 ounces baby carrots, peeled and trimmed

6 ounces asparagus, woody ends trimmed

2 cups broccoli florets

2 cups romanesco or cauliflower florets

½ medium English cucumber

¼ small jícama (4 ounces)

½ large red bell pepper, seeded

Hummus (page 18)

Creamy Caesar Dressing (page 263)

Creamy Ranch Dressing (page 261)

Bring a large pot of water to a rapid boil. Prepare a large bowl of ice water. Add the green beans to the boiling water and cook just until crisp-tender, 30 seconds to 1 minute. Use a skimmer or slotted spoon to quickly remove the green beans and immediately transfer them to the ice water. When they are completely cool, drain them well and set aside.

Return the water to a boil, if necessary, and add more ice to the bowl of ice water. Repeat the steps above to blanch the sugar snap peas, carrots, asparagus, broccoli florets, and the romanesco.

Slice the cucumber into 3- to 4-inch-long spears. Peel the jícama and slice it into 3-inch-long spears. Slice the bell pepper into strips.

When all the vegetables have been prepared, arrange them on a platter, cover with plastic wrap, and refrigerate until ready to serve, or for longer storage, store them in tightly covered individual containers. Let the vegetables stand at room temperature for 15 minutes before serving.

Prepare the hummus, Caesar dressing, and ranch dressing.

When ready to serve, place the hummus, Caesar dressing, and ranch dressing in individual bowls and arrange the vegetables on a platter alongside them.

Romanesco

HUMMUS

From this basic hummus you can make all kinds of delicious variations. Try blending in a minced chipotle chile in adobo or fresh jalapeño or chopped roasted red bell pepper, sun-dried tomatoes, or fresh cilantro. **MAKES 2 CUPS**

1 cup dried chickpeas or 1 (15-ounce) can chickpeas, rinsed and drained

¼ cup fresh lemon juice (from 2 lemons)

2 tablespoons extra-virgin olive oil

1½ tablespoons tahini

2 garlic cloves, crushed

½ teaspoon kosher salt, or to taste

⅛ teaspoon freshly ground black pepper, or to taste

If using dried chickpeas, pick over them and discard any debris or stones; rinse the chickpeas thoroughly. Place them in a bowl and pour in enough cold water to cover by 2 inches. Let stand overnight.

Drain the soaked chickpeas and add them to a pot with water to cover by 2 inches. Bring to a boil over medium-high heat. Reduce the heat and simmer, partially covered, until very tender, about 2 hours, depending on the age of the chickpeas. Add additional water as needed during cooking. Drain thoroughly and let cool completely.

Combine the cooked chickpeas or canned chickpeas, lemon juice, ¼ cup water, olive oil, tahini, and garlic in the work bowl of a food processor. Process until very smooth, about 3 minutes.

Add the salt and pepper and taste for seasoning. Store in a tightly covered container in the refrigerator for up to 3 days.

Beer-Steamed Shrimp
with Avocado-Citrus Vinaigrette and Mixed Greens

Steamed spiced shrimp always remind me of my childhood in Maryland, where I grew up. Shrimp was definitely a luxury for my family since money was tight, but occasionally my father, Lloyd Rucker, would gather the family and we would go out for an all-you-can-eat shrimp feast. Basket after basket would be poured onto the newspaper-covered table and I would do my best to keep up with my dad, but I never could. SERVES 4

1 (12-ounce) can or bottle Pilsner beer

1 tablespoon white vinegar

2 tablespoons Old Bay seasoning

12 jumbo (16 to 20 count) shell-on shrimp (10 to 12 ounces)

Avocado-Citrus Vinaigrette (page 253)

4 cups field greens or mesclun

Pinch of salt, or to taste

Pinch of freshly ground black pepper, or to taste

4 lime wedges, for serving

1 avocado, pitted, peeled, and diced, for serving (optional)

Combine the beer, vinegar, and 1 tablespoon of the Old Bay seasoning in the bottom pot of a steamer or in a pot fitted with an expandable steamer basket. Bring to a simmer.

In a bowl, toss the shrimp with the remaining tablespoon Old Bay seasoning and transfer the shrimp to the steamer or steamer basket. Cover and steam until the shrimp are pink and cooked through, about 5 minutes. Remove the shrimp from the steamer and let stand until cool enough to handle. Peel the shrimp, leaving the tail shell intact, devein, and set aside.

Prepare the avocado-citrus vinaigrette.

In a large bowl, toss the greens with ½ cup of the vinaigrette and a pinch each of salt and pepper, if desired. Divide among four salad plates or chilled martini glasses. If using plates, place 3 shrimp next to or on top of each salad. If using martini glasses, arrange 3 shrimp over the edge of each glass, with the tails hanging over the outside. Drizzle over a little more dressing and garnish with lime wedges and diced avocado, if desired.

CONTINUES ON PAGE 21

CONTINUED FROM PAGE 19

Beer-Steamed Shrimp Cocktail

This recipe is dedicated to the memory of Dad, for whom steamed shrimp would not be complete without a Maryland-style cocktail sauce. Skip the avocado dressing above and toss the greens with the juice of 1 lemon, 1 tablespoon extra-virgin olive oil, and a pinch of salt and pepper. Place the shrimp on top and serve with this simple cocktail sauce.

½ **cup ketchup**

1 **tablespoon prepared horseradish**

1½ **teaspoons Worcestershire sauce**

1½ **teaspoons fresh lemon juice**

1 **teaspoon Old Bay seasoning**

In a medium mixing bowl, whisk together the ketchup, horseradish, Worcestershire sauce, lemon juice, and Old Bay seasoning. Serve with steamed shrimp.

Spiny Lobster and Mango Gazpacho Shooters

A creamy sweet mango and citrus puree is studded with crisp vegetables and succulent lobster. Serve in shot glasses as individual "shooters" or in bowls as the soup course to the meal. The lobster can be replaced by 12 ounces shrimp, steamed, shelled, and chopped. **MAKES 20 (2½-OUNCE) SERVINGS; OR SERVES 6 AS A FIRST COURSE**

1 (1½-pound) live Spiny or Maine lobster, or 6 to 8 ounces shelled cooked lobster meat (1¼ to 1½ cups)

1 large mango, peeled and diced (2 cups)

2 cups fresh orange juice (from 6 oranges)

3 teaspoons fresh lime juice (from 2 limes)

2 tablespoons extra-virgin olive oil

1 medium cucumber, peeled, seeded, and finely diced (1¼ cups)

1 small red bell pepper, seeded and finely diced (1 cup)

1 medium red onion, finely diced (1½ cups)

1 small serrano chile, seeded and minced (1 tablespoon)

2 garlic cloves, minced

2 tablespoons chopped fresh cilantro leaves

1½ teaspoons sriracha or Vietnamese chile-garlic sauce, or a few dashes of hot pepper sauce (optional)

½ teaspoon kosher salt, or to taste

⅛ teaspoon freshly ground black pepper, or to taste

Pea shoots, for serving

In a large saucepan, bring 3 quarts of lightly salted water to a boil. Put the lobster into the pot head first and lightly simmer, covered, until the lobster turns bright red, 11 to 13 minutes. (If the lobster is boiled too harshly, it will make the delicate meat tough.) Transfer the cooked lobster to a bowl of ice water to cool.

When cool enough to handle, twist the claws off the body if using Maine lobster. Crack open the claws and slice open the joints that connected the claws to the body and dice the meat. Twist the tail to separate it from the body. Split the tail open lengthwise and remove the meat. If serving shooters, dice the tail meat; set aside about ⅓ cup for garnish and add the rest of the diced tail meat to any claw meat. If serving in soup bowls, slice the tail meat crosswise into ¼-inch-thick slices and set aside for garnish. If desired, use a skewer to push meat out of the legs and to pull it out of the rounded flippers at the bottom of the tail. You may lift off the hard shell from the body and find meat there. Refrigerate the lobster meat until ready to serve.

In a blender, combine the mango, orange juice, lime juice, and olive oil and process until smooth, about 1 minute. Transfer the puree to a medium bowl and stir in the cucumber, bell pepper, onion, serrano, garlic, cilantro, sriracha, salt, and pepper. Refrigerate for at least 3 hours and up to 6 hours.

When ready to serve, stir the diced lobster meat (except the meat reserved for garnish) into the gazpacho. If serving shooters, divide the gazpacho among twenty chilled shot glasses. Top each shooter with 1 scant teaspoon of diced lobster and a pea shoot. Arrange the shooters on a platter and serve.

If serving as a soup course, divide the soup among six chilled soup bowls. On top of each bowl, arrange a few slices of tail meat in a fan and top with a few pea shoots.

Baked Artichoke Spinach Dip *with Corn Crisps*

This dip is very similar in taste and texture to a full-fat version that calls for lots of sour cream and mayonnaise. My recipe scrimps on fat and calories but definitely not on taste. Be sure to use a small-holed microplane grater to grate Parmesan. Serve garnished with diced tomato, chopped scallions, and a drizzle of good extra-virgin olive oil, if desired. If you don't feel like baking your own crisps, serve with store-bought baked tortilla chips, crusty baguette, or crudité vegetables. This is elegant served in individual ramekins and more rustic when served in a single, large dish. **SERVES 8**

Olive oil spray

4 (5-inch) thin corn tortillas

2 pounds fresh spinach

1 lemon

4 large fresh artichokes

2 tablespoons thinly sliced shallots

2 teaspoons minced garlic

⅓ cup dry white wine

4 sprigs fresh thyme

1 bay leaf

1½ cups low-fat cottage cheese

1 ounce Parmesan cheese, grated
(1 cup)

¼ teaspoon kosher salt, or to taste

⅛ teaspoon freshly ground black pepper,
or to taste

Preheat the oven to 400°F. Line two baking sheets with parchment paper and spray them lightly with olive oil, or use nonstick baking sheets.

Cut each tortilla into eight triangles. Spread the corn tortilla triangles on the prepared baking sheets and spritz them lightly with olive oil. Bake for 10 to 12 minutes, until light golden brown and crisp. Set aside to cool. Leave the oven on.

Meanwhile, prepare the dip. Trim the tough stems from the spinach and rinse the leaves and tender stems well in a sink or bowl of cold water. Transfer the leaves with water still clinging to them to a large skillet with a lid. Place the pan over medium-high heat and cook, covered, until the spinach has wilted, 3 to 4 minutes. If the pan cannot hold all the spinach at first, cover and cook as much as can fit in the pan, and then add the remaining leaves after the first leaves have wilted sufficiently to make room in the pan. Transfer the spinach to a strainer and let stand until cool enough to handle. Place it in a clean kitchen towel and twist the towel around the spinach as hard as you can to wring out excess liquid. Chop the spinach (you should have about 2 cups) and set aside.

Squeeze the juice from the lemon. Set aside 1 tablespoon juice. Fill a large bowl with cold water and add the remaining lemon juice and the lemon halves. This acidulated water will prevent the trimmed artichokes from discoloring.

Bend and snap off the tough outer leaves of the artichoke until you reach the leaves that are yellow at the base end and slightly green toward the tip. Remove several layers of these leaves until you reach the tenderest ones at the center of the artichoke. Use a sharp knife to trim the stem to about 1 inch long. Peel off the tough, outer layer from the stem with the knife. Cut off the central cone to remove the leaves. Use the tip of a knife or a small spoon to scoop away all the remaining leaves and the furry choke. Cut the heart lengthwise in half. Place each half cut side down on the cutting board and thinly slice it. Drop the slices in the acidulated water. Repeat with the remaining artichokes.

Spray a large saucepan with olive oil and heat over medium heat. Add the shallots and garlic and cook, stirring, until slightly translucent and fragrant but not at all brown, about 2 minutes. Add the artichokes and stir for 30 seconds.

Add the white wine and simmer briskly until it is reduced by half, 5 to 10 minutes. Add ¾ cup water along with the thyme and bay leaf, and bring to a gentle simmer. Cover and continue to cook for 10 to 12 minutes, until the liquid is reduced and the artichokes are tender. Remove from the heat and let cool slightly. Remove and discard the thyme and bay leaf.

In the bowl of a food processor, combine the artichoke mixture, the spinach, the reserved 1 tablespoon lemon juice, the cottage cheese, 1 tablespoon of the Parmesan, the salt, and pepper. Process in batches if necessary until the mixture is creamy but not completely pureed—there should be small pieces of spinach and artichoke interspersed—20 to 30 seconds, scraping down the sides of the bowl as needed.

Scrape the artichoke dip into eight individual ramekins or a 5- to 6-cup oven-proof serving dish. Level the top so the dip is flat and sprinkle the remaining Parmesan over the top. Bake until the dip is hot and the cheese is light golden brown and slightly crisp, about 20 minutes for individual ramekins and 30 minutes for a single, large dish.

Serve the dip hot with the corn crisps.

Coriander-Crusted Tuna on Wonton Crisps
with Sesame Slaw and Wasabi Cream

A harmony of textures and flavors is created when silky tuna is coated in a flavorful crust and served with crisp, tangy slaw and velvety wasabi cream on top of a crunchy wonton crisp.

The wonton crisps are versatile and store well. To make your own signature crisps, after brushing with egg white, sprinkle the wonton wrappers with sesame, poppy, or other seeds or crushed spices before baking. They can be stored in an airtight container at room temperature for several days and make a pleasing, crunchy addition to chicken salad or are nice as a light snack on their own. **MAKES 12 PIECES; SERVES 4 TO 6**

FOR THE WONTON CRISPS

Grapeseed oil spray

6 wonton wrappers

1 large egg white

FOR THE WASABI CREAM

¼ cup plain nonfat yogurt

¼ teaspoon wasabi paste

¼ teaspoon mirin or honey

Pinch of kosher salt, or to taste

FOR THE SESAME SLAW

2 cups shredded Chinese cabbage

1 small carrot, cut into matchsticks (¼ cup)

¼ cup bean sprouts

2 tablespoons thinly sliced scallions (white and green parts)

Prepare the crisps. Preheat the oven to 350°F. Line a baking sheet with parchment paper and spray it lightly with oil.

Cut each wonton wrapper diagonally in half to make two triangles. Beat the egg white with 1 tablespoon water and lightly brush both sides of the wonton triangles with the egg white. Place them on the baking sheet. Bake until golden brown, 6 to 7 minutes. Transfer the wonton triangles to a cooling rack and let cool completely.

Meanwhile, prepare the wasabi cream. Combine the yogurt, wasabi paste, mirin, 2 teaspoons water, and salt. Whisk to combine. Set aside.

Prepare the slaw. In a large bowl, combine the cabbage, carrot, bean sprouts, scallions, and sesame seeds. Cover and refrigerate. In a small bowl, whisk together the mirin, rice vinegar, lime juice, and sesame oil. Cover and refrigerate.

Prepare the tuna. Combine the coriander seeds and peppercorns in a spice grinder and coarsely grind, 5 to 10 seconds. Transfer the crushed seeds to a small mixing bowl and stir in the salt.

CONTINUES ON PAGE 28

Toasting Sesame Seeds

Put the sesame seeds in a small cast-iron or other heavy skillet over medium-high heat. Cook, shaking the pan continuously, until the seeds smell fragrant and toasted and release their oils, 2 to 3 minutes. Immediately transfer the seeds to a plate to cool.

Mango-Avocado Summer Rolls *with Sweet and Sour Dipping Sauce*

Filled with sweet mango, rich avocado, crunchy vegetables, and fresh herbs, these rolls burst with flavor. To kick up the protein, add to each roll 1 to 2 tablespoons of shredded, roasted chicken or cooked shrimp, lobster, or crab meat.

Rice paper wrappers can be found in the Asian food aisle of your local supermarket, or at Asian specialty markets, or online. When working with the wrappers, make sure not to place all of them in the water at once; prepare just one roll at a time.

MAKES 6 ROLLS; SERVES 6

FOR THE DIPPING SAUCE

¼ cup low-sodium soy sauce

¼ cup fresh lime juice (from 2 to 3 limes)

¼ cup packed light brown sugar

1½ teaspoons minced peeled fresh ginger

1 teaspoon sriracha or Vietnamese chile-garlic sauce

FOR THE SUMMER ROLLS

1 red bell pepper, seeded

½ English cucumber, halved lengthwise and seeded

1 medium avocado, pitted and peeled

1 mango, peeled and pitted

4 cups shredded romaine lettuce hearts

3 tablespoons fresh cilantro leaves

3 tablespoons torn fresh mint leaves

3 tablespoons torn fresh basil

6 (8-inch) rice paper wrappers

Prepare the dipping sauce. In a small bowl, combine the soy sauce, lime juice, brown sugar, ginger, and sriracha. Whisk until the sugar is completely dissolved, about 1 minute. (The sauce can be made up to 4 days in advance and stored in the refrigerator, tightly covered.)

Prepare the summer rolls. Slice the red pepper and cucumber into 24 (2-inch-long) strips. Slice the avocado lengthwise into 24 strips. Slice the mango into 48 (2-inch-long) strips. In a large bowl, toss the romaine with the cilantro, mint, and basil.

Place one rice paper wrapper in tepid water until softened, 1 to 1½ minutes. Remove it from the water and pat both sides dry with a paper or clean kitchen towel. Lay the wrapper flat on a work surface or clean kitchen towel. Across the center of the wrapper, arrange in a line 4 strips each of red pepper, cucumber, and avocado and 8 strips of mango, leaving bare about 1 inch on either side. Spoon about ⅓ cup of the romaine mixture on top of the vegetables.

Fold the bottom third of the wrapper over the ingredients. While holding the very top of the wrapper steady, use the fingertips of your other hand to pull the rolled part back firmly toward you to tighten the roll. Fold in the sides, and roll the wrapper forward to create a tight, sealed roll. Set the roll on a platter and cover with a damp kitchen towel. Repeat with the remaining wrappers and ingredients.

To serve, slice each roll diagonally in half and place two halves on each of six plates. Divide the dipping sauce among six small serving bowls, or pass a single bowl of the sauce so that your guests may serve themselves.

tips from the golden door
eight steps to mindful eating

For most of us, emotions are almost always involved with eating, even when we have a healthy relationship with food. A particular dish or flavor can immediately elicit an unsolicited memory—good or bad. It is easy to overindulge in unhealthful food when we eat on the run, absentmindedly keeping our mouths busy while we cope with the stresses and strains of everyday life. A pint of ice cream can lure even the strongest among us right off course when we are tired, lonely, stressed, or otherwise vulnerable. To diminish the inevitable pull of emotions on your eating habits, Cindi Peterson, Golden Door's resident behavioral therapist, and Dr. Wendy Bazilian, the nutrition specialist at the Golden Door, advocate "mindful eating." Mindful eating is not about strict diets; it has nothing to do with deprivation. Instead, mindful eating encourages you to approach the emotions that affect eating in a new way, so that you can develop a healthier relationship with food. Here are the eight steps to mindful eating:

1. Identify food cravings. Learn to recognize the difference between a craving for spinach and a craving for ice cream. A hankering for spinach likely means your body needs iron or another nutrient found in leafy greens. A craving for ice cream, on the other hand, does not mean your body is in dire need of butterfat, but may be caused by fatigue or even stress, which can send very real chemical signals to eat food. When you don't know why you are eating, it can be hard to assess what an appropriate alternative response might be. Often, if you are eating for any reason other than to satisfy hunger, whatever relief you gain is temporary, at best, and ultimately can lead to less clarity rather than more. Think of food as energizing fuel for the body instead of as a source of comfort. When you feel hunger, ask yourself if you are actually hungry or are instead craving something. If hungry, use the scale in step 3 to assess your level of hunger. If experiencing a craving, evaluate its intensity—from mild to somewhat strong to extreme. Check your watch: is it time for a snack or a meal? Honor your body with healthy choices when you are physically hungry. If not truly hungry, try to find something besides food that can satisfy your needs.

2. Practice managing your stress and learn to relax. When we are under stress our bodies react with what's known as the "stress response," releasing cortisol, the stress hormone, and other chemicals. These hormonal changes can stimulate cravings for simple carbohydrates or sugars, found in foods such as bread, pasta, muffins, pretzels, candies, and cookies. Furthermore, the release of cortisol makes it easier for us to make and store fat deep in the abdominal region. This is the type of fat that is particularly hard to lose and is associated with increased risk of diabetes, heart disease, and other chronic diseases. In a sense, our unresolved, chronic stress can literally make us fat.

There are many ways to manage stress over the long term, including exercise (page 184), meditation (page 236), and keeping a food diary (page 212). But to successfully practice mindful eating, it's important to manage stress in the moment, before the stress response is triggered. The simplest and most effective first step is to learn how to breathe fully. Deep abdominal breathing can help bring the body away from the stress response and induce the relaxation response, which slows your heart rate and breathing, relaxes muscle tension, decreases blood pressure, and increases chemicals associated with healthy well-being. To practice, place your hands one on top of the other over your navel and begin breathing. Take in air slowly and deeply through the nose and feel your hands move outward as you picture moving the air in and down toward the belly. Breathe out slowly through your mouth, feeling your hands relax and come inward as your abdominal cavity deflates. Repeat this nine more times. Practice this simple exercise several times a day and you'll train yourself to breathe deeply even when you're not specifically focusing on it.

3. Use the hunger scale. The hunger scale goes from 0 to 10, where 0 is truly physically hungry and empty and 10 is really stuffed. Check in with your stomach and your brain several times throughout the day and before and during each meal. Try to stop eating when you are satisfied (7 to 8), before you are full. Being aware of your level of hunger can help you avoid ever getting to 0 and can also help you learn to stop when you reach a maximum level of 7 or 8. Use a food diary (page 212) to track your hunger, your intake, and the physical feelings associated with both.

4. Always eat sitting down. Acknowledging and honoring the meal can help you avoid mindless eating.

Never eat out of boxes or bags. Whether for a full meal or a simple snack, set the table, even if it's just a placemat and utensils. Put your feet on the floor, face forward, sit up straight, and look at your food. This simple practice makes a big impact on your overall mindfulness—and satiety—over the course of the day.

5. Use the One-Minute Rule. Before eating anything, whether you are sitting down to a full meal or a snack, wait one full minute before putting any food in your mouth. Take inventory of the quality and portion size of the food. Note what your food looks like and how it smells. Put your hand on your stomach and establish your hunger level using the hunger scale in step 3. Take three deep breaths (see step 2) to help you relax your body and focus on the food. Finally, taste the food that you have so carefully observed.

6. Slow down. It takes up to 20 minutes for the message to go from your stomach to your brain that you have food "on board." The best way to eat just enough is to chew slowly. This can be hard to remember if you've never done it before, so try it for one meal a day at first. Consistent practice will help make it a new positive habit. Other simple ways to slow down include eating with your nondominant hand or with chopsticks; setting down your fork or taking a sip of

water after every bite; or dining with a friend and talking while you eat—the more controversial or exciting the topic, the better!

7. Drink plenty of water. Your body is nearly 60 percent water and your brain is almost 70 percent water. Staying hydrated at all times is good for your skin, joints, muscles, and circulation. Make it a goal to drink six or more glasses of water everyday, eight or more if you are more active. Try to get at least 80 percent of your daily intake of liquid in the form of flat or bubbly water—add a squeeze of fresh lemon or orange juice if desired—and consume good amounts of fruits and vegetables. Green or black tea is also a good water source, and tea provides some other health-promoting properties.

8. Practice radical self-acceptance. Above all, be kind to yourself and stop beating yourself up about overeating. The next time you get feelings that usually lead you to eat for reasons other than hunger, say to yourself, "I must need something. What am I feeling and how can I meet that need differently?" Practice some of the many strategies above, and also practice accepting and loving yourself. Feel proud with every success—large or small.

salads

Avocado, Orange, and Jícama *with Coriander Dressing*

The grounds around the Golden Door were the inspiration for this salad. The Door is surrounded by orange groves, and some of the hiking trails that snake away from the valley lead to a huge, mountaintop avocado grove. Tangy citrus and floral coriander are perfect foils for buttery avocado in this cool, refreshing salad. SERVES 4

2 to 3 large oranges

3 tablespoons plus 2 teaspoons fresh
    lime juice (from 2 limes)

1 tablespoon extra-virgin olive oil

1 teaspoon coriander seeds, crushed
    with a mortar and pestle or in a
    spice grinder

1 garlic clove, minced

2 tablespoons fresh cilantro leaves

Pinch of kosher salt, or to taste

Pinch of freshly ground black pepper,
    or to taste

¼ small jícama (about 4 ounces)

⅛ teaspoon cayenne pepper

6 cups field greens or mesclun

1 medium avocado, pitted, peeled, and
    sliced

Peel and section one orange as directed on page 51. You should have 1 cup of segments. If not, peel and section another orange.

Squeeze the remaining juice from the membranes and discard them. Pour the collected orange juice into a glass measuring cup. Slice another orange in half and squeeze enough of the juice to make ⅓ cup total. Pour the orange juice in a blender and add 3 tablespoons of the lime juice, the olive oil, coriander seeds, and garlic. Blend for 10 seconds, until well combined. Add the cilantro leaves and pulse for 5 seconds so that the cilantro is chopped but not pureed. Add a pinch of salt and pepper and taste for seasoning. Set the dressing aside.

Peel the jícama and cut it into ½-inch dice; you should have ¾ cup. Toss the jícama with the remaining 2 teaspoons lime juice and the cayenne pepper.

Toss the greens with half of the reserved dressing and a pinch each of salt and pepper, if desired. Divide the greens among four plates, mounding them in the center of the plate. Arrange the avocado slices and orange segments over each salad. Scatter the jícama over each salad and drizzle each with additional dressing. Serve.

Sugar Snap and Snow Pea Salad *with Orange Sesame Vinaigrette*

Fresh orange juice is flavored with ginger, rice wine vinegar, and a little toasted sesame oil and then drizzled over a crispy pea and cabbage salad. Whenever we serve this salad someone inevitably asks, "What is in that dressing? I actually want to drink it!"

In this recipe I use one of my favorite methods for getting maximum flavor out of fresh ginger without the laborious peeling, slicing, and mincing: grate the unpeeled ginger and then squeeze out the juice. This little trick works beautifully to quickly add fresh ginger flavor to tea, steamed rice, marinades, and dressings with half the work. It only takes 2 to 3 inches of fresh ginger to get enough juice for this recipe, but trying to grate a piece that small can be dangerous. Instead just grate the whole ginger root until you have enough (as you would for cheese). **SERVES 4**

4 ounces sugar snap peas, trimmed
   (1½ cups)

4 ounces snow peas, trimmed (1½ cups)

Large knob of fresh ginger

1 medium orange, peeled (see page 51)

½ cup fresh orange juice (from 2 oranges)

2 tablespoons unseasoned rice vinegar

1 tablespoon mirin

1 teaspoon toasted sesame oil

Pinch of kosher salt and pinch of
   freshly ground pepper, or to taste

3 cups shredded napa cabbage

½ medium red bell pepper, seeded and
   thinly sliced (½ cup)

¼ cup thinly sliced scallions (white
   and green parts)

2 teaspoons black sesame seeds, toasted
   (see page 27)

2 teaspoons white sesame seeds, toasted
   (see page 27)

Bring a pot of water to a boil. Fill a large bowl with ice water. Submerge the sugar snap peas in the boiling water for 30 seconds. Use a slotted spoon to transfer the snap peas directly into the ice water for 2 minutes to cool. Submerge the snow peas in the boiling water for 10 seconds. Use a slotted spoon to transfer the snow peas to the ice water for 2 minutes to cool. Drain the peas well and set aside.

Grate the ginger on the large-holed side of a box grater until you have about ¼ cup. Collect the grated ginger in your hand and squeeze over a bowl to extract the juice. You should have about 2 teaspoons of juice; if you don't, grate more ginger and squeeze out the liquid until you do. Pour the ginger juice into a blender. Discard the grated ginger.

Cut the peeled orange into four wedges and add them to the blender. Add the orange juice, rice vinegar, mirin, and sesame oil, and puree until smooth. Strain through a medium strainer and season with a pinch each of salt and pepper. If the dressing separates before serving, just whisk it again or put it in a jar and shake.

Toss the cabbage, bell pepper, and scallions with ¼ cup of the dressing and a pinch each of salt and pepper, if desired. To serve, spoon the cabbage mixture onto each of four plates, top with the peas, and drizzle on more vinaigrette. Sprinkle the toasted sesame seeds over each salad and serve.

Watercress, Strawberry, and Goat Cheese Salad

Here, simple ingredients result in striking flavor. Peppery watercress is foiled by sweet strawberries and the creamy tang of goat cheese. Red wine vinegar is assertive and winey while white balsamic vinegar is milder and sweeter; either is very good in this recipe—choose your vinegar according to which quality you prefer or which vinegar you have in your pantry. Regular balsamic would also be tasty, but will significantly affect the color of the final dish. Whichever vinegar you use, if the strawberries are extremely sweet, you may want to use the greater amount called for below. SERVES 4

1½ pints (12 ounces) fresh strawberries, sliced (2 cups)

1½ teaspoons minced shallot

1½ teaspoons to 1 tablespoon red wine vinegar or white balsamic vinegar

2 tablespoons extra-virgin olive oil

⅛ teaspoon kosher salt, or to taste

⅛ teaspoon freshly ground black pepper, or to taste

4 cups watercress, whole leaves and tender stems (about 1 bunch)

1 ounce fresh or aged goat cheese, crumbled (¼ cup)

Combine half of the sliced strawberries and 2 tablespoons water in a blender. Blend until just pureed, stopping the blender if necessary to push the strawberries down with a spoon a few times. Strain the puree through a mesh strainer set over a medium bowl to remove the seeds.

Add the shallot and vinegar to the strawberry puree and whisk to blend. Whisking constantly, drizzle in the olive oil and continue whisking until well combined. Season with the salt and pepper. (You may prepare the dressing and store it, covered, in the refrigerator for up to 3 or 4 days.)

Arrange 1 cup of watercress on each of four salad plates. Scatter the remaining 1 cup sliced strawberries over the salads. Drizzle 2 tablespoons dressing over each salad. Scatter the goat cheese over each salad and serve.

Heirloom Tomato Salad

Look for a variety of vine-ripened heirloom tomatoes at your local farmers' market. In the summer months you can find red, yellow, green zebra, purple Cherokee, baby tear drop, and many other interesting varieties. All are delicious, ranging in flavor from mild and almost buttery to explosively sweet, and the vibrant colors are absolutely gorgeous. Serve this simple salad on its own as a starter, or as a side dish with pasta, grilled fish, or other grilled seafood. **SERVES 6**

1½ pounds ripe heirloom tomatoes

2 tablespoons white balsamic vinegar

2 teaspoons Dijon mustard

2 teaspoons minced garlic

2 teaspoons chopped fresh oregano leaves

2 tablespoons extra-virgin olive oil

Pinch of kosher salt, or to taste

Pinch of freshly ground black pepper, or to taste

2 tablespoons chopped fresh Italian parsley leaves

Remove the stems from the tomatoes. Slice the larger tomatoes into wedges. Cut the smaller tomatoes in half or leave them whole. Put the tomatoes in a large bowl.

In a medium bowl, whisk together the vinegar, mustard, garlic, and oregano. Whisking constantly, drizzle in the olive oil; continue to whisk until well combined. Season with the salt and pepper. Pour the dressing over the tomatoes and toss gently to coat. Cover and chill for 1 hour.

Remove the tomatoes from the refrigerator and toss in the chopped parsley. Adjust the seasoning with salt and pepper if necessary. Serve cold or at room temperature.

Chopped Vegetable Salad
with White Balsamic Dijon Vinaigrette

This beautiful, marinated summer salad bursts with a rainbow of colors and textures, spiked with the flavors of mustard, garlic, fresh basil, and mild white balsamic vinegar. **SERVES 4**

Kernels from 1 ear of corn (½ cup)

1 medium carrot, diced (½ cup)

¼ small English cucumber, seeded and diced (½ cup)

½ medium red bell pepper, seeded and diced (½ cup)

1 celery rib, diced (½ cup)

½ cup broccoli florets

½ large ripe, red tomato, seeded and diced (½ cup)

¼ cup thinly sliced scallions (white and green parts)

2 tablespoons white balsamic vinegar

1 tablespoon extra-virgin olive oil

1 tablespoon Dijon mustard

½ teaspoon minced garlic

6 fresh basil leaves

2 cups mesclun or field greens

Pinch of kosher salt, or to taste

Pinch of freshly ground black pepper, or to taste

In a large bowl, combine the corn, carrot, cucumber, bell pepper, celery, broccoli, tomato, and scallions. Gently toss to mix the vegetables.

In a blender, combine the vinegar, olive oil, mustard, garlic, and ¼ cup water. Blend for 10 seconds to combine. Add the basil leaves and pulse until the basil is well chopped but not pureed. Set aside ¼ cup of the dressing. Pour the remaining dressing over the chopped vegetables and toss to combine. Cover and refrigerate for 30 minutes to lightly marinate the vegetables.

When ready to serve, pour the reserved ¼ cup dressing over the mixed greens, season with the salt and pepper, and toss together to coat. Divide the greens among four salad plates. Toss the marinated vegetables and spoon them over the mixed greens. Serve.

Shaved Fennel *with Parmesan Shavings and Lemon*

Very thinly sliced fennel is the key to this simple salad. Many swear by authentic French slicing tools called mandolines to slice this thin. These are excellent tools, to be sure, but even better, I think, are Japanese ones, which are less expensive and do just as excellent a job. Check one out in your local kitchen or cooking supply store, or online.

Serve this on its own for a first course, or alongside simply grilled or broiled salmon. **SERVES 4**

1 large or 2 medium bulbs fennel

2 cups loosely packed arugula

2 tablespoons extra-virgin olive oil

2 tablespoons fresh lemon juice
   (from 1 lemon)

Pinch of kosher salt

Pinch of freshly ground black pepper

¾ ounce Parmesan cheese, thinly
   shaved (¼ cup; see Note),
   for serving

NOTE: *You can shave the cheese with a mandoline, a vegetable peeler, or a cheese slicer.*

Prepare a large bowl of ice water. Trim the fronds and thin stems from the top of the fennel bulb and cut off the base. Cut the fennel in half lengthwise and remove the core. Use a mandoline to thinly slice 1 fennel half at a time, placing it either top or base down on the blade. Alternatively, use a very sharp knife to thinly slice the fennel. You should have 3 cups. Place the cut fennel into the ice water for 5 minutes, to crisp and prevent it from discoloring.

Drain the fennel well and transfer it to a large bowl with the arugula. Add the olive oil, lemon juice, salt, and pepper and toss to combine. Divide the salad among four salad plates, top each serving with Parmesan shavings, and serve.

Citus Salad
with Extra-Virgin Olive Oil and Cracked Black Pepper

This is a refreshing winter salad full of vitamin C. The contrasts of the sweet oranges, tart blood oranges, and bittersweet grapefruit create a delicious harmony of citrus flavors. The olive oil mixes with the citrus juices to form a light and savory vinaigrette that rounds out the dish. **SERVES 6**

1 ruby red grapefruit

1 pomelo or 1 additional grapefruit

2 navel oranges

2 blood oranges

2 tangerines

6 cups mixed salad greens, such as
    arugula, radicchio, and mizuna

3 tablespoons extra-virgin olive oil

Pinch of kosher salt

Pinch of freshly cracked black pepper

1 tablespoon thinly sliced fresh mint
    or basil leaves

Peel the grapefruit as directed below. Turn the peeled grapefruit on its side and cut it crosswise into ¼-inch-thick slices. Place the slices in a shallow pan. Peel and slice the pomelo, navel oranges, blood oranges, and tangerines in the same way. To make it easier to assemble the salads for serving, keep each fruit grouped together in the pan; do not mix them.

Divide the greens among six salad plates. Arrange the citrus slices around the salad on each plate. Pour any accumulated citrus juices from the pan over the greens. Drizzle ½ tablespoon olive oil over each salad and sprinkle lightly with salt, pepper, and mint. Serve.

Peeling and Sectioning Citrus Fruit

To peel citrus fruit, use a sharp, thin-bladed or serrated knife to cut a thin slice off the bottom and top of the fruit. Stand the fruit on one cut end. Starting at the top, follow the curve of the fruit with the knife to cut off the peel and the pith and reveal the fruit. Do this all the way around the fruit to cut away all the pith and peel.

To section the fruit, hold the peeled fruit over a bowl to catch any juices and cut the segments away from the thin membranes holding them together.

Persimmon, Pomegranate, and Tangerine Salad
with Roasted Shallot Balsamic Dressing

In this beautiful, savory fruit salad, pale, orange-colored wedges of crisp persimmon and juicy tangerines are dotted by tiny jewels of sweet-tart pomegranate seeds and dressed with deeply flavorful roasted shallot and balsamic vinaigrette.

The two most common varieties of Oriental persimmons are fuyu and hachiya. Fuyu persimmons are squatter and much less astringent than the oblong hachiya. They are typically eaten when firm like an apple, although they can also be eaten when a little softer. They are sweet and a little less intensely flavored than hachiya. Choose fuyu with deep orange skin. **SERVES 4**

2 large shallots (about 4 ounces total), peeled, trimmed, and quartered

½ cup balsamic vinegar

4 sprigs fresh thyme

1 small pomegranate

1 tablespoon extra-virgin olive oil

Pinch of kosher salt, or to taste

Pinch of freshly ground black pepper, or to taste

6 cups loosely packed field greens or mesclun

1 firm fuyu persimmon, sliced into thin wedges

2 tangerines, peeled (see page 51) and sliced crosswise ¼ inch thick

Preheat the oven to 400°F.

In a nonreactive, ovenproof skillet just big enough to hold the shallots, combine the shallots, vinegar, and thyme sprigs. Cover the pan with aluminum foil and roast until the shallots are softened and the vinegar is reduced by half, about 40 minutes. If the vinegar is not sufficiently reduced and the shallots are still a bit firm, remove the foil and continue to roast, uncovered, for 5 to 10 minutes.

While the shallots are roasting, prepare a large bowl of cold water. Cut the pomegranate in half lengthwise. Holding one half under the water, use your fingers to gently remove the seeds from the fruit. Most of them will float to the top. Repeat with the other half. Drain the seeds well, removing any pith left over. Set aside ⅓ cup. (Store any remaining seeds in the refrigerator for another use.)

When the shallots are ready, remove the pan from the oven and carefully remove the foil. Let cool for 15 minutes. Remove and discard the thyme. Transfer the shallots and vinegar to a blender. Add ½ cup water and blend until the mixture is smooth but slightly chunky, 8 to 10 seconds. Add the olive oil and blend for 5 more seconds. Add the salt and pepper.

Toss the greens with ¼ cup of the dressing and salt and pepper, if desired. Pile the greens high in center of each of four plates. Scatter the persimmon wedges, tangerine slices, and pomegranate seeds over each salad. Drizzle with additional dressing and serve.

Forest Mushrooms and Frisée *with Truffle-Beet Vinaigrette*

This is a supremely elegant warm salad, perfect any time you want to present a beautiful first course with bold yet refined flavor but very little fat. Truffle oil is one of my pantry staples; I often use it to add earthiness to dishes that contain mushrooms, as the oil bolsters the mushrooms' aroma and flavor. **SERVES 4**

8 ounces red beets (about 1 medium-large beet), trimmed

Olive oil spray

Kosher salt and freshly ground black pepper

6 ounces shiitake mushrooms, stemmed and sliced (2 cups)

6 ounces cremini mushrooms, sliced (2 cups)

6 ounces oyster mushrooms, sliced (2 cups)

1 tablespoon minced shallot

1 teaspoon minced garlic

¼ cup dry white wine

1 tablespoon fresh lemon juice

3 teaspoons truffle oil or extra-virgin olive oil

1 to 1½ tablespoons sherry vinegar

4 cups loosely packed baby frisée

Preheat the oven to 375°F.

Scrub the beets under cold running water. Place them in a small, shallow baking pan. Spritz them with olive oil and sprinkle with salt and pepper. Pour ½ inch of water into the pan and cover the pan with aluminum foil. Roast until the beets are tender when pierced with a thin-bladed knife, about 1 hour. Let the beets rest at room temperature until they are cool enough to handle. Use a paring knife to peel the beets; this is easier to do when the beets are still warm. Dice the beets. Set aside ½ cup for the dressing and reserve the rest for garnish.

While the beets are roasting, spray a sauté pan with olive oil and heat it over medium heat. Add the shiitake, cremini, and oyster mushrooms, and cook, stirring occasionally, until slightly softened, about 3 minutes. Add the shallot and the garlic and cook, stirring occasionally, for 2 minutes. Add the wine and simmer until it is reduced by half, about 10 minutes. Season with a pinch each of salt and pepper. Drain off and reserve the liquid for the vinaigrette.

Add the lemon juice and 1 teaspoon of the truffle oil to the mushrooms. Set aside and keep warm.

In a blender, combine the ½ cup beets, the remaining 2 teaspoons truffle oil, the reserved mushroom liquid, 1 tablespoon vinegar, ¼ cup water, and ⅛ teaspoon each salt and pepper. Puree until smooth, 20 to 30 seconds. Taste and add up to ½ tablespoon vinegar if desired. (The dressing can be stored, covered, in the refrigerator for up to 3 days.)

Toss the frisée with the mushrooms and divide among four plates. Drizzle 1 tablespoon of beet vinaigrette around each salad and sprinkle with diced beets. Serve.

Broccoli Almond Salad in Radicchio Cups

Broccoli stems can be a little tough and because of this it's not uncommon for folks to chop off the stem of a head of broccoli and just toss it out. But peel the tough outer layer off that stem and a tasty surprise is revealed: the pale green inner stem is crisp and sweet and perfect in this refreshing salad. Better still, hardly anything is wasted! **SERVES 4**

1 pound broccoli

1 lemon

½ cup low-fat or regular buttermilk

1 tablespoon apple cider vinegar

1 teaspoon honey

½ teaspoon Dijon mustard

Pinch of kosher salt, or to taste

Pinch of freshly ground black pepper, or to taste

2 tablespoons sliced almonds, toasted (see page 135)

1 tablespoon golden raisins

4 radicchio leaves

2 cups shredded romaine lettuce

Cut the florets from the head of broccoli into bite-size pieces. Use a sharp paring knife to peel off the tough outer layer of the stem. Cut the stem lengthwise in half and then slice about ¼ inch thick. You should have about 4 cups florets and sliced stem.

Bring a pot of water to a boil. Fill a medium bowl with ice water. Submerge the broccoli in the boiling water for 10 seconds. Use a slotted spoon to transfer the broccoli directly into the ice water for 2 minutes to cool. This will bring out the vibrant green color but still leave the broccoli fairly raw and crunchy. Drain the broccoli well and set aside.

Grate 1 teaspoon zest from the lemon. Set the zest and the lemon aside.

In a small bowl combine the buttermilk, vinegar, honey, mustard, lemon zest, salt, and pepper. Whisk together until combined.

Stir the almonds and raisins into the broccoli. Add the dressing and toss to combine. Cover and refrigerate for at least 30 minutes and up to 3 hours before serving.

To serve, place 1 radicchio leaf on each of four plates. Fill each radicchio leaf with shredded romaine. Spoon the broccoli salad on top. Squeeze 1 to 2 teaspoons of lemon juice from the reserved lemon over each salad. Serve.

Celery Root and Fuji Apple Slaw *with Cider Dressing*

Versatile celery root has the fresh, concentrated aroma and flavor of celery and is delicious either raw, as in this dish, or cooked. In this wonderful cool-weather salad, it is paired with sweet crisp apples and lightly marinated in light vinaigrette. **SERVES 4**

1 medium head celery root (about 1 pound)

2 medium Fuji apples

2 tablespoons plus 2 teaspoons fresh lemon juice (from 1 lemon)

¼ cup chopped fresh Italian parsley leaves

2 tablespoons apple cider vinegar

1 tablespoon whole-grain mustard

1 tablespoon canola or grapeseed oil

1½ teaspoons honey

1 head Belgian endive

Pinch of kosher salt, or to taste

Pinch of freshly ground black pepper, or to taste

Use a sharp paring knife to peel the celery root. Use a large, sharp knife to cut the peeled celery root into thin matchsticks. Cut 1½ of the apples into matchsticks the same size as the celery root. Put the apples and celery root in a large bowl and toss with the 2 tablespoons lemon juice.

In a medium bowl, combine the parsley, apple cider vinegar, mustard, oil, honey, and ¼ cup water. Whisk until well blended. Pour the dressing over the celery root and apples and toss to combine. Cover and refrigerate for at least 20 minutes and up to 1 hour.

Gently separate the leaves of the Belgian endive. Set 12 whole leaves aside for serving. Stack the remaining leaves and thinly slice them crosswise. Add the sliced endive to the celery root salad. Thinly slice the remaining ½ apple and toss it with 2 teaspoons of the lemon juice. Set aside.

To serve, lay 3 endive leaves on each of four plates. Toss the celery root and apple slaw with a spoon and season with salt and pepper, if desired. Place a mound of slaw on each plate, on top of the endive leaves. Garnish each salad with the apple slices and serve.

*Sweet Corn Soup
with Blue Crab and
Avocado Relish*

soups

Miso Soup

Miso soup, which we serve as the first course to our traditional Bento Box lunch (page 146) every Thursday at the Golden Door, is a soothing, traditional Japanese soup. Kombu, bonito flakes, and miso paste can be found at Asian groceries. To make this a more substantial dish, you can stir in additions such as cooked noodles, cubed tofu, cooked prawns, sliced scallions, or shredded fresh wakame (seaweed). **SERVES 6**

1 (6-inch) square piece kombu (seaweed)

½ cup bonito flakes

¼ cup plus 1 tablespoon white or yellow miso paste

Combine the kombu and 6 cups of water in a medium saucepan and bring to a boil over medium heat. Turn off the heat and stir in the bonito flakes. Cover and let stand for 5 minutes; when the bonito flakes sink the stock—or dashi—is ready.

Strain the dashi, return it to the saucepan, and bring to a simmer. Turn off the heat and whisk in the miso paste. Do not boil the soup once the miso is added, or the flavor will weaken and some of the beneficial enzymes will be destroyed. Keep the soup hot but below the simmering point. Divide among six bowls and serve hot.

Wonton Soup

The Chinese word wonton *literally translates to "swallowing clouds," and I can't think of a better way to describe the experience of eating the best renditions of this soup. This version has all the traditional flavor of a great wonton soup but replaces the traditional ground pork with leaner ground turkey. (It is just as good when the ground turkey is itself replaced by finely chopped shrimp or chicken breast.) Wonton wrappers can be found at Asian groceries. The filling should make enough to fill 18 wontons; be sure to measure the amount you place in each wonton.* **SERVES 6**

1 (3-inch) piece fresh ginger

3 scallions

8 cups Chicken Stock (page 268) or
    store-bought low-sodium broth

4 dried shiitake mushrooms

¾ teaspoon kosher salt, or to taste

2¼ teaspoons cornstarch

4 ounces ground turkey breast

1 tablespoon low-sodium soy sauce

2 teaspoons dry sherry

1 teaspoon toasted sesame oil

⅛ teaspoon sugar

18 wonton wrappers

1 cup spinach leaves, torn

Peel the ginger. Slice 2 inches of it into thin rounds and place them in a large saucepan. Mince the remaining 1-inch piece and set it aside for the wonton filling.

Finely chop the scallions, white and green parts, and set aside 1½ tablespoons for the wonton filling. Place the remaining scallions in the saucepan with the ginger rounds.

Set aside 2 tablespoons of the stock for the filling. Pour the rest of the stock in the saucepan with the ginger and scallions. Add the dried shiitake mushrooms and the salt, and bring to a boil over medium heat. Reduce the heat and simmer for 10 minutes. Remove from the heat, cover the pan, and set aside.

Meanwhile, make the wonton filling. In a small bowl, combine the cornstarch with the reserved 2 tablespoons stock and whisk until dissolved. Add the reserved scallions, minced ginger, the turkey, soy sauce, sherry, sesame oil, and sugar. Use a fork to mix until well blended.

Place a wonton wrapper on a work surface at an angle so that one point is closest to you; keep the remaining wonton wrappers covered with plastic wrap or a towel. Spoon 1½ teaspoons filling in the center of the wrapper. Brush the two top edges lightly with water. Fold the bottom half up and, starting at the top point, run your fingers down the two edges to seal them shut, pressing out any air. You will

CONTINUES ON PAGE 62

CONTINUED FROM PAGE 61

have a broad-based triangle with the flat end closest to you. Brush one of the corners of the base of the triangle with water. Fold the corners in toward each other and press between your index finger and thumb to seal them together. Set the wonton aside and cover it with a towel. Repeat to fill the remaining wonton wrappers.

When all of the wontons have been filled, uncover the broth. Remove and discard the ginger slices. Remove the shiitakes from the broth, slice them, and return them to the broth. Bring the broth back to a boil. Reduce the heat to low so that the broth simmers. Add the wontons and simmer until the filling is firm and the wontons are cooked through, about 5 minutes.

Divide the torn spinach leaves among six warmed bowls. Ladle the hot broth over them and add three wontons per bowl. Serve hot.

Truffled Mushroom Soup *with Popped Wild Rice*

Rich, earthy mushrooms are the stars of this soup. The popped wild rice is almost as fun to prepare as it is delicious to eat: you make it just as you would popcorn. It adds great crunchy texture and toasted flavor to the soup.

I scrape out the portobello gills, the dark feathery parts on the underside of the caps, because they darken the soup too much if left in. If you can get your hands on pure truffle oil—infused with pure truffle, not with added chemical truffle flavor—use it here to highlight and intensify the flavor of the mushrooms. Truffle oil can be found at specialty food stores and online sources. But don't hesitate to make this recipe if you do not have truffle oil on hand; all those mushrooms and popped wild rice ensure that the soup is delicious no matter what. **SERVES 6**

FOR THE SOUP

Grapeseed oil spray

2 large shallots, thinly sliced
(about ¾ cup)

1½ teaspoons minced garlic

1 pound portobello mushroom caps, gills
scraped out with a spoon, sliced
¼ inch thick (4 cups)

4 ounces shiitake mushrooms, stemmed
and sliced ¼ inch thick (1⅓ cups)

4 ounces oyster mushrooms or white
mushrooms, trimmed and sliced
¼ inch thick (1⅓ cups)

1 teaspoon kosher salt, or to taste

¼ teaspoon freshly ground black pepper

½ cup dry white wine

4 cups Chicken or Vegetable Stock
(pages 268 and 269) or store-bought
low-sodium broth

5 sprigs fresh thyme

1 bay leaf

Prepare the soup. Spray a medium saucepan with grapeseed oil and place the pan over medium heat. Add the shallots and garlic and cook, stirring frequently, until slightly translucent and fragrant but not at all brown, 4 to 5 minutes. Stir in the mushrooms, salt, and pepper, and cook, stirring frequently, until the mushrooms have softened and begun to release their liquid, about 4 minutes. Add the wine and raise the heat to medium-high. Simmer for 5 minutes so that the wine reduces and the mushrooms release their liquid.

Add the chicken stock, thyme, and bay leaf. Simmer for 15 minutes. Remove the saucepan from the heat. Discard the thyme and bay leaf.

Transfer the soup to a blender, working in batches if necessary; fill the blender no more than one-third full. Blend at high speed until creamy, about 30 seconds. Transfer the soup to a clean saucepan and set it over low heat to keep warm while you make the garnish.

CONTINUES ON PAGE 65

FOR THE GARNISH

1 tablespoon grapeseed or canola oil

2 tablespoons uncooked wild rice

¼ cup chives, in ½-inch pieces

Pinch of kosher salt

Pinch of freshly ground black pepper

2 teaspoons white or black truffle oil or
   best-quality extra-virgin olive oil

CONTINUED FROM PAGE 63

Prepare the garnish. Have ready a plate lined with paper towels. Pour the grapeseed oil in a small skillet and heat it over medium-high heat for 1 minute. Add the wild rice and shake the uncovered pan over the heat to toss the rice until most of the rice has puffed up and split open, 1½ to 2 minutes. Transfer the popped rice to the paper towel–lined plate to drain.

When the rice is cool, place it in a small bowl and add the chives, salt, and pepper. Toss with a fork to combine. Bring the soup back to a simmer and stir in the truffle oil. Divide the soup among six warmed bowls, and garnish with the popped wild rice and chive mixture. Serve hot.

Thai Coconut Vegetable Soup

Whether you're craving sweet, salty, sour, or spicy, this soup has a little bit of everything and combines them into a sumptuous whole. Kaffir lime leaves add an exotic, citrus-y aroma and flavor to the soup that can't be duplicated by any substitution. Although the soup is still delicious even without the leaves, it is nonetheless worth a bit of effort to find them. They can be purchased both fresh and frozen at Asian groceries. If you buy fresh, you can freeze whatever you don't use in a tightly sealed zipper-lock bag for many months. Kaffir lime leaves grow in an unusual double leaf configuration with two leaves connected to each other; count connected double leaves as two individual leaves. **SERVES 8**

1 stalk lemongrass

2 (13.5-ounce) cans light coconut milk

3 teaspoons red curry paste, preferably Mae Ploy brand

3 cups Vegetable Stock (page 269) or store-bought low-sodium broth

1 cup shredded green cabbage

1 medium sweet potato, peeled and diced (1 cup)

⅛ fresh pineapple, diced (1 cup)

1 medium carrot, diced (½ cup)

5 fresh or frozen kaffir lime leaves (each about 2 inches long and 1 inch wide)

1 tablespoon Thai fish sauce (nam pla)

16 whole cherry tomatoes

1 cup fresh basil leaves, preferably Thai basil, plus more for serving

2 limes, each cut into 4 wedges, for serving

Trim the lemongrass stalk to about 6 inches, discarding the darker ends. Lay the lemongrass stalk on a cutting board and with the handle of a heavy knife, smash it several times. Set aside.

In a Dutch oven or other large saucepan, bring the coconut milk to a simmer over medium heat. Whisk in the curry paste. Add the crushed lemongrass stalk and simmer for 10 minutes to develop the flavors. Stir in the stock and bring back to a simmer.

Stir in the cabbage, sweet potato, pineapple, carrot, lime leaves, and fish sauce and simmer until the vegetables are tender, 15 to 20 minutes.

Stir in the tomatoes and the basil, and simmer for 1 minute just to warm them through; the tomatoes and basil should retain their shape and bright color.

Divide the soup among eight warmed bowls and garnish each with Thai basil leaves and a lime wedge. Serve hot.

Lemongrass-Ginger Broth *with Shrimp and Snow Peas*

Colorful strips of snow peas, celery, and carrots float in a clear, fragrant broth studded with pink juicy shrimp. Served in its simplest form, this dish is a light starter or midday snack. For a more filling soup, serve over cooked noodles. The dish becomes a festive meal to share with family or guests when served with a platter of brightly colored and aromatic condiments such as fresh cilantro, chopped chiles, and lime wedges. **SERVES 6**

2 stalks lemongrass

6 cups Chicken or Vegetable Stock (pages 268 and 269) or store-bought low-sodium broth

1 (2-inch) piece fresh ginger, peeled and sliced ¼ inch thick

1 teaspoon kosher salt, or to taste

6 ounces peeled and deveined medium shrimp

3 ounces snow peas, thinly sliced lengthwise (1 cup)

1 celery rib, cut into matchsticks (½ cup)

1 small carrot, cut into matchsticks (¼ cup)

12 ounces rice, soba, or udon noodles, cooked according to the package directions (optional)

¼ cup chopped fresh cilantro leaves (optional)

¼ cup sliced fresh basil leaves (optional)

2 tablespoons chopped serrano or Thai bird chiles (optional)

2 tablespoons sriracha or Vietnamese chile-garlic sauce (optional)

1 lime, sliced into 6 to 8 wedges (optional)

Trim the lemongrass to about 6 inches, discarding tops. Lay each lemongrass stalk on a cutting board and with the handle of a heavy knife, smash each stalk several times.

Put the lemongrass in a medium saucepan and add the stock, ginger, and salt. Bring to a boil, and then reduce the heat so the mixture simmers. Cook for 20 minutes to extract the flavor of the ginger and lemongrass and perfume the broth. Remove and discard the ginger and lemongrass.

Add the shrimp to the simmering broth and gently poach for 3 minutes. Stir in the snow peas, celery, and carrot. Remove the pan from the heat. Serve hot as is or, if desired, divide the noodles among six warmed soup bowls and pour the soup on top.

If desired, place each of the garnishes—the cilantro, basil, chopped chiles, chile-garlic sauce, and lime wedges—in individual small bowls and present them on a platter at the table so that guests may garnish their servings as desired.

*Broccoli Basil Soup

This is a Golden Door classic, served at least once every week for many years. Very flavorful and creamy, the soup is nonetheless extremely low in calories and fat. For even more flavor, stir in the optional smoked Cheddar cheese. **SERVES 6**

Olive oil spray

½ medium onion, diced (½ cup)

1 pound broccoli

4 cups Vegetable or Chicken Stock (pages 269 and 268) or store-bought low-sodium broth

½ teaspoon kosher salt, or to taste

¼ teaspoon freshly ground black pepper, or to taste

1 bay leaf

1 cup packed fresh spinach leaves

2 tablespoons sliced fresh basil leaves

2 ounces sharp smoked Cheddar or Gouda, grated (about 1 cup, loosely packed; optional)

Spray a medium saucepan with olive oil and heat over low heat. Add the onion and cook, stirring frequently, until translucent and not at all brown, 4 to 5 minutes.

Meanwhile, peel the woody stems of the broccoli with a paring knife and slice the stems ¼ inch thick. Chop the florets.

Stir the broccoli into the onion. Cook for 1 minute. Add the stock, salt, pepper, and bay leaf. Raise the heat to medium and bring to a boil. Reduce the heat and simmer, uncovered, until the broccoli is tender when pierced with a fork, 10 to 15 minutes.

Remove the pan from the heat and allow to cool for 10 minutes. Remove and discard the bay leaf.

Transfer the soup to a blender or food processor and process until creamy but still slightly chunky, about 30 seconds, working in batches if necessary. Add the spinach and basil to the blender and process for an additional 10 seconds to incorporate.

Return the soup to a clean saucepan and reheat over low heat until gently simmering. If desired, add the grated Cheddar and stir until melted. Remove from the heat and serve hot.

Creamy Cauliflower Soup *with Caramelized Cauliflower*

This silken soup has the rich flavor of a classic, indulgent, cheesy fondue but with none of the guilt. The secret here is to cook the cauliflower until it is very tender and then puree it until smooth and fluffy. The method yields what appears to be a cream-based soup, but which is, in fact, made up almost entirely of good-for-you vegetables and fat-free milk. **SERVES 8**

2 pounds cauliflower, trimmed

Olive oil spray

1 teaspoon sugar

Kosher salt and freshly ground white pepper

½ small leek, sliced (1 cup)

2 cups skim milk

2 cups Chicken Stock (page 268) or store-bought low-sodium broth

1 teaspoon dry mustard

⅛ teaspoon freshly ground nutmeg

2 ounces Gruyère cheese, finely grated (about 1 loosely packed cup)

Parsley Oil (page 272), for serving

Preheat the oven to 400°F.

Chop the cauliflower into enough small florets and stems to equal 2 cups. Coarsely chop the remaining cauliflower and set it aside in a separate bowl. Spray the 2 cups of cauliflower one or two times with olive oil. Add the sugar and a pinch each of the salt and white pepper. Toss the cauliflower with a fork to coat it with the oil and seasonings. Transfer it to a baking dish and spread the cauliflower in a single layer. Bake, stirring once or twice, until the cauliflower is light golden brown, about 25 minutes.

Meanwhile, spray a large saucepan with olive oil and heat over medium heat. Add the leek and cook, stirring, until softened and not at all brown, 4 to 5 minutes. Add the coarsely chopped cauliflower, the milk, stock, dry mustard, nutmeg, and ½ teaspoon salt and ⅛ teaspoon white pepper and stir to combine. Bring the mixture to a gentle simmer and cook, uncovered, stirring occasionally, until the cauliflower is tender when pierced with a fork, about 20 minutes.

Remove the saucepan from the heat and allow the mixture to cool slightly. Transfer the mixture to a blender or food processor and blend until smooth and creamy, working in batches if necessary. Return the soup to a clean saucepan and reheat it over medium-low heat, stirring frequently, until it simmers lightly. Add the Gruyère and stir until it has melted. Remove the pan from the heat.

Ladle the soup into warm bowls. Top each with caramelized cauliflower and drizzle with a little parsley oil. Serve hot.

Garden Vegetable Soup with Pistou

Made from basil, garlic, olive oil, and Parmesan cheese, pistou *is stirred into soups, stews, and pastas to add aromatic flavor and color. Ordinarily, that savory burst comes from a large amount of olive oil and cheese, but my version uses no oil and just a bit of Parmesan. The trick is to puree the* pistou *ingredients with some of the hot soup and then stir this mixture back into the soup. This method gives the soup the extra body and robust flavor of classic* pistou *without the added fat.* **SERVES 8**

1 cup dried flageolet, great northern, or cannellini beans

6 cups Chicken or Vegetable Stock (pages 268 and 269) or store-bought low-sodium broth

1 bay leaf

1 medium carrot, diced (½ cup)

2 celery ribs, diced (1 cup)

1 medium zucchini, diced (1 cup)

4 ounces green beans, cut into 1-inch pieces (1 cup)

½ small leek, thinly sliced (1 cup)

1 teaspoon kosher salt, or to taste

¼ teaspoon freshly ground black pepper, or to taste

1 cup packed coarsely chopped fresh basil leaves

¼ cup chopped fresh Italian parsley

2 tablespoons grated Parmesan cheese

2 teaspoons tomato paste

½ cup sliced scallions (white and green parts)

2 garlic cloves, smashed

½ large ripe red tomato, seeded and diced (½ cup)

Rinse the beans in cold water and pick over them, discarding any stones or debris. Place them in a large bowl and pour in enough cold water to cover by 2 inches. Let stand overnight.

Drain the beans, discarding the water. Transfer the beans to a medium saucepan and add the stock and bay leaf. Bring to a boil and then reduce the heat. Simmer gently, partially covered, until the beans are tender, 40 to 50 minutes.

Stir in the carrot, celery, zucchini, green beans, leek, salt, and pepper and simmer until the vegetables are tender, about 15 minutes. Remove and discard the bay leaf.

Combine the basil, parsley, Parmesan, tomato paste, scallions, and garlic in a blender. Add 2 cups of the hot broth to the blender and process for 20 seconds, until the mixture is well blended and smooth. Pour the blended mixture into the soup and stir to combine. Stir in the diced tomato. Ladle the soup into warm bowls and serve hot.

White Bean, Roasted Tomato, and Rosemary Soup

This savory, satisfying soup is not only delicious but it packs the healthy punch of three of the SuperFoods (see page 81) in one bowl: beans, tomatoes, and spinach. If you make the soup ahead or are not necessarily going to serve it all during one meal, place some fresh spinach and scallions into each bowl and ladle the hot soup over, instead of adding these to the whole batch. The soup will store and reheat better without these ingredients.

Note that the cooking time for beans can be longer than what is given below if they are old—which you can't know when you buy them. This soup should be quite brothy, so have extra stock on hand if necessary to thin it after cooking. **SERVES 6**

---

2 cups dried cannellini beans

1 (28-ounce) can whole Italian plum tomatoes

6 garlic cloves, peeled

2 tablespoons olive oil

1 medium onion, diced (1 cup)

4 cups Chicken or Vegetable Stock (pages 268 and 269) or store-bought low-sodium broth, plus more if needed

½ teaspoon kosher salt, or to taste

⅛ teaspoon freshly ground black pepper, or to taste

4 sprigs fresh rosemary

4 sprigs fresh thyme

1 bay leaf

2 cups fresh spinach leaves, chopped

½ cup thinly sliced scallions (white and green parts)

Rinse the beans in cold water and pick over them, discarding any stones or debris. Place them in a large bowl and pour in enough cold water to cover by 2 inches. Let stand overnight. Drain the beans and set aside.

Preheat the oven to 400°F.

In a 2-quart baking dish, pour in the tomatoes with their juice and add the garlic. Drizzle with 1 tablespoon of the olive oil. Roast, uncovered, until the tomatoes and garlic are slightly browned in spots and the liquid has reduced, about 45 minutes. Transfer the tomatoes, garlic, and pan juices to a blender or food processor and blend just until the mixture is slightly chunky, working in batches if necessary. Set the mixture aside.

In a 3-quart saucepan, heat the remaining 1 tablespoon olive oil over medium heat. Add the onion, reduce the heat to medium-low and cook, stirring occasionally, until the onion is translucent, 4 to 5 minutes.

Stir in the beans, stock, and a pinch each of the salt and pepper. Raise the heat to medium-high and bring the mixture to a simmer. Tie the rosemary and thyme sprigs and bay leaf in cheesecloth and add them to the pot. Reduce the heat and simmer, covered, until the beans are tender, 1 to 1½ hours.

Remove and discard the herb bundle. Stir the roasted tomato puree into the soup and bring it back to a simmer. Add more stock if necessary so the soup has a brothy texture. Stir in the remaining salt and pepper. Remove the pan from the heat, and stir in the spinach and scallions. Serve hot.

Roasting Peppers

Position a rack about 6 inches from the broiler and preheat the broiler to high.

Line a rimmed baking sheet with foil. Place the peppers on the baking sheet and mist them with olive oil. Broil until the skins of the peppers are lightly charred all over, using tongs to turn the peppers as necessary, about 10 minutes for poblano chiles and about 20 minutes for bell peppers. (Alternatively, you may blacken the peppers over a hot grill, or use tongs to hold the peppers directly over a gas burner.)

To help loosen the skins and make them easy to peel, place the peppers in a bowl, cover with plastic wrap, and allow to steam in the bowl until cool enough to handle, about 15 minutes. Remove the peppers from the bowl and place plastic wrap over a cutting board to catch the pepper peelings and make them easier to gather and discard. Remove the stems of the peppers and split the peppers in half. Use a paring knife to scrape out seeds and peel away the skins; it's okay if a little of the skin remains. Don't rinse the peppers, as that will wash away the roasted flavor.

Roasted Poblano, Corn, and Potato Soup

Spicy, smoky, and creamy, this soup is boldly flavored yet comfortingly smooth and rich. Potatoes give the soup body without the excess fat that cream would give. **SERVES 6**

Grapeseed or canola oil spray

1 large onion, diced (1½ cups)

1 teaspoon chili powder

1 teaspoon ground cumin

1 teaspoon dried oregano

¾ teaspoon kosher salt, or to taste

1 pound russet or Yukon Gold potatoes, peeled and sliced

4 to 5 cups Chicken or Vegetable Stock (pages 268 and 269) or store-bought low-sodium broth

1½ cups corn kernels (from about 2 ears of corn)

2 poblano chiles, roasted (page 74), peeled, seeded, and diced or 1 can (4 ounces) green chiles, drained and diced

½ cup light sour cream

½ cup chopped fresh cilantro leaves

Spray a large saucepan with grapeseed oil and heat over medium-low heat. Add the onion and cook, stirring, until translucent but not at all brown, 4 to 5 minutes. Stir in the chili powder, cumin, oregano, and salt, and cook, stirring, for 20 seconds. Add the potatoes and stock and bring to a boil. Reduce the heat to low and simmer, partially covered, until the potatoes are tender, about 20 minutes.

Spray a medium skillet with oil and heat over medium-high heat until hot but not smoking. Add the corn and cook, stirring occasionally, until lightly browned, about 3 minutes.

Transfer the potato mixture to a blender and process until smooth, about 20 seconds, working in batches if necessary. Return the soup to the saucepan. Stir in the chiles and corn. Bring back to a simmer and remove the pan from the heat. Whisk in the sour cream and chopped cilantro. Serve hot.

Spicy Chicken and Hominy Soup *with Crisp Tortilla Strips*

This savory, spicy, tangy soup is especially delicious when finished with the crisp corn tortilla strips, cilantro leaves, and some crumbled queso fresco, a mild Mexican cheese. To learn about chipotles in adobo, see page 29. Boneless chicken breast can be used to make this soup, but using chicken on the bone gives more flavor. **SERVES 8**

Grapeseed or canola oil spray

2 medium carrots, diced (1 cup)

1 medium onion, diced (1 cup)

2 celery ribs, diced (1 cup)

2 garlic cloves, minced

2 teaspoons ancho chile powder

1 teaspoon ground cumin

1 teaspoon dried oregano

1 teaspoon kosher salt, or to taste

6 cups Chicken Stock (page 268) or
    store-bought low-sodium broth

1 (12-ounce) skinless chicken breast
    on the bone or 7 ounces boneless
    skinless chicken breast

2 (5-inch) thin corn tortillas

1 (15.5-ounce) can hominy, drained

1 cup crushed tomatoes

1 chipotle in adobo, chopped

1 medium avocado, diced

1 cup chopped fresh cilantro leaves,
    plus more for serving

Juice of 1 lime

1 ounce crumbled (¼ cup) queso fresco,
    for serving

Preheat the oven to 400°F.

Spray a medium saucepan with oil and heat it over medium heat. Add the carrots, onion, celery, and garlic and cook, stirring, until the vegetables are slightly softened but not at all brown, 4 to 5 minutes. Add the chile powder, cumin, oregano, and salt and cook, stirring, for 1 minute. Add the stock and bring to a boil. Add the chicken breast and reduce the heat. Simmer, covered, until the chicken is cooked through, about 15 minutes.

Meanwhile, lay the tortillas on a cutting board and lightly spray them on both sides with oil. Use a sharp knife to slice them into ½-inch-wide strips and lay the strips in a single layer on a baking sheet. Bake until the strips are lightly browned and crisp, 6 to 8 minutes. Remove the tortilla strips from the baking sheet and set them aside to cool.

Remove the chicken breast from the soup and let stand for 5 minutes (remove the soup from the heat and let it stand, covered, during this time). Pull or cut the meat from the bone and cut it into bite-size pieces. Return the meat to the soup.

Stir in the hominy, crushed tomatoes, and chipotle and simmer for 5 minutes. Remove the pan from the heat. Stir in the avocado, cilantro, and lime juice. Ladle the soup into eight serving bowls and top each serving with a few tortilla strips, chopped cilantro, and some queso fresco. Serve hot.

Sweet Corn Soup *with Blue Crab and Avocado Relish*

Sweet corn, sweet crab, and rich avocado are a match made in heaven; for the creamiest, sweetest results use summer corn in season. I like to serve this soup chilled on a hot summer day, but it is also excellent served hot. (Photograph on page 58.)

SERVES 6

FOR THE CORN SOUP

6 ears corn

2 teaspoons grapeseed oil

½ medium onion, coarsely chopped (½ cup)

1 small carrot, coarsely chopped (¼ cup)

½ celery rib, coarsely chopped (¼ cup)

1 bay leaf

1 teaspoon kosher salt, or to taste

¼ teaspoon freshly ground white pepper, or to taste

FOR THE CRAB AND AVOCADO RELISH

8 ounces lump or backfin blue crab meat, picked over to remove any bits of shell or cartilage

1 medium avocado, diced

1 ripe, plum tomato, seeded and diced

2 tablespoons fresh lemon juice (from 1 lemon)

½ teaspoon Old Bay seasoning

½ cup fresh basil leaves

Use a sharp, thin knife to cut the corn kernels from the ears. You should have 5 cups of kernels; set them aside. Place the ears in a large soup pot and cover with 8 cups of cold water. Bring to a boil over medium heat. Reduce the heat and simmer, uncovered, for 40 minutes. Strain and discard the ears. Set the corn stock aside.

In a large saucepan, heat the grapeseed oil over medium-low heat. Add the onion, carrot, celery, and bay leaf and cook, stirring frequently, until the onion is translucent but not browned, 4 to 5 minutes. Stir in the corn and cook, stirring, for 3 minutes. Stir in 5 cups of the corn stock along with the salt and pepper. Bring to a boil, then reduce the heat, and simmer, uncovered, for 30 minutes. Remove the pan from the heat, discard the bay leaf, and let the soup cool.

Transfer the soup to blender, in batches if necessary. Blend on a low speed until creamy. Strain through a medium-mesh sieve set over a bowl and use the back of ladle to push the soup through. You should have about 6 cups of soup. Add a bit more corn stock or water if the soup is too thick. Refrigerate until chilled, 1 to 3 hours. Season to taste with pepper.

When ready to serve, prepare the crab and avocado relish. Put the crab in a medium bowl and use a fork to break up the meat slightly. Add the avocado, tomato, lemon juice, and Old Bay seasoning. Tear the basil leaves and add them. Stir gently to combine.

Divide the soup among six chilled bowls and place a generous dollop of crab and avocado relish in the center of each bowl. Serve.

tips from the golden door
superfoods

For generations the Golden Door has advocated a diet based on whole foods and plants, served in reasonable portions. Finally nutrition science has caught up with this commonsense, life-enhancing approach to eating, and *SuperFoods* has become the movement's unofficial watchword. But what is a SuperFood? To Wendy Bazilian, the nutrition specialist at the Golden Door, a doctor of public health, and the author of *The SuperFoodsRx Diet,* the term *SuperFoods* is simply a way of drawing attention to a group of foods whose compounds and nutrients have been shown to promote good health and have the potential to reduce the risk of many chronic diseases associated with aging. Some of these compounds, such as certain antioxidants, help repair cellular damage associated with regular, daily exposure to the environment. Others can reduce inflammation. Still others help regulate blood sugar or fat metabolism. Crucially, it has been discovered that these compounds work together *synergistically* in the SuperFoods; the emphasis in a healthy diet should be on eating food, not consuming supplements.

The specific SuperFoods were first widely introduced as a group of fourteen foods in 2004, followed by a list of several more, plus dozens of "sidekicks," or foods that can be substituted for the SuperFoods (see Resources, page 283). As Dr. Wendy likes to say, SuperFoods provide the greatest nutritional bang for the caloric buck. These tasty and nutrient-dense whole foods are already familiar to most of us and can be found in any grocery store, critical factors for making healthy eating with SuperFoods easy to embrace. A stroll down any supermarket aisle can expose us to a mountain of packaged foods emblazoned with empty promises of "good health," all of which just add to the cacophony of confusing messages about what and how we should—and should not—eat. A diet based on SuperFoods, however, is not about falsely promising a magic bullet, nor is it about exclusion or elimination of any foods. Instead it's about *adding* to your diet, choosing from a short list of whole, wholesome, delicious foods—with no labels to read! The SuperFoods, SuperSpices, and their sidekicks are listed here. Asterisks (*) denote the original fourteen SuperFoods.

- Apples; sidekick: pears
- Avocados
- *Beans; sidekicks: all dried beans (such as black beans, kidney, pinto, navy, great northern, white, garbanzo, lentils) plus green beans, sugar snap peas, green peas, and canned, low-sodium beans
- *Blueberries; sidekicks: purple grapes, cranberries, boysenberries, raspberries, strawberries, fresh currants, blackberries, cherries, and all other varieties of fresh or frozen berries
- *Broccoli; sidekicks: Brussels sprouts, cabbage, kale, turnips, cauliflower, collard greens, bok choy, mustard greens, Swiss chard
- Dark chocolate
- Dried SuperFruits: dried cherries, raisins, blueberries, prunes, apricots, cranberries, currants, figs
- Extra-virgin olive oil
- Honey
- Kiwi; sidekicks: pineapple, guava

- *Oats; sidekicks: wheat germ, ground flaxseed, brown rice, barley, wheat, buckwheat, rye, millet, bulgur wheat, amaranth, quinoa, triticale, kamut, yellow corn, wild rice, spelt, whole wheat couscous
- Onions; sidekicks: garlic, scallions, shallots, leeks, chives
- *Oranges; sidekicks: lemons, white and pink grapefruit, kumquats, tangerines, limes
- Pomegranates; sidekick: plums
- *Pumpkin; sidekicks: carrots, butternut squash, sweet potato, orange bell pepper
- *Soy; sidekicks: tofu, soymilk, soy nuts, edamame, tempeh, miso
- *Spinach; sidekicks: kale, collard greens, Swiss chard, mustard greens, turnip greens, bok choy, romaine lettuce, orange bell peppers
- SuperSpices; sidekicks: cinnamon, cumin, oregano, thyme, turmeric, plus red pepper, ginger, and rosemary
- *Tea: green and black

- *Tomatoes; sidekicks: watermelon, pink grapefruit, Japanese persimmons, red-fleshed papaya, strawberry guava
- *Turkey; sidekick: skinless chicken breast
- *Walnuts; sidekicks: almonds, pistachios, pumpkin and sunflower seeds, macadamia nuts, pecans, hazelnuts, cashews, Brazil nuts, peanuts (although technically a legume, like beans, peanuts' nutritional profile and health benefits are similar to tree nuts.)
- *Wild salmon; sidekicks: chunk light tuna, sardines, herring, trout, bass, oysters, clams
- *Yogurt; sidekick: kefir

In addition, there are a good number of fresh and good-quality dried herbs and spices—many of which are likely already in your kitchen cabinets or refrigerators—that not only enhance the flavor of dishes without the use of excess salt, fat, or sugar, but are actually antioxidant-packed powerhouses themselves. For example, 1 teaspoon of ground

cinnamon is as high in antioxidants as ½ cup of fresh blueberries. Add cinnamon to oatmeal, yogurt, or muffins, mix it with ground coffee before brewing, or stir it into tea with honey.

Dr. Wendy calls oregano—one of the highest sources of antioxidants among dried herbs—a "mini salad." Sprinkle it into homemade or store-bought pasta sauce, on vegetables or meat, or in a grilled cheese sandwich made with whole-grain bread, a modest amount of delicious cheese, and thick slices of tomatoes.

Ground dried red peppers, whether hot cayenne or sweet paprika, are sources of capsaicin, a compound that has been shown to have metabolism-boosting properties as well as fat-burning potential. And there's promising research on other herbs and spices, including turmeric (commonly found in yellow curry), thyme, rosemary, cumin, and fresh or dried ginger.

It is important to note that while SuperFoods feature prominently in the

Golden Door diet and in the recipes in this book, they're not the only foods that are on the menu. Above all, Dr. Wendy maintains that the emphasis of the Golden Door diet is on regularly eating fresh fruits and vegetables, whole-grains, and lean meat- and plant-based proteins such as fish, poultry, beans, soy, nuts, and seeds. Whether you are trying to resize your body and lose excess weight or are simply looking to change your eating habits, you don't want to sacrifice your health, taste buds, or wallet in the process. Rather than concentrating on cutting foods out of your diet, focus on *adding* nutritious foods (which are, conveniently, also quite filling). No food should be eliminated from your diet altogether if you truly enjoy it—especially when you eat well most of the time. And don't forget that good health isn't only about what you eat. Along with SuperFoods and a healthy diet, exercise, stress management, and sleep are all vital elements of a super, healthy life.

vegetarian main dishes

Carrot-Walnut Pâté and Whole Wheat Chapati Wrap

Carrots and walnuts—the main players in this tangy, nutty pâté—pack a one-two SuperFoods punch (see page 81). The pâté is so incredibly flavorful that it is actually the star of these wraps. If you don't have time to make the chapati, use the excellent whole-grain tortillas that are commonly available at the supermarket and warm them in the microwave or in a dry skillet for a few seconds before filling them. You may also use warmed whole wheat pitas or flatbreads, or toasted whole-grain bread. Serve with Dressed Field Greens (page 110), if desired.

The carrot-walnut pâté is also really good as an appetizer: serve as a dip with crudités or spoon the pâté on cucumber slices, endive leaves, or crackers. **SERVES 4**

⅓ cup walnuts

2 medium carrots, grated (1 cup)

1 celery rib, diced (½ cup)

½ cup thinly sliced scallions (white and green parts)

1 garlic clove, crushed

Juice of 1 lemon

Pinch of kosher salt, or to taste

Pinch of freshly ground black pepper, or to taste

4 (8-inch) Whole Wheat Chapati (opposite)

4 teaspoons Dijon mustard

4 lettuce leaves

1 ripe, red tomato, sliced

4 slices red onion

¼ small English cucumber, thinly sliced (½ cup)

4 pepperoncini peppers, sliced

1 kosher dill pickle, sliced

Put the walnuts in a small bowl and add enough cold water to cover. Refrigerate overnight.

Drain the walnuts and transfer them to the work bowl of a food processor, along with the carrots, celery, scallions, garlic, and lemon juice. Process for about 2 minutes, until the mixture is a thick paste with visible bits of walnut, carrot, and scallion; stop the food processor occasionally to scrape down the sides of the bowl. Season with salt and pepper. Cover and refrigerate while you make the chapatti, or for up to 2 days.

On a work surface, lay out the warm chapati. Spread a little Dijon mustard in a straight left-to-right line across the center of each, stopping 2 inches from both sides. Divide the carrot-walnut pâté among the chapati and spread it out on top of the mustard. Lay a lettuce leaf across the pâté, followed by the sliced tomato, onion, cucumber, pepperoncini, and pickle. Fold the sides over by 2 inches and then fold the bottom of the wrap over the filling and roll into a tight wrap. Cut each in half on the bias. Serve.

WHOLE WHEAT CHAPATI

Chapati, also known as roti, is unleavened, whole wheat Indian flat bread. It is also one of the easiest to make breads under the sun, from a dough of nothing more than whole wheat flour, water, and salt. There's no rising, very little shaping, and no baking—just a quick browning in a skillet, like a pancake. Make them just once and I believe that these chewy, nutty flatbreads will become a staple in your home, as they have in the Golden Door kitchen. Formed into large rounds, they make great sandwich wraps; shaped into small rounds, they are the perfect accompaniment to Quinoa Tabbouleh with Spinach and Feta Hummus (page 88) or other salads, dips, or curry dishes. MAKES 6 (3-INCH) CHAPATI; MAKES 4 (8-INCH) CHAPATI IF THE RECIPE IS DOUBLED; SEE NOTE

½ cup whole wheat flour, plus more for rolling out the dough

Pinch of kosher salt

¼ cup warm water

Canola or grapeseed oil, for the dough and for cooking

NOTE *If making chapati big enough for wraps, use 1 cup flour, ½ cup water, and 2 pinches of salt. Divide the dough into four equal pieces and roll each into an 8-inch round. Cook one chapati at a time in a large skillet. Stack them on a large plate as you cook them. Do not place them in a warm oven, or they will become too crisp and brittle.*

In a bowl combine the flour and salt. Stir in the warm water with your hand or a wooden spoon until the mixture becomes a sticky dough. Put a few drops of oil on the dough and your hands and bring the dough together into a ball. Lightly dust the work surface with flour. Transfer the dough to the counter and divide it into six equal pieces. Form each piece into a ball. Roll each ball into a 3-inch circle.

Pour a small amount of oil on a cast-iron skillet or griddle and use a paper towel to spread it around and soak up excess oil. Heat the pan over medium-high heat until a few droplets of water dropped on the pan hop and sizzle. If the water stays in one place and boils slowly, the pan is too cold; if it steams away immediately, the pan is too hot.

Place two to three chapati in the skillet; you will need to cook them in two to three batches. Cook until the chapati start to steam and puff up in spots and their undersides are golden brown, about 1 minute. Flip and cook 1 minute or until they have puffed. (They may not all puff, which is fine, but don't cook beyond 1 minute or the chapati will become too crisp.) Stack the cooked chapati and cover with a clean kitchen towel to keep warm while you prepare the remaining chapati. Serve warm as soon as all the chapati are ready.

Quinoa Tabbouleh
with Spinach and Feta Hummus and Whole Wheat Chapati

Although it is cooked and served like a grain, quinoa is not technically a grain, which is most strictly defined as the seed of a cereal grass (quinoa, on the other hand, is the seed of a plant related to beets, spinach, and Swiss chard). True grain or not, quinoa is a nutritional powerhouse, high in protein, an excellent source of iron, magnesium, and potassium, and a good source of calcium. Quinoa also provides vitamin E, several B vitamins, and an excellent balance of amino acids, making it the most complete protein source among the grains. Best of all, quinoa cooks in less than 20 minutes and is as versatile as rice.

In this dish quinoa replaces the cracked wheat usually used to make the parsley and mint salad known as tabbouleh, for an even more nutrient-rich version than the original. The lemony tabbouleh is paired here with spinach- and feta-spiked hummus and warm chapati. **SERVES 6**

FOR THE QUINOA TABBOULEH

1 cup quinoa

1 medium ripe, red tomato, seeded and
   diced (1 cup)

1¼ cups finely chopped fresh parsley
   leaves

¼ cup finely chopped fresh mint leaves

¼ cup fresh lemon juice (from 2 lemons)

2 tablespoons extra-virgin olive oil

1 teaspoon minced garlic

½ teaspoon kosher salt

½ teaspoon freshly ground black pepper

Prepare the tabbouleh. Place the quinoa in a large bowl and cover with cold water. Use your hand to swish the quinoa around a few times. Drain and repeat until the water in the bowl is clear; you may need to do this several times. Drain well. In a medium pot, combine the quinoa with 1¼ cups of water. Bring just to a boil. Reduce the heat and simmer, covered, for 15 minutes. Remove the pan from the heat and let stand, covered, for 5 minutes to steam and finish cooking. Transfer the quinoa to a large bowl and cool to room temperature.

Add the tomato to the bowl with the cooled quinoa. Add the parsley, mint, lemon juice, olive oil, garlic, salt, and pepper, and stir gently until well combined. Cover and set aside in the refrigerator. (The tabbouleh will keep for 2 to 3 days in the refrigerator.)

FOR THE SPINACH AND FETA HUMMUS

1 (15-ounce) can chickpeas, rinsed and drained

1 ounce feta cheese, crumbled (¼ cup)

2 tablespoons extra-virgin olive oil

1 tablespoon tahini

2 garlic cloves, minced

1 cup chopped fresh spinach

¼ teaspoon kosher salt, or to taste

Pinch of freshly ground black pepper, or to taste

6 (3-inch) Whole Wheat Chapati (page 87)

Prepare the hummus. In the work bowl of a food processor combine the chickpeas, feta, olive oil, tahini, garlic, and 3 tablespoons water. Process until the mixture is very smooth, about 2 minutes. Use a rubber spatula to scrape down the sides of the bowl and add the spinach. Pulse just to combine; there should be bits of spinach throughout the hummus. Season with salt and pepper. Cover and set aside in the refrigerator. (The hummus will keep in the refrigerator for 3 to 4 days.)

Prepare the chapati and keep warm. To serve, divide the tabbouleh and the hummus among six plates, arranging a spoonful of each side by side on each plate. Place a chapati on each plate and serve.

Individual Vegetable Pizzetta

Pizza has long been a Wednesday lunch favorite at the Golden Door. A crisp semolina crust—to achieve crisp-yet-chewy crust perfection at home, bake the crust halfway before assembling the pizza—is topped with zesty tomato sauce, fresh vegetables laced with garlic, and sweet caramelized onions. The toppings give these individual pizzettas such bold flavors that there's no need for a thick layer of cheese. Don't let yourself be limited by the ingredients listed here, however. Pizza invites improvisation: devise your own exciting and healthful toppings. In fact, pizza making is a great way to get the whole family in the kitchen, and to get kids to eat things they might not otherwise. Set up a pizza bar with the half-baked crusts and sauce ready to go, along with bowls of thinly sliced portobello mushrooms or seasoned and grilled or seared meat or poultry, onions, peppers, tomatoes, fresh basil, fresh mozzarella, and a little grated Parmesan cheese. Bake the pizzettas as directed below. SERVES 6

Cornmeal, for rolling out the dough

Semolina Dough for Pizzettas (page 274)

Olive oil spray

6 ounces portobello mushroom caps, gills scraped out with a spoon, diced small (2 cups)

1 large zucchini, diced (1½ cups)

2 garlic cloves, minced

Pinch of kosher salt, or to taste

Pinch of freshly ground black pepper, or to taste

Golden Door Pizza Sauce (page 92)

3 plum tomatoes, cut into 18 thin slices

2 tablespoons grated Parmesan cheese

1 cup Caramelized Onions (page 273)

4 ounces fresh mozzarella cheese, diced (1 cup)

Fresh baby basil leaves or chopped fresh basil, for serving (optional)

If using pizza stones, place two in the oven. Preheat the oven to 450°F.

Dust the work surface with cornmeal. Divide the pizza dough into six equal balls (each about ¼ cup). Roll each ball into a 6-inch circle. (Alternatively, to make two large pies, divide the dough in half and roll each portion into a 12-inch circle.) Prick the dough all over with the tines of a fork to prevent large bubbles from forming. Transfer the rolled-out dough to nonstick baking sheets or pizza pans or a regular baking sheet sprinkled with a little cornmeal. If using pizza stones, use a rimless cookie sheet to slide them onto the hot stones. Bake until the bottom of the crust is just light golden, about 8 minutes. Remove the dough from the oven.

Spray a sauté pan with olive oil and heat over medium-high heat. Add the mushrooms and cook, stirring, for 1½ minutes. Add the zucchini and the garlic and cook, stirring, for 1½ minutes. The vegetables should be cooked no more than halfway through. Remove the pan from the heat. Season with salt and pepper.

Spread a scant 2 tablespoons of pizza sauce on each crust. Arrange three tomato slices on each and sprinkle with 1 teaspoon Parmesan. Divide the caramelized onions and the mushroom mixture among the crusts. Divide the mozzarella chunks among the pizzas.

Bake until golden brown on the bottom and edges and the cheese is melted, 10 to 12 minutes. Serve hot, garnished with fresh basil, if desired.

FOR THE SANDWICHES

½ small English cucumber, thinly sliced (1 cup)

½ medium red onion, thinly sliced (1 cup)

1 yellow bell pepper, seeded and thinly sliced

1 ripe, red tomato, thinly sliced

1 medium carrot, thinly sliced (½ cup)

¼ cup pitted kalamata olives, chopped

4½ teaspoons red wine vinegar

4½ teaspoons extra-virgin olive oil

1 tablespoon fresh lemon juice

2 teaspoons chopped fresh oregano leaves

Pinch of kosher salt, or to taste

Pinch of freshly ground black pepper, or to taste

4 (4-inch) square focaccia or other rustic bread

2 tablespoons Dijon mustard

1 medium avocado, pitted, peeled, and cut into quarters

1 cup alfalfa, broccoli, or sunflower sprouts

CONTINUED FROM PAGE 93

Spread the focaccia with the mustard. Divide the avocado quarters among the four bottom slices and use a fork or knife to smash and spread the avocado across the focaccia. Arrange the bean sprouts on top of the avocado. Toss the vegetables to coat them with the marinade and divide them among the four bottom slices, layering the vegetables so they lie flat. Place the remaining focaccia slices on top and press down to flatten slightly. Cut diagonally in two and place two halves on each of four plates. Divide the white bean salad among the plates. Serve.

Baked Falafel

with Grilled Eggplant Puree and Cucumber, Tomato, and Yogurt Salad

Classic falafel is a delicious blend of mashed chickpeas and spices, formed into balls and deep fried. The Golden Door version is merely browned on each side and then baked, drastically reducing the fat but certainly not the flavor. You can serve this with whole wheat pita or chapati (page 87, or use store-bought). Grilling the eggplant gives the puree a delicious, smoky flavor. Roasting also works very well, so don't worry if you don't have access to a grill. A cool, clean-tasting yogurt salad rounds out this meal inspired by the flavors of the Middle East. SERVES 4

FOR THE EGGPLANT PUREE

1 large eggplant

Grapeseed oil spray

1 tablespoon drained capers, chopped

1 tablespoon fresh lemon juice

1 tablespoon extra-virgin olive oil

1½ teaspoons balsamic vinegar

1½ teaspoons chopped fresh Italian parsley leaves

½ teaspoon ground cumin

1 garlic clove, minced

½ teaspoon freshly ground black pepper

Prepare a hot grill or preheat the oven to 350° F.

Pierce the eggplant a few times with a thin-bladed knife and spray it lightly with oil. Place the whole eggplant directly on the grill or in a shallow baking dish and in the oven. Grill on all sides until the eggplant chars on the outside, softens, and starts to collapse, about 20 minutes, or roast until soft, about 1 hour.

If grilling, remove the eggplant from the grill, place it in a bowl, and cover the bowl with plastic wrap. Let stand for 15 minutes before splitting the eggplant in half. If roasting, split the eggplant lengthwise and let cool.

Scrape out the eggplant pulp and transfer it to a blender or food processor. Add the capers, lemon juice, olive oil, balsamic vinegar, parsley, cumin, garlic, and pepper. Pulse until creamy but slightly coarse, scraping down the sides if necessary; do not puree until smooth. Set aside.

Place an empty baking dish in the oven. If necessary, preheat the oven to 350°F.

Prepare the falafel. Put the chickpeas in the work bowl of a food processor or a large bowl. Process or mash with a potato masher to break up the chickpeas. Add the onion, parsley, cilantro, tahini, cumin, coriander, baking powder, garlic, and salt. Pulse or mash to make a thick paste.

1 (15-ounce) can low-sodium chickpeas, rinsed and drained

¼ medium onion, diced (¼ cup)

2 tablespoons chopped fresh Italian parsley leaves

2 tablespoons chopped fresh cilantro leaves

1 tablespoon tahini

1½ teaspoons ground cumin

1 teaspoon ground coriander

½ teaspoon baking powder

2 garlic cloves, minced

¼ teaspoon kosher salt

Grapeseed or canola oil spray

1 tablespoon olive oil

FOR THE CUCUMBER, TOMATO, AND YOGURT SALAD

¾ small English cucumber, seeded and thinly sliced (1½ cups)

1 cup cherry tomatoes, halved

½ cup nonfat or low-fat Greek-style yogurt

1 tablespoon chopped fresh mint leaves

2 teaspoons fresh lemon juice

Pinch of kosher salt, or to taste

Pinch of freshly ground black pepper, or to taste

Scoop up golf ball–size balls of the mixture and flatten them slightly into 12 patties. Spray a nonstick pan with grapeseed or canola oil and heat the pan over medium-high heat until hot but not smoking. Add the patties to the pan and cook until golden brown on each side, about 2 minutes per side. Add the olive oil to the hot baking dish and transfer the patties to the dish. Bake until the patties are slightly puffed and deep golden brown, about 20 minutes, turning them over halfway through cooking.

Meanwhile, prepare the salad. Put the cucumber in a medium bowl along with the cherry tomatoes, yogurt, mint, lemon juice, salt, and pepper. Stir gently to combine. Cover and refrigerate until serving.

To serve, place three falafel patties on each of four plates. Divide the eggplant puree and salad among the plates, placing a spoonful of each alongside the patties. Serve while the falafel is still warm.

Red Lentil Veggie Burgers
with Garlicky Yam Fries and Spicy Mango Ketchup

Here you get your burger, fries, and ketchup with no meat and none of the guilt! I admit that the list of ingredients appears daunting, but the burgers are not hard to make. Each ingredient adds its own vital flavor and nutrients, and they all add up to the best veggie burgers I've had. To speed things up, pulse the vegetables one at a time in a food processor just until finely chopped. Once formed, the patties freeze very well, so it's well worth making a double batch and freezing the individually wrapped patties until you're ready for them; let the frozen patties stand on the counter for 1 hour before cooking.

When making the mango ketchup, if you want more heat, leave the seeds in the serrano; for a milder ketchup, remove the seeds. The ketchup is also very good with grilled fish and vegetable chili. **SERVES 8**

FOR THE MANGO KETCHUP

1 large or 2 medium mangoes

1 tablespoon fresh lime juice

¼ cup chopped fresh cilantro leaves

1 tablespoon diced red onion

1 tablespoon diced red bell pepper

1 serrano chile, seeded, if desired, and minced

Pinch of kosher salt, or to taste

Pinch of freshly ground black pepper, or to taste

FOR THE BURGERS

½ cup brown rice

1 cup red lentils, picked over and rinsed

Canola or grapeseed oil spray

½ medium onion, finely diced (½ cup)

1 teaspoon minced garlic

Prepare the mango ketchup. Peel the mango and cut the flesh off the pit. Dice half of the mango and set it aside; you should have about 1 cup or so. Coarsely chop the remaining mango and put it in a blender. Add the lime juice and puree until the mixture is smooth and thick, stopping the blender a few times and using a rubber spatula to push the mixture down. Transfer to a bowl. Stir in the reserved mango along with the cilantro, red onion, bell pepper, and serrano chile, and stir to combine. Season with a pinch of salt and pepper and set aside in the refrigerator. (The ketchup is best served the day it is made but will keep for up 2 days.)

Prepare the burgers. Put the rice in a small saucepan and add 1 cup water. Bring to a boil over medium heat. Reduce the heat and simmer, covered, until the rice is tender, about 35 minutes. Remove the pan from the heat and let stand, covered, for 5 minutes. Uncover the pan and use a fork to fluff the rice. Set aside until cool.

Meanwhile, put the lentils in a medium saucepan and add 2 cups water. Bring to a boil over medium heat. Reduce the heat to low and simmer gently, covered, until the lentils are slightly mushy, like a thick paste with a few whole lentils, 18 to 20 minutes, stirring once or twice during cooking. Set the lentils aside until cool.

Spray a large nonstick skillet with canola or grapeseed oil and heat over medium

CONTINUES ON PAGE 100

5 ounces broccoli, florets and peeled stems finely chopped (1½ cups)

2 medium carrots, finely chopped (1 cup)

2 medium potatoes, peeled and grated (1 cup), squeezed to remove excess liquid

3 ounces shiitake mushrooms, stemmed and finely chopped (1 cup)

2 ounces fresh or defrosted frozen shelled edamame beans, finely chopped (½ cup)

1½ teaspoons yellow curry powder

½ teaspoon kosher salt

⅛ teaspoon freshly ground black pepper

FOR THE GARLICKY YAM FRIES

1¼ pounds yams, peeled

2 teaspoons canola or grapeseed oil, plus more in spray bottle for finishing the fries

Kosher salt and freshly ground black pepper

¼ cup chopped fresh Italian parsley leaves

2 teaspoons minced garlic

½ cup cornmeal, for cooking

Leaf lettuce, for serving

Thinly sliced red onion, for serving

Thinly sliced tomatoes, for serving

Pickles, for serving

CONTINUED FROM PAGE 98

heat. Add the onion and garlic and cook, stirring, until slightly translucent and fragrant but not at all brown, about 3 minutes. Add the broccoli, carrots, potatoes, shiitake mushrooms, and edamame beans and cook, stirring, until the vegetables are fragrant but still crunchy, 2 minutes. Add the curry powder and cook, stirring, for 30 seconds. Remove the pan from the heat and stir in the salt and pepper. Let cool slightly. Transfer the rice, lentils, and vegetables to a large bowl and mix until well combined.

Scoop out ½ cup of the mixture and with wet hands, pack it firmly into a tight ball as if forming a meatball. Form the ball into a 3-inch patty about 1 inch thick. Place the patty on a baking sheet and repeat to make eight burgers in all. Chill for 30 minutes to 1 hour.

Prepare the garlicky yam fries. Preheat the oven to 400°F.

Cut the yams into sticks approximately ½ inch wide by 3 to 4 inches long, depending on the length of the yams. Place the yams in a large bowl and add the canola oil and a pinch each of salt and pepper. Use your hands or a wooden spoon to gently toss the yams and coat them with oil. Spread the yams in a single layer on a baking sheet and bake until golden brown and cooked through, 25 to 30 minutes, turning once halfway through cooking. Transfer the fries to a bowl and spritz them with canola oil. Add the parsley and garlic and toss to coat evenly. Serve hot.

While the fries are baking, cook the burgers. Have ready a nonstick baking sheet or line a regular baking sheet with parchment paper and spray with oil. Spread the cornmeal on a plate. Dredge each patty in cornmeal. Spray a large skillet with canola oil and heat over medium-high heat until hot but not smoking. Place the burgers in the pan without crowding (work in batches if necessary) and sear until they are light golden on both sides, 2 to 3 minutes per side. Transfer the burgers to the prepared baking sheet and bake for 12 minutes to warm through completely.

To serve, place a lettuce leaf on each of eight plates. Top the leaf with a burger, sliced red onion, and tomato. Divide the yam fries among the plates, placing them alongside the burger. Divide the mango ketchup among the plates, spooning it on top of the burgers. Serve with pickles on the side.

Vegetable Stir-Fry *with Caramelized Tofu and Forbidden Rice*

Stir-frying is a wonderful technique for maximizing flavor without using much fat. The key to successful stir-fry cooking is to have all the ingredients sliced, chopped, or mixed and in easy reach when you begin cooking. Read through the recipe, and as you prepare the ingredients, group those that are to be added to the pan at the same time on the same plate or bowl. It's also important that once cooked, the stir-fry be served right away. The very first time you make this, wait until the rice is almost cooked before you start the stir-fry. It's far better to let the rice wait for the stir-fry to be complete than for the stir-fry to wait for the rice.

Pressing as much moisture from the tofu as possible really helps when it comes time to brown it; if there's too much moisture, the tofu steams instead of browning. During cooking the soy sauce and sugar caramelize, creating a salty-sweet glaze that coats the tofu and commingles with the toasty flavor of peanuts in this very tasty dish.

Forbidden Black Rice is short-grained, heirloom, whole-grain rice that is high in fiber and contains a number of important minerals, including iron. It's also a good protein source. Black rice has a delicious nutty flavor and very pleasant light, chewy texture. Once reserved for Chinese emperors, this purplish-black rice and many others are readily available today and make an interesting, tasty alternative to white or brown rice. SERVES 4

FOR THE TOFU AND RICE

1 (12-ounce) package firm tofu, drained

¾ cup Forbidden Black Rice or other Chinese black rice

1½ teaspoons peanut, canola, or grapeseed oil

¼ cup low-sodium soy sauce, plus more if needed

2 tablespoons light brown sugar

2 tablespoons raw, unsalted peanuts

1 tablespoon thinly sliced scallions (white and green parts)

2 teaspoons minced peeled fresh ginger

½ teaspoon minced garlic

Prepare the tofu and rice. Snugly wrap the block of drained tofu in a clean kitchen towel and place it on a dinner plate. Place another dinner plate on top of the tofu and let stand for 30 minutes to 1 hour to squeeze out the excess moisture. Cut the tofu into ¾-inch cubes and set aside.

Put the rice in a medium saucepan and add 1½ cups of water. Bring to a boil over medium-high heat. Reduce the heat, cover, and simmer for 20 minutes. Remove the pan from the heat and let stand, covered, for 5 minutes to finish cooking. Use a fork to fluff the rice. Keep warm until serving.

To caramelize the tofu, heat the peanut oil in a nonstick pan or wok over medium-high heat until hot but not smoking. Add the tofu to the hot pan and cook, tossing with a spatula or spoon, until excess moisture is removed and the tofu is golden brown, 10 to 12 minutes. Add the soy sauce and sugar and cook, tossing, for 1 minute;

CONTINUES ON PAGE 103

FOR THE VEGETABLE STIR-FRY

2 tablespoons low-sodium soy sauce, plus more if needed

1½ teaspoons cornstarch

2 teaspoons peanut, canola, or grapeseed oil

1 tablespoon thinly sliced scallion (white and green parts)

2 teaspoons minced peeled fresh ginger

1 teaspoon minced garlic

3 ounces shiitake mushrooms, stemmed and quartered (1 cup)

1 cup broccoli florets

1 medium carrot, halved and sliced on the bias (½ cup)

3 ounces fresh snow peas, trimmed (1 cup)

½ medium red bell pepper, seeded and thinly sliced (½ cup)

2 cups chopped Chinese, napa, or green cabbage

1 cup whole spinach leaves

¼ cup sliced scallions (white and green parts), for serving

Fresh cilantro sprigs, for serving

1 lime, quartered, for serving

CONTINUED FROM PAGE 101

add a touch more soy sauce and 1 to 2 teaspoons water if the tofu becomes too dry too quickly. As the soy sauce reduces and the sugar caramelizes, it will coat the tofu with a salty, sweet glaze. Add the peanuts, scallions, ginger, and garlic and cook, tossing, for 30 seconds. Transfer the tofu to a warm bowl and set aside to keep warm. Wipe out the pan with a paper towel.

Prepare the vegetable stir-fry. In a small bowl, stir together the soy sauce and cornstarch. Set this slurry aside. Add the peanut oil to the skillet and heat over medium-high heat until hot but not smoking. Add the scallion, ginger, and garlic and cook, stirring until fragrant but not brown, about 30 seconds. Add the shiitake mushrooms, broccoli, and carrot and cook, stirring, for 2 minutes; add 1 tablespoon water if the mixture becomes too dry. Add the snow peas and bell pepper and cook for 1 to 2 minutes more. Add the cabbage and spinach and cook for 1 to 2 minutes more. The vegetables should be vibrant and still crunchy, and the spinach wilted. Add 3 tablespoons water to the slurry and stir to loosen the cornstarch. Make a well in the center of the vegetables and pour in the cornstarch slurry. Cook for about 30 seconds, tossing to coat the vegetables with the sauce as it thickens.

To serve, place a spoonful of vegetable stir-fry on each of four plates. Place a scoop of rice alongside the stir-fry and spoon the caramelized tofu alongside or on top of the rice. Sprinkle the sliced scallions over the top and garnish with cilantro sprigs and a lime wedge. Serve.

Soft Rosemary-Lemon Polenta
with Sweet Corn, Oyster Mushrooms, and Rainbow Chard

Creamy, soul-satisfying polenta is flavored with lemon and rosemary, paired with sweet corn, meaty oyster mushrooms, and earthy chard. Further enhanced with roasted tomato sauce and a sweet drizzle of balsamic reduction, this is a warm, soothing meal on a cold evening. SERVES 4

FOR THE POLENTA

4 cups Vegetable Stock (page 269) or store-bought low-sodium broth

Olive oil spray

½ small onion, diced small (¼ cup)

2 garlic cloves, minced

1 cup coarse stone-ground cornmeal

2 tablespoons grated Parmesan cheese

1 tablespoon extra-virgin olive oil

1½ teaspoons finely chopped fresh rosemary leaves

1 teaspoon finely chopped fresh thyme leaves

1 teaspoon grated lemon zest

½ teaspoon kosher salt, or to taste

¼ teaspoon freshly grated black pepper, or to taste

Prepare the polenta. Bring the vegetable stock to a boil in a medium saucepan. Meanwhile, spray a small sauté pan with olive oil and heat over medium-high heat. Add the onion and garlic and cook, stirring, until slightly translucent and fragrant but not at all brown, about 2 minutes. Scrape the onion and garlic into the stock. Whisking constantly, pour in the cornmeal in a slow, constant stream. Reduce the heat and cook at a low simmer, stirring often, until thick and creamy, 10 to 20 minutes. Stir in the Parmesan, olive oil, rosemary, thyme, and lemon zest. Season with the salt and pepper. Cover and set aside.

While the polenta is cooking, prepare the vegetables. Spray a large skillet with olive oil and heat over medium-high heat. Add the mushrooms, corn, and red onion and cook, stirring occasionally, until the mushrooms soften and the corn is cooked through, 4 to 5 minutes. Add the chard and cook until just wilted and beginning to release its liquid, about 2 minutes. Remove the pan from the heat and stir in the lemon juice and olive oil. Season with a pinch each of salt and pepper, or to taste.

To serve, divide the polenta among four plates or wide, shallow bowls. Spoon the sautéed mushroom, corn, and rainbow chard mixture on top or alongside the polenta. Spoon 2 tablespoons of tomato sauce on top of the polenta or vegetables. Drizzle a little balsamic reduction on top of the polenta and vegetables. Serve.

FOR THE VEGETABLES

Olive oil spray

9 ounces oyster mushrooms, cleaned
and sliced (3 cups)

1 cup fresh corn kernels (from about
2 ears corn)

¼ small red onion, diced (¼ cup)

4 ounces rainbow chard, leaves cut bite-
size and stems thinly sliced (2 cups)

2 teaspoons fresh lemon juice

1½ teaspoons extra-virgin olive oil

Pinch of kosher salt, or to taste

Pinch of freshly ground black pepper,
or to taste

½ cup Roasted Tomato Sauce (page 106),
warmed

Balsamic Reduction (page 270),
for serving

ROASTED TOMATO SAUCE

Slow-roasting the tomatoes for this sauce concentrates all of their flavor and sweetness, which are further enhanced by blending with balsamic vinegar and olive oil. Use this sauce for grilled fish and chicken, pasta, and pizza. It's even delicious stirred into soups. **MAKES 1 TO 1½ CUPS**

6 plum tomatoes, halved

½ teaspoon dried oregano

½ teaspoon dried basil

¼ teaspoon kosher salt, or to taste

¼ teaspoon freshly ground black pepper, or to taste

Olive oil spray

2 teaspoons balsamic vinegar

1 head garlic, roasted (page 111; optional)

¼ large ripe, red tomato, seeded and diced (¼ cup)

2 tablespoons chopped mixed fresh herbs, such as basil, oregano, and Italian parsley leaves

Preheat the oven to 400°F.

Arrange the tomato halves cut side up on a baking sheet. Sprinkle the tomatoes with the dried oregano, dried basil, salt, and pepper. Spray with olive oil. Bake until the tomatoes are slightly shriveled and dark brown and crisp on the edges, about 45 minutes.

Combine the roasted tomatoes and any juices in a blender along with the balsamic vinegar. Squeeze in the roasted garlic pulp, if using. Blend until smooth, 10 to 15 seconds. Push the mixture through a strainer into a saucepan; discard the seeds and skin. Season to taste with salt and pepper if needed. (If not using immediately, store in a tightly covered container in the refrigerator for up to 3 days.)

When ready to use, bring to a simmer over low heat. Remove from the heat and stir in the diced fresh tomatoes and fresh herbs.

Pinto Bean and Vegetable Chili Tostada
with Salsa Fresca and Avocado-Cilantro Cream

Meaty portobello mushrooms and rich spices fortify this bold chili. Stacked between layers of a crispy tostada, garnished with a generous serving of fresh salsa, and drizzled with avocado-cilantro cream, a tasty but humble bowl of chili is easily transformed into an elegant vegetarian meal. And it's a meal with some serious nutritional chops: pinto beans are a good source of protein and are an excellent source of fiber. A mere ½ cup has 6 grams of fiber—nearly one-quarter of your daily fiber needs.

Use very thin corn tortillas for the tostadas—they are usually marked "for chips" on the package. Regular, thicker corn tortillas harden in the oven and are unpleasant to eat. SERVES 8

1 cup dried pinto beans, picked over and rinsed, or 1 (15-ounce) can pinto beans, rinsed and drained

1 (3-inch) cinnamon stick

1 bay leaf

FOR THE SALSA FRESCA

1 large ripe, red tomato, diced (1¼ cups)

½ small red onion, diced (½ cup)

1 jalapeño chile, seeded and minced

¼ cup coarsely chopped fresh cilantro leaves

2 tablespoons fresh lime juice (from 1 lime)

½ teaspoon kosher salt

½ teaspoon freshly ground black pepper

FOR THE AVOCADO-CILANTRO CREAM

½ medium avocado

¼ cup light sour cream

Prepare the beans. If using dried beans, place the pinto beans in a bowl and cover with cold water by 2 inches. Let stand overnight. Drain the soaked beans and transfer the beans to a medium saucepan. Add the cinnamon stick, bay leaf, and cold water to cover by 2 inches, and place over medium heat. Bring to a boil, reduce the heat, and simmer until tender, about 1 hour. Drain if necessary, reserving ½ cup of the cooking liquid. Set the beans aside with the cinnamon stick and bay leaf.

While the beans are cooking, prepare the salsa fresca. In a large bowl, combine the tomato, red onion, jalapeño, cilantro, lime juice, salt, and pepper. Stir until well combined. Cover and refrigerate for at least 1 hour or up to 1 day before serving.

Prepare the avocado-cilantro cream. Combine the avocado, sour cream, lime juice, 2 tablespoons water, the garlic, salt, and pepper in a blender. Blend until smooth, about 30 seconds. Add the cilantro and blend until chopped, about 5 seconds more. The cream should be the consistency of mustard; add a small amount of water if necessary to achieve this consistency. Transfer the cream to a squeeze bottle. Alternatively the cream can be placed in a plastic zipper-lock bag, and when ready to serve, cut off one corner of the bag. (The cream can be covered and stored in the refrigerator for up to 3 to 4 hours before serving.)

CONTINUES ON PAGE 109

1½ teaspoons fresh lime juice

1 garlic clove, minced

¼ teaspoon kosher salt

⅛ teaspoon freshly ground black pepper

1 tablespoon chopped fresh cilantro leaves

FOR THE PINTO BEAN AND VEGETABLE CHILI

Canola oil spray

1 medium onion, diced (1 cup)

½ medium red bell pepper, seeded and diced (½ cup)

1 tablespoon minced garlic

1 serrano chile, seeded and minced

1 medium zucchini, diced (1 cup)

1 cup fresh corn kernels (from about 2 ears corn)

12 ounces portobello mushroom caps, gills scraped out with a spoon, diced (4 cups)

1 tablespoon chili powder

1½ teaspoons ground cumin

½ teaspoon kosher salt

1 (14-ounce) can crushed tomatoes

1 (8-ounce) can tomato sauce

FOR THE TOSTADAS

8 (5-inch) thin corn tortillas or whole wheat flour tortillas

Canola oil spray

CONTINUED FROM PAGE 107

Prepare the pinto bean and vegetable chili. Spray a heavy-bottomed saucepan with oil and heat over medium-high heat. Add the onion, bell pepper, garlic, and serrano chile, and cook, stirring, until soft, about 3 minutes. Add the zucchini, corn, and mushrooms and cook, stirring, until the vegetables are slightly soft and give off liquid, about 5 minutes. Add the chili powder, cumin, and salt and cook, stirring, until fragrant, about 30 seconds. Add the crushed tomatoes and stir well. Add the tomato sauce, the cooked, drained beans or canned beans, the reserved ½ cup bean cooking liquid or ½ cup water, and the cinnamon stick and bay leaf, if not already added. Stir well and bring to a boil. Reduce the heat to medium-low and simmer, stirring occasionally, for about 20 minutes. Remove and discard the cinnamon stick and bay leaf. Set aside.

While the chili is cooking, prepare the tostadas. Preheat the oven to 375°F. Have ready two nonstick baking sheets or line two regular baking sheets with parchment and spray lightly with oil.

Cut the tortillas in half. Place the half-moons on the baking sheet and bake for 10 minutes. Turn the tostadas over and bake until very crisp, 5 to 10 minutes.

To serve, spoon ½ cup vegetable chili into each of eight shallow bowls. Place a tostada on top of the chili, and then add another small scoop of chili. Place another tostada on top of the chili and top with a generous spoonful or two of salsa fresca. Squeeze the avocado-cilantro cream over the entire dish. Serve.

Vegetable Pavé *with Roasted Garlic Lentils and Dressed Field Greens*

This dish was born one summer day when I was faced with what seemed like mountains of eggplant, zucchini, and tomatoes from the Golden Door garden. By thinly slicing all the vegetables (use a serrated bread knife for best results), layering them, and then weighting them down before baking, they stick firmly to each other to form a firm, layered cake. This cake can be sliced into beautiful little squares, which is where this method gets its name: pavé is French for "cobblestone," and the word is used in cooking to describe both sweet and savory square-shaped delicacies. **SERVES 8**

FOR THE VEGETABLE PAVÉ

Olive oil spray

4 medium plum tomatoes, very thinly sliced

½ large eggplant (½ pound), very thinly sliced

1 medium onion, very thinly sliced

½ ounce Parmesan cheese, grated (½ cup)

½ cup chopped fresh basil leaves

3 teaspoons minced garlic

1 teaspoon dried thyme

1 teaspoon kosher salt, or to taste

½ teaspoon freshly ground black pepper, or to taste

1 large zucchini (½ pound), very thinly sliced

2 small carrots (¼ pound), very thinly sliced

Spray an 11 x 17 x 2-inch or similar-size baking pan with olive oil. Have ready another ovenproof pan that fits inside the baking pan. Set aside about 24 slices of tomato, depending on the size of your pan, to form an attractive top layer.

Using about half of the eggplant, cover the bottom of the pan with a layer of eggplant, slightly overlapping the slices if necessary. Cover with a thin layer of about one-sixth of the onion. Sprinkle a scant 1½ tablespoons of Parmesan over the top along with a scant 1½ tablespoons of the chopped basil, a little garlic, and a pinch each of dried thyme, salt, and pepper. Arrange one-fifth of the remaining tomato slices on top.

Using about half of the zucchini, arrange a single layer of zucchini on top, overlapping the slices slightly if necessary. Cover with another layer of onion, sprinkling with the cheese, basil, garlic, thyme, salt, and pepper and arranging some slices of tomato as before. Arrange half of the carrots on top. Cover with a thin layer of onion, and sprinkle over the cheese, basil, garlic, thyme, salt, and pepper, and a sparse layer of tomato slices as before. Repeat the entire process once more to use the remaining ingredients. Use the reserved tomatoes to form the top layer.

Cover with parchment paper. Place a pan that is slightly smaller than the baking pan holding the pavé on top of the parchment and fill it with 1 to 2 pounds of canned goods to weight the vegetables down. Refrigerate for at least 2 hours or overnight.

1 cup black, green, or brown lentils

2 heads garlic, roasted (below)

1¾ cups Vegetable Stock (page 269), store-bought low-sodium broth, or water

1 bay leaf

1 tablespoon balsamic vinegar

2 teaspoons extra-virgin olive oil

Pinch of kosher salt

Pinch of freshly ground black pepper

FOR THE GREENS

8 cups field greens or mesclun

¼ cup fresh lemon juice (from 2 lemons)

3 tablespoons extra-virgin olive oil

Pinch of kosher salt

Pinch of freshly ground black pepper

Preheat the oven to 375°F.

Remove the vegetable pavé from the refrigerator. Remove the cans but leave the pan in place. Bake until the vegetables are tender enough that a sharp knife slides through with little resistance, about 1 hour. Allow to rest with the pan in place for 10 minutes.

Meanwhile, prepare the lentils. In a medium saucepan, combine the lentils, roasted garlic, stock, and bay leaf. Bring just to a boil over medium heat. Reduce the heat and simmer gently, covered, until the lentils are tender and most of the liquid is absorbed, 30 to 45 minutes. Remove the pan from the heat. Stir in the balsamic vinegar, olive oil, salt, and pepper. Keep warm aside.

When ready to serve, toss the field greens with the lemon juice and olive oil, and season with salt and pepper. Use a sharp knife to cut the pavé into eight equal squares. Arrange a nice mound of dressed greens on each of eight plates. Place a square of pavé next to the greens and a spoonful of lentils alongside. Serve.

Roasting Garlic

Preheat the oven to 375°F.

Use a sharp knife to cut the top quarter off the heads of garlic to expose the cloves. Place the heads on a large sheet of aluminum foil. Spray the heads with olive oil, sprinkle with a little salt and pepper, and wrap them tightly in the foil. Bake until soft, about 45 minutes. Remove from the oven, unwrap the garlic, and let cool. When cool enough to handle, squeeze the roasted garlic from the husk.

Whole Wheat and Flax Fettuccine
with Asparagus and Porcini-Shiitake Cream

A velvety cream of porcini and shiitake mushrooms lightly coats fresh asparagus, spinach, and thyme tucked among long strands of flavorful fettuccine. At once luxurious and rustic, this dish also provides a powerful nutritional boost.

Basic pasta dough is a pretty straightforward affair: flour, eggs, water, and a little oil is all it takes to make one of the most popular foods in the world. At the Golden Door, I've tweaked that simple formula to make it one of the most healthful as well. I replace the standard white flour with whole wheat flour, which is more nutritious overall and is especially high in fiber and other micronutrients. I also add to each serving about 1 teaspoon ground flaxseed, high in fiber and, importantly, the best plant-based source of omega-3 fatty acids, which may help reduce the risk of heart disease. The health benefits of the shiitake mushrooms, too, should not be overlooked. They contain nearly all of the essential amino acids and provide a good vegetarian source of protein, too. **SERVES 6**

FOR THE FETTUCCINE

2 large eggs

1 tablespoon extra-virgin olive oil

2 cups whole wheat flour, plus more for kneading

2 tablespoons ground flaxseed

¼ teaspoon kosher salt

Cornmeal, for dusting

Make the pasta. In a medium bowl, whisk together the eggs, olive oil, and ⅓ cup water. In the work bowl of a food processor, combine the flour, flaxseed, and salt. With the processor running, pour the egg mixture through the feed tube. Process until the mixture comes together into a ball. If the dough seems too dry, add a few teaspoons of water and process for an additional 10 seconds. Remove the dough from the food processor. Dust the work surface with a little flour and knead the dough until smooth and elastic, about 4 to 5 minutes; add a little more flour as you knead if the dough is too sticky. Wrap the dough tightly in plastic wrap and place in refrigerator for 1 hour to rest.

Divide the dough into four equal pieces. Working with one piece at a time—keep the remaining dough covered with a towel to keep it from drying out—flatten each piece into an approximately 3 x 5-inch rectangle. Run the dough through the thickest setting of the pasta maker. Sprinkle the dough with a little flour if it sticks. If it falls apart, fold it in half or in thirds, like a business letter, and run it through the maker again. Repeat as necessary until the dough comes out in a fairly smooth

CONTINUES ON PAGE 114

Fresh shiitake mushrooms

FOR THE PORCINI-SHIITAKE CREAM

Olive oil spray

1 medium shallot, thinly sliced (¼ cup)

3 garlic cloves, thinly sliced

1 ounce dried porcini mushrooms (1 cup)

¼ ounce dried shiitake mushrooms (½ cup)

1 tablespoon unsalted butter

2 teaspoons fresh lemon juice

½ teaspoon kosher salt

¼ teaspoon freshly ground black pepper

12 ounces asparagus, woody ends trimmed and cut into 1-inch pieces (2 cups)

2 cups chopped spinach leaves

1 teaspoon chopped fresh thyme leaves

1 ounce Parmesan cheese, thinly shaved (⅓ cup; see Note), for serving

½ cup chopped fresh Italian parsley leaves, for serving

1 whole lemon, cut into 6 wedges, for serving

NOTE: *You can shave the cheese with a mandoline, a vegetable peeler, or a cheese slicer.*

CONTINUED FROM PAGE 112

sheet. Reduce the pasta maker's setting by one notch and run the sheet of pasta through one time. Continue to reduce the setting until you reach the second to last setting; you will have a very long, thin sheet of pasta. Cut the sheet crosswise in half.

Attach the fettuccine cutter to the pasta maker and run the sheet through it to cut into fettuccine. Alternatively, use a very sharp knife to cut crosswise into ¼-inch-wide strips.

Spread the fettuccine out on a sheet pan and toss with cornmeal to keep it from sticking. Repeat until all the dough is cut.

Bring a large pot of lightly salted water to a boil.

While the water is coming to a boil, prepare the porcini-shiitake cream. Spray a medium saucepan with olive oil and heat over medium-high heat. Add the shallot and garlic and cook, stirring, until tender and fragrant, 2 to 3 minutes. Add 2½ cups water and the dried porcini and shiitake mushrooms and bring just to the boil. Reduce the heat and simmer for 20 minutes.

Pour the mushroom mixture, including all of the liquid, into a blender—work in batches if necessary. Add the butter, lemon juice, salt, and pepper. Puree until smooth, about 1 minute. Set aside.

When water has come to a boil, prepare a bowl of ice water. Add the asparagus to the boiling water and cook for 1 minute. Use a slotted spoon to transfer the asparagus to the ice water. When completely cool, drain the asparagus well and set aside. Return the water in the pot to a boil if necessary. Stir in the pasta and cook until it is tender but still has bite, 2 to 4 minutes. Drain well.

Spray a large, nonstick skillet with olive oil and place over medium heat. Add the pasta, asparagus, spinach, and thyme. Toss to combine and cook until warmed through, about 1 minute. Add half of the porcini-shiitake cream and cook and toss for 1 to 2 minutes longer to heat through.

Mound the pasta in the center of six pasta bowls. Spoon the remaining porcini-shiitake cream on top of and around the pasta. Scatter the Parmesan and parsley over each serving. Place a lemon wedge on the side of each bowl and serve.

tips from the golden door
simple vegetable preparations

At the Golden Door we are extremely lucky to have a copious organic vegetable garden about thirty yards from the kitchen. And while I enjoy the praise heaped on us by guests after they eat the vegetable dishes we serve, I certainly can't take all the credit. A tasty dressing or sauce with the right balance of acidity, sweetness, and proper seasoning can heighten the best qualities of any dish, but when it comes down to it, the freshness and quality of the vegetables themselves are what make the difference. When the lettuce was picked just a few hours before it reaches the table and the tomato is still warm from the sun, my primary job is really to get out of the way of what the earth has given us. I need only highlight something that is already great.

I know, of course, that not everyone has access to an abundant vegetable garden, but in almost every part of the country you can find a local farmers' market where there will be a much wider array of vegetables and fruits than at the supermarket. The offerings at farmers' markets are usually mostly if not entirely organic, which is better for the farmers, the earth, and our bodies. Everything you find at a farmers' market in your area is by definition local and seasonal, which means it has been picked or harvested when fully ripe—not when it's firm enough to ship hundreds or thousands of miles, like most supermarket produce. At many markets you can also sign up for regular produce deliveries from local farms. These community supported agriculture farms, or CSAs, allow you to buy a seasonal share in a farm's harvest, guaranteeing you a season's worth of the freshest possible produce. Just as important, shopping at a local farmers' market or joining a CSA means that you are helping your local farmers and community and, therefore, your local economy. To find a farmers' market or CSA in your area, check out www.localharvest.org.

Portion control is one of the keys to eating healthy and light, but no one wants to eat a full meal and leave the table still hungry. By eating smaller portions of protein and starches and filling up on vegetables, you can significantly reduce your caloric and fat intake, get much-needed nutrients, and, no less important, leave the table satisfied. That's why vegetables are the stars of almost every meal or snack served at the Golden Door. Following are some quick and easy ideas for preparing vegetables. Serve a big platter of vegetables family-style so that each diner can have as much or as little as she or he wants. Or make the vegetables the highlight of the meal: serve them with whole-grains such as quinoa, brown rice, whole wheat couscous, or polenta; then drizzle over some good-quality extra-virgin olive oil, fresh lemon juice, and a pinch of salt for a satisfying light meal.

SIMPLEST COOKED VEGETABLES SERVES 4

This quick method takes off the raw edge but retains the crispness and vibrant color of fresh vegetables. Note that firmer vegetables such as carrots, cauliflower, turnips, and kohlrabi will take 1½ to 2 minutes, while more delicate snow peas or tender, thin asparagus may take only 30 seconds. If cooking a few different kinds of vegetables in the same pot, start the firmer vegetables first and add the fast-cooking ones a minute or so later. To check doneness, carefully fish a vegetable out of the water while cooking and taste it.

Choose seasonings depending on what else you are serving. For example, to serve vegetables with an Italian-inspired pasta dish, add extra-virgin olive oil, lemon juice, and some fresh basil; for an Asian meal, drizzle over some sesame oil, squeeze in a little lime juice, and toss in some chopped fresh cilantro leaves and scallions; for a Mediterranean meal, add a little olive oil, a squeeze each of lemon and orange juices, and some chopped fresh mint leaves.

1 pound fresh vegetables such as cauliflower, broccoli, or romanesco florets; diced carrots, turnips, or kohlrabi; trimmed snow peas, asparagus, or green beans; or shelled English peas

2 teaspoons extra-virgin olive or other oil

Juice of ½ lemon, 1 lime, or ¼ orange (optional)

1 to 2 tablespoons chopped fresh herbs such as basil, cilantro, parsley, savory, or thyme leaves

Pinch of kosher salt

Pinch of freshly ground black pepper

Bring a large pot of water to a rapid boil. Add the prepared vegetables to the boiling water and cook just until crisp-tender.

While the vegetables are cooking, heat a dry, heavy-bottomed sauté pan or saucepan (not nonstick) over medium-high heat. Use a skimmer or small strainer to remove the vegetables from the boiling water and immediately transfer them to the hot pan. Toss for about 30 seconds to evaporate the excess water from the vegetables. Remove the pan from the heat and add the oil, any other desired seasonings, and a pinch each of salt and pepper. Transfer the vegetables to a serving platter or individual plates and serve.

Maryland Crab Cakes with Caramelized Pineapple
and Roasted Red Pepper Remoulade

seafood

Teriyaki Black Cod

with Sticky Rice Cakes and Seared Baby Bok Choy

A staple of classic Japanese cooking, teriyaki is wonderful with not only seafood but also poultry, beef, vegetables, and tofu. Often, however, this versatile sauce can be quite sweet. My version uses fresh orange juice, which adds just a touch of natural sweetness as well as some acidity to temper the sweet mirin. Pouring some of the teriyaki sauce into the hot pan with the fish further reduces it so the sauce really coats the fish with a deep, caramel glaze that enhances the delectable moist, buttery, and tender qualities of black cod perfectly. Other good fish for this dish are Alaskan cod, true cod, sablefish, or wild salmon.

Searing each side of the sticky rice cake gives a nutty flavor and crisp texture. I also like to serve these rice cakes with vegetable stir-fries in place of plain rice. If you have a rice cooker, use it to prepare the rice according to the manufacturer's directions. If not, follow the instructions in the recipe to prepare it in a saucepan. **SERVES 6**

9 baby bok choy, halved lengthwise

FOR THE STICKY RICE CAKES

¾ cup sushi rice

Grapeseed or canola oil spray

2 tablespoons sliced scallions (white and green parts)

1 teaspoon minced garlic

1 tablespoon minced peeled fresh ginger

1 tablespoon unseasoned rice vinegar

1½ teaspoons mirin

Pinch of kosher salt

Pinch of freshly ground black pepper

Bring a large pot of water to a rapid boil. Prepare a bowl of ice water. Add the bok choy to the boiling water and cook for 30 seconds. Drain the bok choy and immediately transfer it to the ice water for 2 minutes to cool. Drain the bok choy and set aside on a clean kitchen towel to soak up excess moisture.

Prepare the sticky rice cakes. Put the rice in a large bowl and cover with cold water. Use your hand to swish the rice around a few times. Drain and repeat until the water in the bowl is clear; you may need to rinse it several times.

Put the rice in a small, heavy-bottomed saucepan and add water to cover by 1 inch. Cover the pan; for best results, do not uncover the pan at any time during cooking. Bring to a boil over medium-high heat, 4 to 5 minutes; you will be able to tell the water is boiling by the large amount of steam pouring out from under the lid. Reduce the heat to low and simmer, covered, for 10 minutes. Remove the pan from the heat and let stand, covered, for 15 minutes.

Spray a small sauté pan with grapeseed oil and heat over medium heat. Add the scallions, garlic, and ginger and cook, stirring, until just softened and fragrant, about 30 seconds. Fold the scallion mixture into the warm, cooked rice along with the vinegar, mirin, salt, and pepper.

CONTINUES ON PAGE 124

FOR THE BLACK COD

½ cup low-sodium soy sauce

¾ cup fresh orange juice (from 3 oranges)

¼ cup mirin

1 teaspoon minced peeled fresh ginger

½ teaspoon cornstarch

6 (4-ounce) skinless black cod fillets, each 1 inch thick

¼ teaspoon freshly ground black pepper

Grapeseed or canola oil spray

½ cup thinly sliced scallions (white and light green parts), for serving

1 tablespoon sesame seeds, toasted (see page 27), for serving

CONTINUED FROM PAGE 122

Line a platter or baking sheet with parchment paper sprayed with oil or with waxed paper. Have a separate bowl of water ready. Dip your hands into the water and scoop up ¼ cup rice. Form it into a tightly packed cake about 2 inches thick and place the cake on the platter. Repeat with the remaining rice to form five more cakes. Set aside in the refrigerator.

Meanwhile, in a small saucepan, combine the soy sauce, orange juice, mirin, and ginger. Bring to a boil and reduce the heat to low. Simmer just until reduced by half, 30 to 40 minutes. In a small dish, mix the cornstarch and 1 teaspoon water and stir this slurry into the simmering sauce. Simmer 30 seconds and remove the pan from the heat.

Preheat the oven to 400°F.

Season each fillet with pepper. Spray an ovenproof sauté pan (preferably non-stick) with grapeseed oil and heat over medium-high heat until hot but not smoking. Lay the fish in the pan flesh side down (not the side where the skin was); you should hear a sizzle. Cook until golden brown, about 3 minutes. Turn the fish over and place the pan in the oven. Cook until the fish is just cooked through, 6 to 8 minutes. Pour half of the teriyaki sauce over the fish. The sauce will bubble and simmer. Gently turn the fish over and gently swirl the pan to coat the fish. Turn the fish over again.

While the fish is cooking, finish the bok choy: spray a nonstick skillet with grape-seed oil and heat over medium-high heat until hot but not smoking. Place the bok choy in the pan cut side down and cook until deep brown, 3 to 4 minutes. Turn the bok choy over and cook 1 minute. Remove the bok choy from the pan.

To finish the rice cakes, spray a nonstick skillet with oil and heat over medium heat until hot but not smoking. Add the rice cakes and cook until heated through and golden on both sides, 2 to 3 minutes per side.

Divide the bok choy halves among six plates. Place a rice cake and a fillet of teriyaki cod next to the bok choy and drizzle teriyaki sauce around the plate and over the fish. Sprinkle each serving with sliced scallions and sesame seeds. Serve.

Miso-Glazed Mero

with Shiitake Mushroom Quinoa and Grilled Pineapple and Mango Salsa

We serve a lot of fish and shellfish at the Golden Door because it is a delicious and versatile source of lean protein and other valuable nutrients, but I, like many others, am always concerned about how the seafood we serve is raised and caught. The excellent Seafood Watch program, run by the Monterey Bay Aquarium, recommends which fish and shellfish to buy and which to avoid, based on whether or not they are raised and/or fished under sustainable conditions. The information is regularly updated and can be accessed on its website (see Resources, page 283). It also offers pocket-size guides that target specific regions of the country and are very useful to have when shopping.

Mero, used in this recipe, is a species of grouper fished using sustainable practices in deep waters off the coast of the northwest Hawaiian Islands, between Hawaii and Japan. This mero is rated "good" by the Seafood Watch program. The origin of the mero you buy is important because mero from the main Hawaiian Islands, the U. S. Atlantic, the Gulf of Mexico, or the Pacific off the coast of South America is on Seafood Watch's "avoid" list.

Mero is sometimes confused with Chilean sea bass, which should be avoided because it has been grossly overfished using less-than-sustainable practices. If you cannot find mero, black cod, Pacific halibut, or striped bass are good substitutes. The miso marinade is also very tasty on wild salmon. **SERVES 6**

FOR THE MISO-GLAZED MERO

Large knob of fresh ginger

¼ cup mirin

¼ cup white or light yellow miso paste

¼ cup sake or dry white wine

1 tablespoon low-sodium soy sauce

6 (4-ounce) skinless mero fillets

Prepare the mero. Grate the unpeeled ginger on the large-holed side of a box grater until you have about ⅓ cup. Collect the grated ginger in your hand and squeeze over a bowl to extract the juice. You should have 1 tablespoon juice; if you don't, grate more ginger and squeeze out the juice until you do. Discard the grated ginger.

Pour the ginger juice into a small bowl along with the mirin, miso, sake, and soy sauce. Whisk together until well blended. Place the mero fillets in a shallow dish or pan big enough to hold the fish in a single layer. Pour the marinade on top and turn the fish over so it is completely coated. Cover the pan and refrigerate for at least 2 hours and up to 24 hours; the longer the fish marinates, the better. Remove the pan from the refrigerator about 30 minutes before cooking the fish.

CONTINUES ON PAGE 127

FOR THE GRILLED PINEAPPLE AND MANGO SALSA

6 (¼-inch-thick) slices fresh pineapple

4 (¼-inch-thick) slices red onion

¼ large mango, diced (½ cup)

2 tablespoons coarsely chopped fresh cilantro leaves

½ serrano or jalapeño chile, seeded and minced (optional)

1 to 2 tablespoons fresh lime juice, to taste

Pinch of kosher salt, or to taste

Pinch of freshly ground black pepper, or to taste

FOR THE QUINOA

1 cup quinoa

Grapeseed or canola oil spray

⅓ cup thinly sliced scallions (white and green parts)

2 garlic cloves, minced

2 teaspoons minced peeled fresh ginger

10 ounces shiitake mushrooms, stemmed and diced (3 cups)

¼ teaspoon kosher salt, or to taste

Pinch of freshly ground black pepper, or to taste

CONTINUED FROM PAGE 125

Prepare the salsa. Prepare a medium-hot grill or heat a grill pan over medium-high heat. Spray the pineapple and onion slices on both sides with grapeseed oil. Grill 2 minutes per side, until there are grill marks on both sides and the onion is softened. Remove the pineapple and onion from the grill and let cool to room temperature.

Dice the pineapple and onion and transfer to a large bowl. Add the mango, cilantro, serrano, lime juice, salt, and pepper. (The salsa may be made several hours in advance, covered, and stored in the refrigerator. Serve at room temperature.)

Prepare the quinoa. Place the quinoa in a large bowl and cover with cold water. Use your hand to swish it around a few times. Drain and repeat until the water in the bowl is clear. In a medium pot, combine the quinoa with 1¼ cups of water. Bring just to a boil. Reduce the heat and simmer, covered, for 15 minutes. Remove the pan from the heat and let stand, covered, for 5 minutes to steam and finish cooking.

Spray a large skillet with grapeseed oil and heat over medium-high heat. Add the scallions, garlic, and ginger to the pan and cook, stirring, until fragrant, about 30 seconds. Add the mushrooms and cook until the mushrooms soften slightly, 3 to 4 minutes, adding 1 to 2 teaspoons water if necessary to prevent sticking. Scrape the mixture into the quinoa and use a fork to fluff the quinoa and incorporate the mushrooms. Season with salt and pepper.

Position an oven rack at the highest level and preheat the broiler to high; the broiler should be just above the fish so it caramelizes nicely.

Arrange the fish in a shallow pan and top each fillet with a teaspoon of marinade. Broil the fish, checking it often and turning the pan occasionally to prevent burning. When the top of the fish is dark caramel brown, after 5 to 6 minutes, remove the pan from the oven and pierce the fish with a toothpick; it should pass with no resistance. If the fish is not done, reduce the oven temperature to 450°F. Return the fish to a low rack in the oven to finish cooking, 3 to 5 minutes.

To serve, divide the quinoa among six plates. Lay a piece of fish on top of or alongside the quinoa. Top the fish with a generous spoonful of salsa. Serve, passing the remaining salsa at the table.

Tuna Niçoise *with Lemon-Caper Vinaigrette*

Classic Niçoise salad is one of my favorite salads; my version is fairly true to the original but with a much lighter vinaigrette. When I have them on hand I like to use imported white anchovies, but any high-quality anchovies packed in pure olive oil are delicious in this dish.

Although tuna is traditional, at the Golden Door we often replace the seared tuna with other seafood such as grilled, seared, or poached prawns, halibut, salmon, sea bass, cod, or seared sea scallops. Any of these will make a wonderful salad, so if your market does not have tuna, just go with the freshest catch of the day.

I like to serve this salad family-style, which is fun and informal and allows each diner to take as much or as little of each component as desired. For individual servings, arrange the ingredients on six separate plates. **SERVES 6**

18 ounces baby red or fingerling potatoes

3 large eggs

8 ounces haricots verts or other thin green beans (3 cups)

1½ pounds 2-inch-thick tuna steak, preferably ahi

½ teaspoon kosher salt

¼ teaspoon freshly ground black pepper

Grapeseed oil spray

Lemon-Caper Vinaigrette (page 252)

1 heart of romaine lettuce, chopped (6 cups)

1 head red leaf lettuce, such as red romaine, lolla rosa, or red oak, chopped (6 cups)

1½ pints cherry tomatoes, halved (3 cups)

12 anchovy fillets

⅓ cup chopped pitted Niçoise or kalamata olives

Place the potatoes in a medium saucepan and add enough cold water to cover by 2 inches. Bring just to a boil over medium-high heat. Reduce the heat and simmer until the potatoes are tender when pierced with a knife or fork, about 25 minutes. Drain and let cool to room temperature. Use a sharp knife to cut the potatoes lengthwise in half. Set aside.

Put the eggs in a small saucepan and add enough cold water to cover by 1 inch. Bring to a boil over high heat. Immediately turn down the heat and cook at a very low simmer for 10 minutes. While the eggs are simmering, prepare a bowl of ice water. As soon as the eggs are cooked, transfer them to the ice-water bath until cool. Peel the eggs and set them aside.

Add more ice to the ice-water bath if it has melted. Bring a large saucepan of water to a boil. Add the haricots verts to the boiling water and cook for 1 minute. Use a slotted or mesh spoon to immediately transfer the beans to the ice water until cool. Drain thoroughly and set aside.

Season the tuna on all sides with salt and pepper. Spray a cast-iron skillet with grapeseed oil and heat it over high heat until hot but not smoking. Add the tuna to the pan; you should hear a sizzle. Sear until nicely browned on both sides and rare in the center, 2 minutes per side. To cook the tuna to medium, lower the heat to medium-high and cook 3 to 4 minutes on each side. Transfer the tuna to a cutting board.

Prepare the lemon-caper vinaigrette.

In a large bowl, toss the romaine heart and red lettuce with ¾ cup of the dressing and a pinch each of salt and pepper. Transfer the dressed greens to the center of a large platter.

Arrange the potatoes, eggs, green beans, tomatoes, and anchovies in separate piles around the greens. Use a very sharp knife to slice the tuna into ⅛-inch-thick slices and fan them on top of the greens. Sprinkle the chopped olives on top of the tuna and drizzle a small amount of dressing over the tuna and the remaining dressing over the vegetables. Serve.

Sesame-Crusted Wild Salmon Salad *with Creamy Miso Dressing*

A sprinkling of sesame seeds adds great flavor and crunch to wild salmon fillets served with a crisp, tangy Asian-style slaw and creamy miso dressing. **SERVES 4**

1 cup fresh or frozen shelled edamame beans

1 small napa or savoy cabbage, quartered lengthwise and shredded (6 cups)

1 small English cucumber, peeled, seeded, and cut into matchsticks (2 cups)

2 medium carrots, cut into matchsticks (1 cup)

1 red bell pepper, seeded and cut into matchsticks (2 cups)

1 cup (about 2 ounces) bean sprouts

2 tablespoons unseasoned rice vinegar

2 tablespoons mirin

2 tablespoons fresh lime juice (from 1 lime)

1 teaspoon toasted sesame oil

Creamy Miso Dressing (page 262)

4 wonton wrappers

Grapeseed or canola oil spray

4 (4-ounce) skinless, wild salmon fillets, each 1 inch thick

½ teaspoon kosher salt

¼ teaspoon freshly ground black pepper

4 teaspoons sesame seeds

Fresh cilantro leaves, for serving

4 lime wedges, for serving

Bring a small pot of water to a rapid boil. Prepare a bowl of ice water. Add the edamame beans to the boiling water. Bring the water back to a boil and cook for 3 minutes. Drain the edamame and immediately transfer them to the ice water to cool. Drain thoroughly and set aside.

In a large bowl, combine the edamame, cabbage, cucumber, carrots, bell pepper, and bean sprouts. In a small bowl whisk together the rice vinegar, mirin, lime juice, and sesame oil until well blended. Pour over the cabbage mixture and toss to coat evenly. Cover and refrigerate until ready to serve.

Prepare the creamy miso dressing.

Preheat the oven to 350°F.

Thinly slice the wonton wrappers. Spread out in a single layer on baking sheet and spray with oil. Bake for 10 minutes. Use a spatula to turn the wonton strips over and bake until golden brown, about 5 minutes. Remove from the oven and let cool.

Increase the oven temperature to 400°F.

Spray an ovenproof skillet (preferably nonstick) with grapeseed oil and heat it over medium heat until hot but not smoking. Season each salmon fillet with salt and pepper and sprinkle the sesame seeds on one side of the fillets. Place the fillets seeded side down in the hot pan; you should hear a sizzle. Sear until the seeds are golden brown, about 3 minutes. Turn the salmon over and place the pan in the oven. For medium-rare, cook until the salmon is opaque on the outside and dark pink and slightly raw in the very center, 5 to 6 minutes. Remove the pan from the oven.

Divide the cabbage salad among four plates. Arrange a salmon fillet, seeded side up, next to the salad and drizzle creamy miso dressing over the fish and around the plate. Top each serving with wonton crisps, cilantro leaves, and a lime wedge. Serve.

Wild Salmon *with Quick-Preserved Lemon Mashed Potatoes and Asparagus Vinaigrette*

True preserved lemons must be brined in salt, sugar, and lemon juice for weeks before they can be used. The quick method used here instead yields soft, fragrant, lemon peels without bitterness or acidity that can be used to give delightful lemon flavor and perfume to mashed potatoes, polenta, or risotto. It is important that the lemony milk be ready by the time the potatoes are cooked, for the potatoes must be mashed when hot.

This springtime dish is a perfect marriage of bright colors and aromas. Serve with sautéed spinach, roasted asparagus, or English peas (pages 117 and 118), if desired. **SERVES 6**

Asparagus Vinaigrette (page 255)

FOR THE MASHED POTATOES

1¼ **pounds russet or Yukon Gold potatoes, peeled and diced (3 cups)**

3 **lemons**

1 **tablespoon plus ½ teaspoon kosher salt**

1 **tablespoon sugar**

1 **cup 2% low-fat milk**

⅛ **teaspoon freshly ground white pepper**

FOR THE SALMON

6 **(4-ounce) skinless wild salmon fillets, each 1 inch thick**

½ **teaspoon kosher salt**

¼ **teaspoon freshly ground white pepper**

Olive oil spray

Prepare the asparagus vinaigrette and set aside.

Prepare the potatoes. Put the potatoes in a large saucepan and add enough cold water to cover by 1 inch. Bring to a boil and simmer just until fork-tender, about 25 minutes. Drain and return the potatoes to the saucepan. Place the pan over medium heat and shake and toss the potatoes until any excess moisture has evaporated, about 1 minute. If you have a ricer or food mill, press or mill the potatoes back into the pan.

While the potatoes are cooking, use a vegetable peeler to remove the yellow zest from the lemons, removing as little of the bitter, white pith as possible. Put the zest in a small saucepan with 1 tablespoon salt, the sugar, and 2 cups cold water. Bring to a boil, and boil for 5 minutes. Drain. Return the lemon peel to the saucepan and add 2 cups fresh, cold water. Bring to a boil, and boil for 5 minutes. Drain. Transfer the peels to a blender.

Pour the milk into a small saucepan and set over medium-low heat. Bring just to a simmer and add to the blender with the lemon peel. Blend until smooth, 30 seconds. Pour the lemony milk into the hot potatoes. If the potatoes have been riced or milled, fold the milk in; if not, use a potato masher to mash the potatoes while slowly pouring in the hot milk. Season with ½ teaspoon salt and the white pepper. Cover and keep warm.

Preheat the oven to 400°F.

Prepare the salmon. Season each salmon fillet with the salt and white pepper. Spray an ovenproof sauté pan with olive oil and heat over medium-high heat until hot but not smoking. Place the salmon in the pan flesh side down (not the side where the skin was); you should hear a sizzle. Cook until golden brown, 2 to 3 minutes. Turn the salmon over and place the pan in the oven. For medium-rare, cook until the salmon is opaque on the outside and dark pink and slightly raw in the very center, 4 to 6 minutes. Remove the pan from the oven.

To serve, place a spoonful of potatoes on each of six plates. Arrange a salmon fillet next to the potatoes on each plate and drizzle the asparagus vinaigrette over and around the fish. Serve.

Barramundi *with Butternut Squash Risotto and Citrus-Almond Salsa*

Warm creamy risotto and sweet, tender butternut squash create a tasty palette of flavors to accent barramundi, a mild, moist fish. Barramundi farmed in the United States is an excellent seafood choice as it is raised using the most sustainable farming practices, recycling and purifying 99 percent of the water used and discharging almost no waste. It has a clean, mild taste and naturally high oil content so it cooks up moist. Use barramundi in place of overfished species such as most snappers, grouper, or Chilean sea bass. It makes a good substitute for most medium-firm, mild white fish and is available year-round. Avoid imported barramundi as it is not raised as responsibly as in the United States and is not of the same high quality.

I use the more tender flesh from the neck of the squash for the risotto because it's easier to dice small than is the firmer flesh from the bulb end.

Serve with wilted spinach, kale, or chard, or blanched asparagus or romanesco (page 16), if desired. **SERVES 4**

FOR THE SALSA

1 orange

1 lemon

1 lime

2 tablespoons fresh orange juice

1 tablespoon fresh lemon juice

2 tablespoons sliced almonds, toasted (page 135) and coarsely chopped

1 tablespoon extra-virgin olive oil

Pinch of kosher salt, or to taste

Pinch of freshly ground white pepper, or to taste

Prepare the salsa. Following the instructions on page 51, peel and section the orange, lemon, and lime, holding the fruit over a medium bowl to catch the fruit sections. Add the orange and lemon juices, the almonds, olive oil, salt, and pepper. Toss until well combined. Cover and refrigerate up to 3 hours.

Prepare the risotto. Pour the stock into a small saucepan and bring just to a simmer over low heat. Reduce the heat to very low to keep it hot.

Pour the olive oil into a heavy-bottomed saucepan and heat over medium-high heat. Add the onion and cook, stirring, until just softened but not brown, 2 to 3 minutes. Add the rice and cook, stirring, until the rice has absorbed the oil and is shiny and smells slightly toasted, about 2 minutes. Add the wine and cook, stirring, until the liquid is almost completely absorbed.

Reduce the heat to medium. Add ⅓ cup of the hot chicken stock and cook, stirring constantly, until the stock is absorbed. Continue to add the stock ⅓ cup at a time, stirring constantly until it is absorbed, until the rice is cooked a little more than halfway, about 15 minutes. Stir in the butternut squash and continue to cook, adding stock and stirring constantly until the rice has formed a starchy sauce and

2 cups Chicken Stock (page 268) or store-bought low-sodium broth

2 teaspoons olive oil

¼ medium onion, cut into ⅛- to ¼-inch dice (¼ cup)

½ cup arborio rice

½ cup dry white wine

1 cup diced butternut squash, in ¼-inch pieces

¼ cup thinly sliced scallions (white and green parts)

¼ teaspoon kosher salt, or to taste

⅛ freshly ground white pepper, or to taste

FOR THE BARRAMUNDI

4 (4-ounce) skinless barramundi fillets

¼ teaspoon kosher salt

¼ teaspoon freshly ground white pepper

Grapeseed oil spray

1 tablespoon fresh lemon juice

1 tablespoon fresh lime juice

1 tablespoon thinly sliced scallions (white and green parts)

the grains are tender but still have a little bite, about 5 minutes. The squash should be tender but not mushy. You may not need all of the stock. Remove the pan from the heat and stir in the scallions, salt, and white pepper.

Preheat the oven to 400°F.

Once you've started the risotto, prepare the fish. Season each fillet with the salt and pepper. Spray an ovenproof skillet with grapeseed oil and heat it over medium-high heat until hot but not smoking. Lay the fish in the pan flesh side down (not the side where the skin was); you should hear a sizzle. Shake the pan a few times to prevent the fish from sticking. Cook until golden brown, 3 to 4 minutes. Turn the fish over and place the pan in the oven. Cook until the fish is just barely opaque in the center when pierced with a thin-bladed knife, 6 to 8 minutes, depending on the thickness of the fish. Squeeze the lemon and lime juices over the fish.

To serve, stir the scallions into the salsa. Divide the risotto among six shallow bowls. Place a barramundi fillet on top of or alongside each serving of risotto. Top the fish with a spoonful of salsa. Serve.

Toasting Almonds

Put the almonds in a small cast-iron skillet or other small, heavy skillet over medium heat. Cook, stirring occasionally, until the almonds are golden and fragrant, about 4 minutes. Immediately transfer the almonds to a plate to cool.

Pan-Roasted Halibut
with Crab Mashed Potatoes, Spinach, and Gazpacho Vinaigrette

This beautiful dish is especially welcome during the summer months when all the ingredients are at peak season. Unfortunately, Atlantic flat-fish populations have been overfished, so wild-caught Pacific halibut is the best option for this dish. If it is not available where you are, use black bass, sablefish, black cod, Alaskan cod, or barramundi in its place. **SERVES 6**

Gazpacho Vinaigrette (page 256)

FOR THE CRAB MASHED POTATOES

1¼ pounds Yukon Gold, russet, or red potatoes, peeled and diced (3 cups)

1 cup 2% low-fat milk

½ teaspoon kosher salt

⅛ teaspoon freshly ground white pepper

Olive oil spray

6 ounces crab meat, preferably fresh blue or Dungeness in season or good-quality canned lump, picked over to remove any bits of shell or cartilage (1 cup)

2 tablespoons chopped fresh Italian parsley leaves

1½ teaspoons grated lemon zest

1 teaspoon fresh lemon juice

¼ teaspoon Old Bay seasoning

Prepare the gazpacho vinaigrette.

Prepare the potatoes. Put the potatoes in a large saucepan and add enough cold water to cover by 1 inch. Bring to a boil and simmer until fork-tender, about 25 minutes. Drain and return the potatoes to the saucepan. Place the pan over medium heat and shake and toss the potatoes until any excess moisture has evaporated, about 1 minute. If you have a ricer or food mill, press or mill the potatoes back into the pan.

While the potatoes are cooking, prepare the garnish. In a small bowl, stir together the cucumber, tomato, red bell pepper, olive oil, lemon juice, salt, and pepper. Set aside.

Preheat the oven to 350°F.

To finish the potatoes, heat the milk in a small saucepan just until it comes to a simmer. Pour the milk into the hot potatoes. If the potatoes have been riced or milled, fold the hot milk in; if not, use a potato masher to mash the potatoes while slowly pouring in the hot milk. Season with salt and pepper.

Spray a small skillet with olive oil and heat over medium heat. Add the crab and toss until just warmed through. Remove the pan from the heat and gently stir in the parsley, lemon zest, lemon juice, and Old Bay seasoning. Fold the crab into the potatoes. Cover and keep warm.

CONTINUES ON PAGE 138

FOR THE GARNISH

¼ small English cucumber, seeded and diced (½ cup)

¼ large ripe, red tomato, seeded and diced (¼ cup)

¼ medium red bell pepper, seeded and diced (¼ cup)

2 teaspoons extra-virgin olive oil

2 teaspoons fresh lemon juice

Pinch of kosher salt, or to taste

Pinch of freshly ground black pepper, or to taste

FOR THE HALIBUT

6 (4-ounce) skinless halibut fillets

½ teaspoon kosher salt

¼ teaspoon freshly ground white pepper

Olive oil spray

FOR THE GARLIC-LEMON SPINACH

Olive oil spray

3 bunches whole fresh spinach, trimmed, rinsed, and drained

2 garlic cloves, sliced

½ medium lemon

Pinch of kosher salt, or to taste

Pinch of freshly ground black pepper, or to taste

CONTINUED FROM PAGE 136

Prepare the halibut. Season each of the halibut fillets with salt and pepper. Spray an ovenproof sauté pan (preferably nonstick) with olive oil and place over medium-high heat until hot but not smoking. Add the halibut fillets flesh side down (not the side where the skin was); you should hear a sizzle. Cook until golden brown, about 3 minutes. Flip the fillets and place the pan in the oven until the fish is just cooked through, 6 to 8 minutes.

Prepare the spinach. While the halibut is roasting, spray a large sauté pan with olive oil and heat over medium-high heat until hot but not smoking. Add the spinach with water still clinging to its leaves and the garlic and use tongs to toss the leaves. When the spinach is half cooked—some raw leaves should be visible—squeeze in the juice of the lemon and add the salt and pepper. Toss quickly and remove the pan from the heat.

To serve, stir the gazpacho vinaigrette and pour ¼ to ⅓ cup onto each of six plates or into six large, shallow bowls, spreading it on part of the plate or across the bottom of each bowl. Divide the mashed potatoes among the plates or bowls, spreading it evenly on top of the vinaigrette. Arrange the spinach next to or on top of the potatoes. Top with the fish and a dollop of the garnish. Serve.

Pan-Roasted Lobster
with Basil Potato Puree and Warm Tomato-Corn Salad

This dish bursts with summer flavors and textures: succulent lobster, earthy basil, sweet corn, and juicy tomatoes. Use Maine or spiny lobster for this dish, but avoid the spiny lobster imported from the Caribbean, as the industry there is not well regulated. Look for lobster from the northeastern United States and Canada or the Baja peninsula. **SERVES 6**

FOR THE LOBSTER

3 (1½-pound) live lobsters

2 tablespoons olive oil

¼ teaspoon kosher salt

¼ teaspoon freshly ground black pepper

FOR THE BASIL POTATO PUREE

1¼ pounds Yukon Gold, russet, or red creamer potatoes, peeled and diced (about 3 cups)

1 cup 2% low-fat milk

½ cup packed fresh basil leaves

½ cup loosely packed fresh Italian parsley leaves

½ teaspoon kosher salt, or to taste

⅛ teaspoon freshly ground black pepper, or to taste

FOR THE TOMATO-CORN SALAD

Olive oil spray

½ medium onion, diced (½ cup)

2 garlic cloves, minced

Bring a large pot of water to a boil over high heat. Cook the lobsters, in two batches if necessary, until just two-thirds cooked, 8 to 10 minutes.

Put the potatoes in a large saucepan and add enough cold water to cover by 1 inch. Bring to a boil, lower the heat, and simmer until fork-tender, about 25 minutes. Drain and return the potatoes to the saucepan. Place the pan over medium heat and shake and toss the potatoes until any excess moisture has evaporated, about 1 minute. If you have a ricer or food mill, press or mill the potatoes back into the pan.

If using Maine lobsters, remove the claws and knuckles and set aside. Lay one lobster back side down on a cutting board, and cut it lengthwise in half through the soft underside with a sharp knife. Repeat with the remaining lobsters. Brush the claws and lobster halves all over with the olive oil and season with salt and pepper. Heat two large sauté pans over high heat until hot. Place the claws and lobster halves, flesh side down, in the pans; you should hear a sizzle. Cook until golden brown, about 3 minutes. Turn over and cook for 1 more minute (the lobster halves will be shell side down). Remove from the heat, and tent with foil to keep warm.

Finish preparing the potato puree. In a small saucepan, heat the milk just until it reaches a simmer. Combine the basil, parsley, and the scalding milk in a blender and blend for 1 minute, until very well combined. Add the herb-milk mixture, salt, and pepper to the hot potatoes. If the potatoes have been riced or milled, fold the hot milk in; if not, use a potato masher to mash the potatoes while mixing in the hot milk. Cover and keep warm.

CONTINUES ON PAGE 141

1½ cups fresh corn kernels (from about 2 ears of corn)

2 large ripe, red tomatoes, seeded and diced (2 cups)

2 tablespoons extra-virgin olive oil

2 tablespoons fresh lemon juice (from 1 lemon)

1½ teaspoons chopped fresh parsley leaves

1½ teaspoons chopped fresh chives

1½ teaspoons chopped fresh tarragon leaves

1½ teaspoons chopped fresh chervil leaves

Pinch of kosher salt, or to taste

Pinch of freshly ground black pepper, or to taste

Lemon wedges, for serving

CONTINUED FROM PAGE 139

Prepare the tomato-corn salad. Spray a medium skillet with olive oil and heat over medium heat. Add the onion and garlic and cook, stirring, until translucent but not brown, 2 to 3 minutes. Add the corn and cook, stirring, until the corn is warmed through, 2 to 3 minutes. Transfer the onion and corn mixture to a medium bowl. Add the diced tomato, olive oil, lemon juice, parsley, chives, tarragon, chervil, salt, and pepper. Gently toss to combine.

Remove the lobster meat from the shell in one piece. If using Maine lobsters, crack the claws and remove the meat from the claws and knuckles just before serving. Chop the knuckle meat and add it to the warm tomato-corn salad.

Spoon some basil-potato puree onto each of six plates. Place the meat of one lobster half and claw next to the potato puree. Spoon the warm tomato-corn salad on top of or next to the lobster along with some of the juices. Serve with lemon wedges.

Dungeness Crab, Quinoa, and Mango Stack
with Lemon-Tahini Dressing

I was born and raised in Maryland, and I have loved crab for as long as I can remember. Like most native East Coasters, I first favored the blue crab. When I moved to San Francisco as an adult, I discovered the much larger but very delicious Dungeness crab and fell in love all over again.

Fresh-picked crab meat in season is always best, but if it is not available to you locally, you still have some good options. Opt for canned backfin, lump, or jumbo lump crab meat in the refrigerated section of your supermarket. Avoid the shelf-stable canned crab meat stocked in the same section as canned tuna.

This colorful and delicious stack is made by layering the ingredients in individual ring molds. If you don't already have them, there's no need to run out to the kitchen supply store; head to your local hardware store instead. Buy a length of 3-inch PVC pipe and have the store cut it into 3-inch lengths. Just run them through the dishwasher when you get home and they will be ready to use over and over again for this or other savory or sweet stacks. **SERVES 6**

½ cup quinoa

1 pound cooked Dungeness, King, or blue crab meat, picked over to remove any bits of shell or cartilage

2 tablespoons white wine vinegar

½ cup chopped fresh Italian parsley leaves

1 tablespoon grated lemon zest

2 teaspoons Old Bay seasoning

Lemon-Tahini Dressing (page 259)

1 avocado, peeled and cut into ¼-inch dice

½ small English cucumber, peeled, seeded, and cut into ¼-inch dice (1 cup)

1 large ripe, red tomato, seeded and cut into ¼-inch dice (¼ cup)

Put the quinoa in a large bowl and cover with cold water. Use your hand to swish the quinoa around a few times. Drain and repeat until the water in the bowl is clear; you may need to rinse it several times. In a small saucepan, combine the quinoa with ¾ cup water. Bring just to a boil. Reduce the heat and simmer, covered, for 15 minutes. Remove the pan from the heat and let stand, covered, for 5 minutes to steam and finish cooking. Transfer the quinoa to a large bowl and let cool; transfer to the refrigerator until cold.

In a medium bowl combine the crab, vinegar, ¼ cup of the parsley, the lemon zest, and Old Bay seasoning. Gently toss with a fork until well combined. Cover and refrigerate until needed.

Prepare the lemon-tahini dressing.

When the quinoa is completely cool, add the avocado, cucumber, tomato, chives, 2 tablespoons of the lemon juice, 2 teaspoons of the olive oil, and a pinch each of salt and pepper to the bowl. Toss gently until well combined.

2 tablespoons finely chopped fresh
chives

3½ tablespoons fresh lemon juice
(from 2 lemons)

4 teaspoons extra-virgin olive oil

Kosher salt and freshly ground black
pepper

1 large ripe mango, peeled and cut into
¼-inch dice

1 tablespoon fresh lime juice

Olive oil spray

6 cups mixed leaf lettuce

In a small bowl, combine the mango and lime juice. Toss gently to combine. Cover and refrigerate the quinoa mixture and the mango separately until needed, or for up to 3 hours.

Lightly spray with oil the inside of six 3-inch ring molds. Place a ring mold on each of six plates. Divide the crab mixture evenly among the molds. Use a flat-bottomed water glass to pack down the crab to make a firm base. Divide the quinoa salad evenly among the ring molds and use the water glass to pack it down. Divide the mango among the molds and spread it evenly to make a top layer.

Slowly lift each ring to unmold the salad. In a large bowl, combine the remaining ¼ cup parsley, 1½ tablespoons lemon juice, 2 teaspoons olive oil, and a pinch each of salt and pepper. Add the lettuce and toss to coat the leaves with the vinaigrette. Divide the salad among the plates, placing it alongside the crab stack. Drizzle the lemon-tahini dressing around the crab stack and on top of the green salad. Pass additional dressing at the table if desired. Serve.

Maryland Crab Cakes
with Caramelized Pineapple and Roasted Red Pepper Remoulade

Summertime is crab time in Maryland, which has some of the best crab cakes in the country. This recipe has all the flavor of a classic Maryland crab cake, but with less mayonnaise and egg and very little filler. (Photograph on page 120.) **SERVES 6**

Roasted Red Pepper Remoulade
(page 265)

Olive oil spray

6 (¼-inch-thick) fresh pineapple rings

1 pound jumbo lump blue crab meat

¼ cup plain dry bread crumbs

2 tablespoons chopped fresh Italian parsley leaves

1 tablespoon mayonnaise

2 teaspoons Dijon mustard

¼ cup plus 2 teaspoons fresh lemon juice (from 2 lemons)

1½ teaspoons Worcestershire sauce

1½ teaspoons Old Bay seasoning

2 tablespoons extra-virgin olive oil

1 garlic clove, minced

Pinch of kosher salt

Pinch of freshly ground black pepper

12 cups field greens or mesclun

2 ripe red tomatoes, each sliced into 6 wedges

1 avocado, peeled and sliced into 12 wedges

Prepare the roasted red pepper remoulade.

Position the top oven rack about 6 inches below the broiler. Preheat the broiler to high. Line two baking sheets with foil and spray with oil.

Arrange the pineapple rings on one of the baking sheets. Spray them with olive oil. Broil for about 12 minutes until browned. Flip them over and broil for about 6 minutes to brown the other side. Remove from the oven.

Put the crab meat in a strainer to drain excess moisture. Pick through the meat to remove any bits of shell or cartilage. Transfer the crab to a large bowl. Add the bread crumbs and parsley and use a fork to toss gently just until combined.

In a small bowl whisk until well blended the mayonnaise, mustard, 2 teaspoons lemon juice, the Worcestershire sauce, and Old Bay seasoning. Add to the crab meat and stir with a fork to combine, gently breaking up about one-quarter of the crab (to help the crab cakes hold together) and leaving the rest of the lumps intact.

Divide the crab meat mixture into six equal balls, pressing each ball tightly until it holds together and flattening it very slightly between your hands. Place them on the prepared baking sheet. Broil until the crab cakes are deep, golden brown on top and hot throughout, about 8 minutes.

While the crab cakes are cooking, in a large bowl whisk together the ¼ cup lemon juice, the olive oil, garlic, salt, and pepper. Add the greens and toss gently to coat.

Divide the salad among six plates. Set the pineapple rings alongside the salad and place the hot crab cakes on top. Arrange the tomato wedges and avocado next to the crab cakes. Spoon a dollop of the roasted red pepper remoulade on top, if desired; pass the remaining remoulade at the table. Serve.

the golden door *bento box*

The bento box is a longtime tradition at the Golden Door, served for lunch every Thursday. Like so much of what we do here, the bento box was inspired by ancient Japanese tradition. The original *bento*, or box lunch, can be traced to the Kamakura Period in Japan, from the late twelfth to early fourteenth centuries, when it was no more than a simple rice meal in a small bag called a *hoshi-ii*. As the popularity of portable meals grew, the bento box became a substantial work of art. Lacquered wooden boxes were the height of fashion at sixteenth-century *hanami*, or tea parties. A century later, fans of the Noh and Kabuki theatre enjoyed intermission with their *makuno-uchi*, or between-act, bento. The *koshibento*, or waist bento, was carried by travelers and sightseers—perhaps even inspiring the "fanny pack" nearly four centuries later. Today, train stations all across Japan pride themselves on their signature *ekiben*, or station bento, often filled with a feast of flavors and colors reflecting the local cuisine and culture.

Here are the six core recipes that we include, along with Miso Soup (page 60), in our Thursday bento box. Our boxes do change throughout the year, depending on what is in season, but we always serve a sushi roll, fresh fish, a noodle salad, a pickled vegetable salad, shiitake mushrooms, and a seasonal fruit salad. I offer these recipes only as suggestions; feel free to use them or other recipes in this book, or experiment with your own seasonal combinations for your bento boxes. If you happen to have compartmentalized bento boxes, by all means use them. Most have about four individual compartments, so feel free to place some elements together in a single compartment. If you don't have a bento box, each element is easily served in its own small dish, either collected onto one larger dish or simply placed in a group in front of each diner. Above all, the key is to have fun!

SESAME-SCALLION CRAB SALAD MAKI SERVES 6 AS PART OF A BENTO BOX

Bamboo sushi mats are an essential tool for making rolls like these. Fortunately there are many inexpensive types available at Asian markets and many natural foods grocery stores, where you'll also find nori, thin sheets of seaweed that are used for wrapping. If you have a rice cooker, use it to prepare the rice according to the manufacturer's directions. If not, follow the instructions in the recipe to prepare it in a saucepan.

¾ cup sushi rice

FOR THE PONZU

¼ cup fresh lemon juice (from 2 lemons)

3 tablespoons mirin

2 tablespoons unseasoned rice vinegar

2 tablespoons low-sodium soy sauce

2 tablespoons bonito flakes

FOR THE MAKI

1 tablespoon plus ¼ cup unseasoned rice vinegar

1½ teaspoons mirin, or ¾ teaspoon sugar

Kosher salt and freshly ground black pepper

2 tablespoons fresh lemon juice (from 1 lemon)

1½ teaspoons Dijon mustard

1 teaspoon honey

¼ teaspoon toasted sesame oil

Put the rice in a large bowl and cover with cold water. Use your hand to swish the rice around a few times. Drain and repeat until the water in the bowl is clear; you may need to rinse it several times.

Put the rice in a small, heavy-bottomed saucepan and add enough water to cover by 1 inch. Cover the pan; for best results, do not uncover the pan at any time during cooking. Bring to a boil over medium-high heat, 4 to 5 minutes; you will be able to tell the water is boiling by the large amount of steam pouring out from under the lid. Reduce the heat to low and simmer, covered, for 10 minutes. Remove the pan from the heat and let stand, covered, for 15 minutes.

Prepare the ponzu. In a small mixing bowl, stir together the lemon juice, mirin, rice vinegar, soy sauce, and the bonito flakes. Let stand for 10 minutes. Strain and set aside.

Prepare the maki. In a small bowl or cup, stir together 1 tablespoon rice vinegar, the mirin, and a pinch of salt until well blended (if using sugar, it should be dissolved). Fold the mixture into the hot rice. Set aside to cool to room temperature.

Whisk together the lemon juice, mustard, honey, and sesame oil. Add the crab, scallions, cilantro, and toasted sesame seeds. Use a fork to gently mix until combined. Season with a pinch each of salt and pepper.

In a small bowl, combine the ¼ cup rice vinegar with 1 cup water. This "hand vinegar" is used to prevent the rice from sticking to your dry hands when you form the rolls. Set aside.

8 ounces fresh crab meat, picked over to remove any bits of shell or cartilage (about 1⅓ cups)

2 tablespoons thinly sliced scallions (white and green parts)

¼ cup chopped fresh cilantro leaves

1 tablespoon sesame seeds, toasted (see page 27)

6 whole nori sheets, cut to 5 by 8 inches

Place a sushi mat on the work surface in front of you so that the bamboo runs horizontally. Lay a sheet of nori shiny side down on the mat so that the longer side is closest to you and is flush with the bottom of the mat. Place about 3 heaping tablespoons of rice on the nori. Wet your hands with the hand vinegar and pat the rice out evenly to cover the bottom half of the nori. Spread one-sixth (about ¼ cup) of the crab salad evenly across the bottom two-thirds of the rice.

Roll the bamboo mat away from you to tightly roll up the nori. Moisten the top edge of the nori with a little of the hand vinegar and roll the cylinder to the end to seal it. Repeat with the remaining ingredients.

To serve, cut each roll into eight equal pieces with a sharp knife and arrange them cut sides up in one compartment of the bento box or on a small plate. Serve the ponzu in individual small dishes or pass it in a single dish at the table.

UDON NOODLE VEGETABLE SALAD SERVES 6 AS PART OF A BENTO BOX

Japanese udon are thick, wheat noodles that can be found dried or fresh in Asian markets or well-stocked grocery stores. I use dried here, but if you have fresh noodles, simply follow the directions on the package to cook them. This salad combines these tasty noodles with crisp, colorful vegetables for a beautiful addition to the bento box.

8 ounces dried udon noodles

Grapeseed oil spray

2 tablespoons thinly sliced scallions (white and green parts)

2 teaspoons minced garlic

2 teaspoons minced peeled fresh ginger

½ small head bok choy, sliced (2 cups)

1 small carrot, cut into matchsticks (¼ cup)

¼ medium red bell pepper, seeded and thinly sliced (¼ cup)

½ celery rib, sliced (¼ cup)

3 ounces snow peas, thinly sliced lengthwise (1 cup)

2 tablespoons low-sodium soy sauce

2 tablespoons reserved cooking liquid from Ginger-Soy Shiitake Mushrooms (page 153; optional)

¼ teaspoon freshly ground black pepper, or to taste

In a large saucepan, bring a generous amount of water to a boil. Add the udon noodles and stir with chopsticks or a wooden spoon to keep them from sticking. Cook until the noodles are tender but still have some bite, 8 to 10 minutes, or cook according to the package directions. Drain the noodles and run cold water over them to stop the cooking, raking through them with chopsticks, a spoon, or your fingers, to cool. Let drain thoroughly and set aside to cool completely. Transfer the cool noodles to a large bowl.

Spray a nonstick skillet with grapeseed oil and place it over medium-high heat. Add scallions, garlic, and ginger and cook, stirring, until softened but not at all brown, about 30 seconds. Add the bok choy, carrot, bell pepper, celery, and 1 tablespoon of water and cook, stirring, for 1½ to 2 minutes. Add the snow peas and cook, stirring, for 30 seconds. All of the vegetables should still be crisp. Remove from the heat and let cool.

Add the cooled vegetables, soy sauce, and reserved shiitake mushroom cooking liquid, if using, to the cooled noodles. Stir to combine. Season with pepper and more soy sauce, if desired. Serve immediately or cover and refrigerate for up to 3 hours before serving.

AHI TUNA WITH SESAME SEEDS SERVES 6 AS PART OF A BENTO BOX

The sesame seeds add a delicious nutty flavor and a great crisp texture to the silky tuna. This is the same method I use for the coriander-crusted tuna we serve as an appetizer (page 26). In fact, either version works well in the bento box.

1 pound sushi-quality tuna loin, preferably ahi

1 teaspoon kosher salt

½ teaspoon freshly ground black pepper

1 tablespoon sesame seeds

Grapeseed oil spray

Cut the tuna into two roughly equal pieces to make it easier to handle. Sprinkle all sides of the tuna with salt and pepper. Press each side of the tuna into the sesame seeds.

Spray a skillet with grapeseed oil and heat it over medium-high heat. When the pan just starts to smoke, add the tuna to the pan. Cook on all sides until crusty and golden brown on the outside and pink and rare in the center, being careful not to burn the sesame seeds, 30 seconds to 1 minute per side, depending on the thickness of the tuna.

Remove the tuna from the pan and let stand for 5 minutes.

When ready to serve, use a very sharp knife to thinly slice the tuna. Layer a few slices in one compartment of each bento box or on a small plate.

PICKLED CUCUMBER, DAIKON, AND GINGER SALAD SERVES 6 AS PART OF A BENTO BOX

Pickled vegetables are a traditional accompaniment to a Japanese meal. Sour yet slightly sweet, this pickled vegetable salad enhances the flavors of the other components of the meal and cleanses the palate. Do not let the salad sit longer than 30 minutes or it will become unpleasantly limp and watery. If you'd like to do some of preparation earlier, you may combine everything except the mirin and rice vinegar up to 8 hours in advance. Cover and chill until needed.

1 medium English cucumber, thinly sliced into rounds (3 cups)

½ medium daikon radish, peeled, halved lengthwise, and thinly sliced (1 cup)

¼ small red onion, thinly sliced (¼ cup)

2 tablespoons chopped pickled ginger

3 tablespoons mirin

3 tablespoons unseasoned rice vinegar

1½ teaspoons white sesame seeds, toasted (see page 27)

1½ teaspoons black sesame seeds, toasted (see page 27)

In a large bowl, combine the cucumber, daikon, onion, pickled ginger, mirin, rice vinegar, and the white and black sesame seeds. Toss gently to combine. Cover and chill for 30 minutes before serving.

GINGER-SOY SHIITAKE MUSHROOMS SERVES 6 AS PART OF A BENTO BOX

For fantastic flavor, drizzle some of the broth from these marinated mushrooms into the Udon Noodle Vegetable Salad (page 150). Serve hot or cold.

12 fresh shiitake mushrooms, stemmed

1 (1-inch) knob of fresh ginger, cut into 6 slices

1 garlic clove, sliced

3 tablespoons low-sodium soy sauce

1 tablespoon mirin

In a medium saucepan, combine the mushrooms, ginger, garlic, soy sauce, mirin, and 1 cup water. Bring to a boil. Reduce the heat and cover. Simmer for 12 minutes, until the mushrooms are soft and plump. Serve immediately or store the mushrooms with their liquid in a tightly covered container in the refrigerator for 2 to 3 days.

To serve, use a slotted spoon to place two warm or cold mushrooms in each bento box, in the compartment with the udon noodle vegetable salad, if desired.

FRESH FRUIT

SERVES 6 AS PART OF A BENTO BOX

Use the freshest, most seasonal fruit available for this part of the bento box. At the Golden Door this changes almost weekly, depending on what's best from our garden or locally. Here's a good summertime selection.

6 leaves lettuce

1 medium mango, peeled and diced

¼ papaya, peeled, seeded, and sliced

1 cup peeled and diced pineapple

1 cup blueberries

1 cup strawberries, hulled and sliced

6 lime wedges

Line a compartment of each of six bento boxes or small plates with a lettuce leaf. Decoratively arrange the fruit on top. Garnish with a lime wedge.

Porcini-Crusted Bison New York Strip Steaks with Baked Mushrooms and Worcestershire Jus

poultry and lean meats

Grilled Dijon Chicken Breast Salad *with Pears and Candied Walnuts*

During the fall, when fresh pears are at their peak, I use them in this dish along with dried blueberries and cherries. In late summer, when fresh blueberries and raspberries are ripe and the season's first apples are available, I use those instead of the pears and dried fruit. No matter which way we serve it, this hearty dish is always a very popular Golden Door lunch. **SERVES 4**

1 pound boneless, skinless chicken breasts, preferably 4 (4-ounce) breasts

3 tablespoons plus 2 teaspoons fresh lemon juice (from 2 lemons)

2 tablespoons Dijon mustard

1 tablespoon olive oil

1½ teaspoons minced fresh rosemary leaves

½ teaspoon freshly ground black pepper, or to taste

¼ teaspoon kosher salt, or to taste

Grapeseed or canola oil, for the grill

Whole-Grain Mustard and Honey Vinaigrette (page 257)

12 cups loosely packed field greens or mesclun

1 Bosc pear or other ripe pear or apple

½ cup fresh or dried blueberries

½ cup fresh raspberries or ⅓ cup dried cherries

½ cup Candied Walnuts (page 158)

Arrange the chicken in a shallow dish just big enough to hold it. In a small bowl combine the 3 tablespoons lemon juice, the mustard, olive oil, rosemary, and ¼ teaspoon of the black pepper and whisk until well blended. Pour the marinade over the chicken and turn the chicken to coat. Cover and refrigerate for at least 1 hour and up to 8 hours.

Prepare a grill with medium-high heat on one half and medium heat on the other.

Remove the chicken from the marinade and shake off any excess marinade. Season each chicken piece on both sides with salt and pepper. Soak a paper towel with grapeseed or canola oil and use tongs to rub it on the grill grate to lightly coat it with the oil. Place the chicken on the hottest part of the grill. Grill for 2 minutes, then give the chicken a quarter-turn and grill for 2 minutes. Turn the chicken over and cook for 4 minutes on the other side, again giving the chicken a quarter-turn halfway through cooking. Move the chicken to the medium-hot side of grill. Close the lid and cook until the chicken is opaque all the way through and an instant-read thermometer inserted into the thickest part registers 165°F, 10 to 14 minutes. Transfer the chicken to a platter and tent with foil. Let stand for 10 minutes before slicing.

Prepare the vinaigrette and set aside.

CONTINUES ON PAGE 158

CONTINUED FROM PAGE 156

Put the greens in a large bowl. Cut the pear in half lengthwise and scoop out the seeds with a melon-baller or spoon. Cut the pear into eight wedges and place them in a small bowl. Add the 2 teaspoons lemon juice and toss the pear wedges gently to coat with the juice to keep it from browning. Add the pear to the greens. Pour half of the dressing into the salad and toss to combine. Season with salt and pepper, if desired.

Divide the salad and pears among four chilled plates. Slice the chicken breasts crosswise and place on top of the salad. Scatter the berries and candied walnuts over each salad. Serve, passing additional dressing at the table.

CANDIED WALNUTS

Crispy, sweet, and salty, candied walnuts excite the palate and can turn an ordinary salad into an exciting one. This recipe calls for much less sugar than most. A pinch each of salt and cayenne brings out the flavor and spices things up.

MAKES 1 CUP; SERVES 8

Grapeseed or canola oil spray

1 cup walnut halves and pieces

1 tablespoon pure maple syrup

1 tablespoon light brown sugar

Pinch of cayenne pepper

Pinch of kosher salt

Preheat the oven to 375°F. Line a baking sheet with parchment and spray it with oil.

In a bowl, combine the walnuts, maple syrup, brown sugar, cayenne pepper, and salt. Stir to combine well. Spread the mixture evenly in a single layer on the prepared baking sheet. Bake in the oven until the nuts are toasted and the sugars are caramelized, about 15 minutes, tossing every 3 to 4 minutes to prevent burning. Remove the pan from the oven and let cool completely before using. (The candied walnuts can be stored in a tightly covered container at room temperature for 1 week.)

Pan-Roasted Lemon Chicken *and Marinated Greek Vegetable Salad*

Basic Greek salad has endured the test of time, thanks in large part to a well-balanced essential formula that shows simple, fresh ingredients to good advantage. For my version of this classic, I marinate the vegetables in the dressing, which makes the flavor even bolder and livelier. SERVES 4

FOR THE VEGETABLES

¼ cup red wine vinegar

2 tablespoons extra-virgin olive oil

1½ teaspoons chopped fresh oregano leaves

¼ teaspoon freshly ground black pepper

Pinch of kosher salt

1 large English cucumber, halved, seeded, and sliced (3 cups)

2 ripe, red tomatoes, cut into wedges

1 yellow bell pepper, seeded and cut into ½-inch dice (1½ cups)

1 medium carrot, halved lengthwise and sliced diagonally ¼ inch thick (½ cup)

½ small red onion, halved and thinly sliced (½ cup)

¼ cup pitted kalamata olives

1 tablespoon drained capers

Marinate the vegetables. In a large bowl, whisk together the red wine vinegar, olive oil, oregano, pepper, and salt. Add the cucumber, tomatoes, bell pepper, carrot, red onion, olives, and capers and toss to combine. Cover and chill for at least 1 hour and up to 4 hours, stirring occasionally.

Marinate the chicken. In a large freezer bag, combine the lemon juice, oregano, garlic, and ¼ teaspoon of the pepper. Add the chicken, seal the bag, and turn the chicken over once or twice to coat. Refrigerate for 1 to 3 hours to marinate.

Preheat the oven to 375°F.

Remove the chicken from the bag, reserving ¼ cup marinade. Season each breast on both sides with salt and pepper.

Spray an ovenproof nonstick or cast-iron skillet with olive oil and heat it over medium heat until hot but not smoking. Place the chicken in the pan; you should hear a sizzle. Cook until golden brown, 5 to 6 minutes. Turn the chicken over and add the reserved marinade to the pan. Cover the pan with an ovenproof lid or aluminum foil and place it in the oven until the chicken is opaque all the way through and an instant-read thermometer inserted into the thickest part of the breast registers 165°F, 15 to 20 minutes. Remove from the oven and tent with foil to keep warm. Let rest for 10 minutes.

CONTINUES ON PAGE 161

FOR THE CHICKEN

¼ cup fresh lemon juice (from 2 lemons)

2 teaspoons chopped fresh oregano
    leaves

1 teaspoon minced garlic

½ teaspoon freshly ground black pepper

1 pound boneless, skinless chicken
    breast, preferably 4 (4-ounce) breasts

½ teaspoon kosher salt

Olive oil spray

1 large or 2 small hearts of romaine,
    trimmed

1 ounce feta cheese, crumbled (¼ cup)

CONTINUED FROM PAGE 159

If using one large romaine heart, cut it lengthwise into four wedges. If using two small hearts, slice them lengthwise in half. Place a romaine heart wedge or half on each of four plates. Use a slotted spoon to divide the marinated vegetables among the plates. Slice the chicken breast and divide it among the plates, arranging it in a fan over the bed of vegetables. Spoon the vegetable marinade over the chicken and romaine. Sprinkle crumbled feta over each serving. Serve.

Parmesan Chicken Schnitzel

with Warm Potato and Garden Bean Salad and Creamy Mustard Sauce

Schnitzel *is the German word for a cutlet of meat, and it usually refers to a cutlet—veal in the case of the classic* Wiener schnitzel—*that has been breaded and fried. Of course, breaded and fried chicken cutlets served with cream sauce are not typical spa fare, but you can enjoy this dish without any guilt. The trick to making really crisp schnitzel without frying it in an inch of oil is to use very dry, crunchy bread crumbs.*

The warm potato and bean salad was inspired by the abundant garden here at the Golden Door. It's a riff on the traditional warm German potato salad, but lighter and crunchier than the original. **SERVES 4**

1 pound boneless, skinless chicken breasts, preferably 4 (4-ounce) breasts

1 cup low-fat buttermilk

1 large egg white

3 (½-inch) slices fresh whole wheat bread, cubed (2½ cups)

¼ ounce Parmesan cheese, grated (¼ cup)

½ teaspoon kosher salt

¼ teaspoon freshly ground black pepper

Olive oil spray

FOR THE WARM POTATO AND GARDEN BEAN SALAD

12 ounces fingerling potatoes, baby Yukon Gold, or baby red potatoes, halved (2 cups)

4 ounces fresh yellow wax beans, trimmed and halved if very long (1 cup)

Prepare the chicken. Place one breast of chicken on a cutting board and use a sharp knife held horizontally to slice the chicken in half through the center to form two thin cutlets. Place one cutlet between two sheets of plastic wrap and use the flat side of a meat pounder or a rolling pin to pound it to ¼ inch thick. If the pounded cutlet is very large, cut it in half. Repeat with the remaining chicken.

In a small bowl, whisk together the buttermilk and egg white, and pour it into a large, shallow baking dish. Put the chicken in the buttermilk and turn over to coat. Cover and refrigerate for 1 hour.

While the chicken is marinating, preheat the oven to 275°F.

Process the bread cubes in a food processor until ground to crumbs. Arrange the crumbs on a rimmed baking sheet in a thin layer. Toast in the oven until the crumbs are completely dry and hard, shaking the pan occasionally, about 15 minutes. Set aside 1 cup; reserve any excess for another recipe.

Lower the oven temperature to 200°F.

CONTINUES ON PAGE 164

4 ounces fresh green beans, trimmed and halved if very long (1 cup)

1 tablespoon apple cider vinegar

1 tablespoon extra-virgin olive oil

2 teaspoons whole-grain mustard

FOR THE CREAMY MUSTARD SAUCE

Olive oil spray

1 tablespoon minced shallot or onion

1 garlic clove, minced

⅓ cup evaporated skim milk

⅓ cup light or low-fat sour cream (do not use nonfat)

¼ cup whole-grain mustard

1 teaspoon Worcestershire sauce

⅛ teaspoon freshly ground black pepper (optional)

⅛ teaspoon cayenne pepper (optional)

2 tablespoons chopped fresh Italian parsley leaves

CONTINUED FROM PAGE 162

Prepare the potato and bean salad. Put the potatoes in a large saucepan and add enough cold water to cover by 1 inch. Bring to a boil and simmer, uncovered, until fork-tender, about 20 minutes. Add the yellow and green beans to the saucepan with the potatoes and boil until the beans are crisp-tender, about 2 minutes. Meanwhile, in a large bowl, stir together the vinegar, oil, and mustard. Drain the potatoes and beans and add them to the bowl. Toss to combine. Cover with foil and keep warm in the oven while you cook the chicken.

Mix the 1 cup bread crumbs and the Parmesan on a plate. Remove one piece of chicken from the buttermilk and shake off the excess liquid. Season both sides with salt and pepper and then press each side into the bread crumb mixture. Repeat with the remaining chicken.

Spray two large nonstick or cast-iron skillets with olive oil and heat over medium heat until hot but not smoking. Add as many pieces of chicken as can easily fit; you should hear a sizzle. Cook until the underside is golden brown and crisp, about 4 minutes. Turn and cook until the other side is golden brown and crisp and the chicken is opaque all the way through, about 4 minutes. Transfer to a platter and keep warm in the oven while you cook any remaining cutlets.

Prepare the creamy mustard sauce. Spray a small saucepan with olive oil and heat over medium heat. Add the shallot and garlic and cook, stirring, until slightly translucent and fragrant and not at all brown, 2 to 3 minutes. Stir in the evaporated milk and bring to a simmer. Whisk in the sour cream, mustard, and Worcestershire sauce. Remove the pan from the heat and stir in the black and cayenne peppers, if desired, and the parsley.

To serve, place a mound of warm potato bean salad on each plate. Arrange two pieces of chicken next to the salad. Spoon the sauce around the plate and drizzle a little over the chicken. Serve.

Crispy Duck Breast

with Cracked Wheat, Caramelized Shallots, and Blackberry Gastrique

Although I frequently make use of skinless chicken and turkey breasts, duck is something else entirely. Rich, crisp skin is one of the best things about duck breast. It is true that there is a lot of fat in the skin, but that's where good technique is necessary. By slow-cooking the duck breast on the skin side, most of the fat is rendered, and what's left behind is mahogany-colored, thin, crisp skin. Cracked wheat is enhanced by a generous measure of caramelized shallots and complements the duck with texture and savory flavor. The tangy blackberry gastrique, a vinegar-and-fruit sauce, brings it all together, cutting through the richness while highlighting the earthiness of both the duck and the wheat.

Serve with roasted cauliflower or simple cooked romanesco or turnips (page 117), if desired. **SERVES 4**

FOR THE DUCK

1 large or 2 small boneless duck breasts
    (14 ounces total), trimmed of
    excess fat

1 tablespoon balsamic vinegar

1 tablespoon low-sodium soy sauce

1 tablespoon honey

FOR THE CRACKED WHEAT

¾ cup cracked wheat (bulgur)

Olive oil spray

3 large shallots, finely chopped (1 cup)

2 tablespoons balsamic vinegar

¼ teaspoon kosher salt, or to taste

Pinch of freshly ground black pepper, or
    to taste

Prepare the duck. With a sharp knife, score the skin of the duck in a crosshatch pattern, cutting just three-fourths of the way through the skin (not quite down to the meat). In a small bowl, whisk together the balsamic vinegar, soy sauce, and honey. Pour the marinade into a shallow dish just large enough to hold the duck breast. Place the duck skin side up in the marinade, being careful not to get the marinade on the skin side, or it will burn during cooking. Cover and refrigerate for at least 3 and up to 6 hours.

Prepare the cracked wheat. Bring 1¾ cups of water to a boil in a small saucepan. Stir in the cracked wheat and reduce the heat to low. Simmer, covered, for 25 minutes. Remove the pan from the heat, cover, and let stand for 5 minutes.

Spray a small sauté pan with olive oil and heat over medium-high heat. Add the shallots and cook, stirring occasionally until the shallots are lightly browned, about 5 minutes. Add the balsamic vinegar and cook until the vinegar is reduced and coats the shallots, 1 to 2 minutes. Add the shallots to the cracked wheat and stir to combine. Season with salt and pepper. Keep warm and set aside.

Preheat the oven to 400°F.

CONTINUES ON PAGE 167

FOR THE BLACKBERRY GASTRIQUE

1 tablespoon sugar

½ cup fresh blackberries

4½ teaspoons balsamic vinegar

Pinch of kosher salt

Pinch of freshly ground black pepper

½ cup fresh blackberries, for serving

CONTINUED FROM PAGE 165

Remove the duck from the marinade and pat with a paper towel to remove any marinade or excess moisture. Put the duck skin side down in a medium cast-iron skillet just big enough to hold the breast (it will shrink during cooking) and place the pan over medium-low heat. After about 1 minute, use tongs to move the breasts gently to make sure they are not sticking. Cook for 12 to 15 minutes, carefully pouring out the fat from the pan halfway through cooking, until the skin is deep golden brown and crisp. Check the skin side periodically to make sure it is not burning and adjust the heat if necessary. Pour out the remaining fat from the pan and turn the breasts over. Place in the oven and roast until an instant-read thermometer reads 135°F for medium-rare, 4 to 6 minutes. Transfer the duck breasts to a cutting board and let stand for 10 minutes.

Prepare the blackberry gastrique. Pour off all the fat from the skillet used to cook the duck breast. Add the sugar and 1 tablespoon water to the skillet and place it over medium-high heat. Cook, using a wooden spoon to scrape up the brown bits from the bottom of the skillet, until the sugar starts to caramelize to a light golden brown, 2 to 3 minutes. Add the blackberries, balsamic vinegar, salt, and pepper, and simmer, smashing the berries with the back of a large spoon, until a light, syrupy consistency is reached, 2 to 3 minutes. Remove from the heat and strain through a fine-mesh strainer, using a wooden spoon to force as much sauce through the strainer as possible. You should have about ¼ cup sauce. The sauce will thicken slightly while standing.

Slice the duck breast crosswise ⅛ inch thick. Divide the cracked wheat among four plates. Arrange the duck breasts slices on top of the cracked wheat, layering them like shingles. Drizzle the gastrique over the duck and around the plate, and place a few blackberries on each plate. Serve.

Smoked Paprika Roasted Game Hen
with Spicy Chicken Sausage and Vegetable Pilaf

Look for a spicy chicken sausage that is nitrate- and preservative-free. There are some good brands out there, so be a label reader and find a wholesome one. It's easiest to remove the sausage from its casing and chop it if the sausage is slightly frozen.

SERVES 6

FOR THE GAME HENS

3 (1½-pound) Cornish game hens

¼ cup fresh orange juice (from 1 orange)

¼ cup fresh lemon juice (from 2 lemons)

1 teaspoon minced garlic

1 teaspoon smoked paprika, plus more for cooking

½ teaspoon sweet paprika

½ teaspoon kosher salt

¼ teaspoon freshly ground black pepper

Olive oil spray

FOR THE PILAF

2¾ cups Chicken Stock (page 268) or store-bought low-sodium broth

Olive oil spray

1 medium onion, diced (1 cup)

2 garlic cloves, thinly sliced

8 ounces spicy Italian, jalapeño cilantro, or other spicy chicken sausage, casing removed, chopped

Rinse the game hens in cold, running water and dry them well with paper towels. With poultry shears or a very sharp boning or other sturdy knife, trim off and discard the first joint of the wings. Lay a game hen on the work surface in front of you breast side down. Cut out the backbone by cutting along one side and then the other of the bone. Cut straight through the center of the breast bone to divide the hen in half. Trim away and discard any loose-hanging, excess skin and fat. Set aside and continue with the remaining hens.

In a shallow baking dish just large enough to hold the game hens, combine the orange juice, lemon juice, garlic, smoked paprika, and sweet paprika. Place the game hens in the dish and turn them over a few times to coat with the marinade. Arrange them in the pan skin side down. Cover the pan and refrigerate for 2 to 4 hours.

To prepare the pilaf, pour the chicken stock into a small saucepan and bring to a simmer over medium-low heat; keep hot until needed.

Spray a heavy-bottomed sauté pan with a tight-fitting lid with olive oil over medium-high heat. Add the onion and garlic and cook, stirring, until softened but not at all brown, 4 to 5 minutes. Add the sausage and both bell peppers and cook, stirring occasionally, for 5 minutes. Add the rice and cook, stirring, for 1 minute. Stir in the hot stock, crushed tomatoes, and saffron. Bring to a boil and then reduce the heat. Simmer, covered, until the rice is tender, 40 to 50 minutes.

1 medium green bell pepper, seeded and diced

1 medium red bell pepper, seeded and diced

1 cup long-grain brown Basmati rice

½ cup canned crushed tomatoes

Pinch of saffron threads

1 cup fresh or thawed, frozen peas

¼ cup chopped fresh cilantro leaves

¼ cup sliced scallions (white and green parts)

½ teaspoon kosher salt

¼ teaspoon freshly ground black pepper

Fresh cilantro sprigs, for serving

Lemon wedges, for serving

While the rice is cooking, finish the game hens. Preheat the oven to 375°F.

Remove the hens from the marinade and pat them dry with paper towels. Season each hen all over with salt, pepper, and smoked paprika. Spray a large cast-iron skillet with olive oil (use two pans if necessary), and heat it over medium heat until hot but not smoking. Lay the hens in the pan skin side down and cook until golden brown, 6 to 8 minutes. Turn the hens over, and place the pan in the oven. Cook until an instant-read thermometer inserted in the deepest part of the thigh reads 165°F and the juices run clear when the thigh is pierced, 20 to 25 minutes. Remove the hens from the oven, loosely tent with foil, and set aside for 10 minutes before serving.

Spoon the peas on top of the rice, cover the pan, and remove the pan from the heat. Let stand, covered, for 10 minutes. Add the cilantro and scallions, season with salt and pepper, and use a fork to fluff and incorporate the ingredients.

To serve, divide the pilaf among six plates. Place a roasted game hen half on each bed of rice and garnish with cilantro sprigs and lemon wedges. Serve.

Walnut-Crusted Turkey Scallopini
with Smashed Yams and Cranberry Vinaigrette

Here is a festive fall dish bursting with familiar Thanksgiving dinner ingredients and boasting two SuperFoods: skinless turkey breast is among the leanest meat protein options available and the omega-3 fats in heart-healthy walnuts may help lower your risk of cardiovascular disease. **SERVES 4**

FOR THE YAMS

1 pound yams (2 medium or 1 large), washed and dried

1 teaspoon grated orange zest

1 tablespoon fresh orange juice

½ teaspoon chopped fresh thyme leaves

⅛ teaspoon ground cinnamon

Pinch of freshly grated nutmeg

Pinch of kosher salt, or to taste

Pinch of freshly ground black pepper

FOR THE TURKEY

1 pound turkey breast cutlets

½ cup coarsely ground walnuts

¼ cup dry whole wheat bread crumbs

2 teaspoons chopped fresh thyme leaves

2 teaspoons chopped fresh sage leaves

1 teaspoon chopped fresh rosemary leaves

½ teaspoon kosher salt

¼ teaspoon freshly ground black pepper

Olive oil spray

Cranberry Vinaigrette (page 258)

Preheat the oven to 400°F.

Place the yams directly on the rack in the oven and bake until tender when pierced with a knife, 40 minutes to 1 hour, depending on the size of the yams.

Prepare the turkey. Lay one turkey cutlet between two sheets of plastic wrap and use the flat side of a meat pounder to pound it until ¼ inch thick. Repeat with the remaining turkey cutlets. If the pounded cutlets are very large, cut them in half.

On a large rimmed plate, combine the ground walnuts, bread crumbs, thyme, sage, and rosemary. Season both sides of each cutlet with salt and pepper and then press each side into the nut mixture. Arrange the cutlets on a baking sheet in a single layer. Refrigerate until needed, or for up to 6 hours.

Prepare the cranberry vinaigrette and set aside.

When the yams are done, transfer them to a cutting board. Carefully split the yams in half (they will be hot) and use a spoon to scoop out the flesh and transfer it to a bowl. Discard the skins. Add the orange zest and juice, the thyme, cinnamon, nutmeg, salt, and pepper. Use a fork to mash the yams and combine the ingredients. Keep warm.

Spray a large, nonstick sauté pan with olive oil and heat over medium heat until hot but not smoking. Add the turkey to the pan in a single layer; you should hear a sizzle (cook in batches if necessary; wipe out the pan with paper towels and spray with oil between batches). Cook until deep golden brown on each side and opaque throughout, 3 to 4 minutes per side.

Divide the roasted yams among four plates. Lean 1 or 2 turkey scallopini against the yams and drizzle some cranberry vinaigrette on each plate. Serve.

Turkey Burgers
with Sharp Cheddar Cheese, Caramelized Onions, and Golden Door Ketchup

Turkey burgers have long been a Friday lunch favorite at the Golden Door. My mentor, former Golden Door chef Michel Stroot, had a great signature burger he created during his tenure, featuring pine nuts, sun-dried tomatoes, and a little surprise in the center of each patty—a chunk of Stilton blue cheese. This is a clever way to add a little something special to a simple burger without melting a big slice of cheese over the top. My turkey burger recipe is inspired by the Golden Door original, but it has some different flavors, such as Worcestershire sauce, Dijon mustard, and thyme and a nugget of sharp Cheddar cheese in the middle.

For best results, use finely ground turkey meat, which yields the nicest texture for the burgers. A blend of mostly light with just a bit of dark meat gives a juicy, flavorful burger while keeping the fat content to a modest level. The semolina dough we use for pizza at the Golden Door also makes fantastic burger buns, and you can make and freeze the dough in advance, so all you have to do is shape it. If you don't have time to make buns, however, just buy a nice whole-grain burger bun. **SERVES 6**

Semolina Dough for Burger Buns (page 275)

Olive oil spray

½ medium onion, finely chopped (½ cup)

1 pound finely ground turkey, preferably 70% white meat and 30% dark meat

1 tablespoon Dijon mustard

1 tablespoon Worcestershire sauce

½ teaspoon chopped fresh thyme leaves, or ¼ teaspoon dried

¾ teaspoon kosher salt, or to taste

¼ teaspoon freshly ground black pepper, or to taste

2 ounces sharp Cheddar cheese, cut into 6 cubes

Preheat the oven to 375°F.

Divide the dough into six equal pieces. Roll each portion into a ball and pat down slightly. Arrange the dough rounds on a floured baking sheet. Bake until light golden, about 20 minutes. Remove from the oven and transfer to a rack to cool.

Spray a small sauté pan with olive oil and heat over medium-high heat. Add the onion and cook, stirring occasionally, until lightly browned, about 4 minutes. Remove from the heat and let cool.

Put the turkey in a medium bowl. Add the onion, Dijon mustard, Worcestershire sauce, thyme, salt, and pepper and mix thoroughly. Divide the meat into six equal balls. Push a cube of the Cheddar into the center of each ball and form into a patty, encasing the cube.

Prepare a medium to medium-high grill or spray a grill pan or cast-iron skillet with oil and heat over medium to medium-high heat until hot but not smoking. If using the grill, soak a paper towel with grapeseed or canola oil and use tongs to rub it on the grill grate to lightly coat it with the oil. Cut the buns in half and grill each half cut side down for 30 seconds to 1 minute. Alternatively, lightly toast the buns.

Grapeseed or canola oil

1½ cups Caramelized Onions (page 273)

6 large red leaf lettuce leaves

12 slices ripe, red tomato

2 dill pickles, sliced

Golden Door Ketchup (recipe follows),
    for serving

Mustard, for serving

Cook the turkey burgers until browned on both sides and an instant-read thermometer reads 165°F, 5 to 7 minutes per side.

Place a grilled bun on each of six plates and place a burger on the bottom half. Divide the caramelized onions among the plates, piling them high on top of the burgers. Arrange one lettuce leaf, two tomato slices, and some pickle slices on the top half. Serve ketchup and mustard on the side.

*GOLDEN DOOR KETCHUP

This is the classic Golden Door house-made ketchup that has accompanied the turkey burger for years. Juniper adds a wonderful tangy, piney flavor. Juniper berries can be found in well-stocked grocery stores or through my favorite source for spices, Penzeys Spices (see Resources, page 283). **MAKES 1 CUP; ENOUGH FOR 6 SERVINGS**

1 medium tomato, diced (1 cup)

1 garlic clove, minced

¼ cup plus 2 tablespoons red wine
    vinegar

¼ cup packed light brown sugar

½ teaspoon black peppercorns

1 whole clove

1 fresh or dried juniper berry

1 bay leaf

1 (2-inch) cinnamon stick

2 teaspoons molasses (optional)

1 (8-ounce) can low-sodium tomato sauce

¼ cup Vegetable Stock (page 269) or
    water

In a medium saucepan, combine the tomato and garlic and simmer, covered, over medium heat, until they soften, about 3 minutes.

Stir in the red wine vinegar, brown sugar, peppercorns, clove, juniper berry, bay leaf, cinnamon stick, and molasses. Simmer, uncovered, until reduced by about one-third, 15 to 20 minutes.

Add the tomato sauce and vegetable stock. Simmer until thick and dark red in color, 20 to 25 minutes. Strain and let cool. Serve at room temperature or chilled. Cover tightly and store in the refrigerator for up to 1 week.

Grilled Lamb Chops
with Rosemary Roasted New Potatoes and Apple-Mint Salad

A few years back a longtime Golden Door guest, Bill Anton, shared with me the broad outline of his renowned lamb marinade. It was a "take a bunch of that, a couple cups of this, and a dozen of these" kind of a recipe, and it was an instant hit the first time I made it. Since then I've managed to nail down more precise quantities of all that, this, and these ingredients and cut down on the oil. We've made these chops countless times since that first trial run, and they never fail to please. Double-cut lamb rib chops include two ribs; these thicker chops remain juicier during cooking. Frenched chops have the meat at the top cut away to expose the bone; they're very attractive this way and make an elegant presentation.

For the accompanying potatoes, baking them covered at first steam-cooks them before the lid is removed to brown them. This technique uses very little oil and yet yields potatoes that are light and fluffy inside and crisp outside. To finish off the dish, I like a mint and apple salad, my homage to the mint jelly traditionally served with lamb.

If desired serve a platter of simple cooked summer squash or baby carrots or wilted greens. **SERVES 4**

FOR THE LAMB CHOPS

4 (4-ounce) double-cut Frenched lamb rib chops, trimmed of excess fat

4 lemons

⅓ cup red wine

2 tablespoons olive oil

1½ teaspoons red wine vinegar

2 tablespoons coarsely chopped fresh rosemary leaves, plus several sprigs for serving

1 tablespoon coarsely chopped fresh thyme leaves, plus several sprigs for serving

1 tablespoon coarsely chopped fresh oregano leaves, plus several sprigs for serving

4 garlic cloves, chopped

Prepare the lamb chops. Put the lamb chops in a nonreactive pan just big enough to hold them. Use a vegetable peeler to remove the yellow peel from three of the lemons; leave behind as much of the white pith as possible. Put the peel in a medium bowl. Use a zester to remove several strips of zest from the remaining lemon. Set aside for garnish. Juice all four lemons and add the juice to the bowl along with the wine, olive oil, vinegar, rosemary, thyme, oregano, garlic, and pepper. Whisk to combine and then pour over the lamb chops. Cover and refrigerate for at least 6 hours and up to 24 hours; the longer, the better.

Preheat the oven to 425°F.

Prepare the potatoes. In a baking pan just big enough to hold the potatoes in a single layer, place the potatoes, rosemary, olive oil, salt, and pepper. Toss to coat the potatoes with the seasonings. Cover the pan with foil and bake for 30 minutes. Uncover the pan and toss the potatoes. Bake, uncovered, until the potatoes are golden brown and crisp on the outside and tender inside, about 15 minutes. Remove from the oven and keep warm.

½ teaspoon freshly ground black pepper

½ teaspoon kosher salt

FOR THE POTATOES

12 ounces new potatoes, baby red creamers, German butterball, fingerling, or baby Yukon Gold potatoes, peeled and halved (2 cups)

1 tablespoon chopped fresh rosemary leaves

2 teaspoons olive oil

¼ teaspoon kosher salt

⅛ teaspoon freshly ground black pepper

FOR THE APPLE-MINT SALAD

½ large Fuji, Gala, or other sweet/tart crisp apple, cut into ¼-inch dice (1 cup)

2 tablespoons fresh lemon juice (from 1 lemon)

2 tablespoons extra-virgin olive oil

1 tablespoon chopped fresh mint leaves

Pinch of freshly ground black pepper

While the potatoes are roasting, prepare the apple-mint salad. In a small bowl combine the apple, lemon juice, olive oil, mint, and pepper. Stir to combine. Cover and refrigerate until ready to serve, up to ½ hour.

Prepare a grill with high heat on one half and medium heat on the other.

Remove the lamb chops from the marinade and shake off the excess. Season both sides of each chop with salt. Place the chops on the high-heat side of the grill and grill for about 2 minutes to develop nice grill marks. Give the chops a ¼ turn and grill for about 2 minutes to develop nice diamond-shaped grill marks.

Turn the chops over and grill for about 4 minutes, again giving the chops a quarter turn about halfway through cooking. Check for doneness: an instant-read thermometer should read 135° to 140°F for medium-rare. If the chops are still too rare, move them to the medium side of the grill, close the lid, and cook for a few additional minutes until done. Transfer to a plate and tent with foil. Let rest for 10 minutes.

To serve, divide the potatoes among four plates, placing them in a small mound on each plate. Prop a lamb chop against each mound of potatoes with the bone pointing up. Spoon the apple-mint salad over each chop. Garnish each plate with fresh herb sprigs and a few strips of lemon zest.

Moroccan Spice-Rubbed Lamb Loin *with Chickpeas, Feta, and Olives*

The delicious spice rub used here is a staple in the Golden Door kitchen. Make more than you'll need for this recipe and keep it on hand to add exotic sweet-savory flavor and aroma to poultry, beef, and even grilled or roasted vegetables. In this dish, an easy pan sauce made in the roasting skillet concentrates the flavors of the spices in the rub, creating a delicious balance of salty, sour, and sweet. A warm stew of tender chickpeas, vegetables, and just a touch of briny, creamy feta is a welcome foil for the fragrant lamb. **SERVES 6**

FOR THE LAMB

1 teaspoon coriander seeds

1 teaspoon cumin seeds

1 whole star anise

⅛ teaspoon black peppercorns

⅛ teaspoon fennel seeds

1 teaspoon light brown sugar

1 teaspoon chili powder

⅛ teaspoon ground cinnamon

1 (1¼-pound) boneless lamb loin,
　trimmed of excess fat, tied at
　intervals with butcher's string

½ teaspoon kosher salt

FOR THE CHICKPEA STEW

Olive oil spray

1 medium onion, chopped (1 cup)

2 garlic cloves, minced

½ teaspoon ground cumin

½ teaspoon dried oregano

¼ teaspoon dried thyme

Prepare the lamb. In a small coffee or spice grinder, combine the coriander seeds, cumin seeds, star anise, peppercorns, and fennel seeds. Grind to a coarse powder. Transfer to a small bowl and add the brown sugar, chili powder, and cinnamon. Stir to combine. Season the lamb loin on all sides with the salt. Spread the spice rub all over the lamb, pressing with your hands so it adheres. Set aside at room temperature while you start the chickpea stew.

Prepare the chickpea stew. Spray a large, heavy-bottomed saucepan with olive oil and heat over medium heat. Add the onion and the garlic and cook, stirring, until translucent and fragrant and not at all brown, 4 to 5 minutes. Add the cumin, oregano, and thyme and cook, stirring, for 30 seconds. Add the chickpeas, diced tomato, chicken stock, and cinnamon stick. Bring to a simmer and cook for 15 minutes. Stir in the zucchini and raisins and simmer for 5 minutes. Remove the pan from the heat and remove and discard the cinnamon stick. Cover until just before serving.

Preheat the oven to 400°F.

CONTINUES ON PAGE 178

1 (15-ounce) can chickpeas, rinsed and
   drained

1 (14-ounce) can diced tomato plus liquid

½ cup Chicken Stock (page 268) or
   store-bought low-sodium broth

1 (2-inch) cinnamon stick

1 medium zucchini, diced small (1 cup)

2 tablespoons golden raisins

2 cups loosely packed baby spinach
   leaves

¼ cup halved, pitted kalamata olives

⅛ teaspoon freshly ground black pepper,
   or to taste

FOR THE PAN GLAZE

⅓ cup fresh orange juice (from
   1 to 2 oranges)

⅓ cup Chicken Stock (page 268) or
   store-bought low-sodium broth

1 tablespoon low-sodium soy sauce

1 tablespoon light brown sugar

1 garlic clove, sliced

1 (2-inch) cinnamon stick

2 whole star anise

⅛ teaspoon fennel seeds

1 ounce feta cheese, cut into small cubes
   (¼ cup), for serving

CONTINUED FROM PAGE 176

Spray an ovenproof skillet with olive oil and heat it over medium-high heat until hot but not smoking. Place the lamb in the skillet; you should hear a sizzle. Sear until a dark, crusty brown on all sides, 3 to 4 minutes per side. Place the skillet in the oven and roast until an instant-read thermometer reads 140°F, 12 to 15 minutes. Transfer the lamb to a plate and tent it loosely with foil to rest for 10 minutes before slicing. Do not wash the roasting skillet; you'll need it to make the pan glaze.

Prepare the pan glaze. Place the skillet the lamb was cooked in over medium heat. Add the orange juice, chicken stock, soy sauce, brown sugar, garlic, cinnamon stick, star anise, and fennel seeds. Stir, scraping the bottom of the pan to loosen the cooked bits. Simmer until the liquid is reduced to about 2½ tablespoons and is a syrupy consistency, 5 to 6 minutes.

Stir the spinach and olives into the stew. Season with pepper.

To serve, slice the lamb loin ⅛ to ¼ inch thick. Divide the chickpea stew among six plates or shallow bowls. Divide the lamb slices among the plates, overlapping them on top of the stew. Drizzle the lamb with a bit of the pan glaze and sprinkle a few feta cubes on each dish. Serve.

Adobo-Marinated Grass-Fed Flank Steak
with Spinach Salad and Roasted Poblano Dressing

Cows are ruminants, which means they have more than one stomach and their digestive systems are specifically designed to break down grasses into proteins and fats to meet their nutritional needs. They are not naturally meant to eat corn and other grain. Grain feeding—the fastest, cheapest way to produce the most beef—is not only unnatural for cows but also has profound consequences for us. To counteract and prevent the damage caused by eating food that is difficult for them to digest, coupled with cramped living conditions, feedlot cattle are often routinely fed antibiotics, which can remain in the meat we buy after the cows are slaughtered. It's not any better for us to routinely consume antibiotics than it is for cows.

Thankfully there is an increasingly available alternative across the country: grass-fed beef can now be found in many natural-food markets and even purchased directly from many of the ranchers themselves. Not only is it kinder to the living animals but grass feeding makes for far better tasting beef, with about half the fat of typical grain-fed beef and more omega-3 fatty acids and other nutrients than its feedlot cousin. Check out Eatwild.com online (see Resources, page 283) for a directory of pasture-raised beef available close to your home.

Adobo seasoning is a mixture of onion powder, garlic powder, pepper, cumin, oregano, and cayenne. It is absolutely delicious on beef, poultry, and grilled vegetables. It can be found in the Mexican or Latino foods section of many supermarkets, but my favorite version of adobo seasoning is at Penzeys Spices (see Resources, page 283).

Note that for this recipe you can use the grill to roast the red bell and poblano peppers for the salad and dressing. **SERVES 4**

FOR THE STEAK

1 pound grass-fed flank, skirt, or strip steak (about ½ inch thick)

¼ cup fresh orange juice (from 1 orange)

2 tablespoons fresh lime juice (from 1 lime)

2 teaspoons adobo seasoning

2 tablespoons chopped fresh cilantro leaves

1 garlic clove, chopped

¼ teaspoon kosher salt

Prepare the steak. Place the steak in a shallow pan just big enough to hold it. Whisk together the orange juice, lime juice, adobo spice, cilantro, and garlic. Pour over the steak and turn the steak over to fully coat with the marinade. Cover and refrigerate for 1 hour.

Prepare the pickled red onions. Place the red onion in a small bowl and add the sherry vinegar and sugar. Stir to combine. Cover the bowl and refrigerate for at least 30 minutes and up to 8 hours.

Prepare a medium-high grill or set a grill pan over medium-high heat.

CONTINUES ON PAGE 181

FOR THE PICKLED RED ONIONS

¼ small red onion, thinly sliced (¼ cup)

1 tablespoon sherry vinegar

Pinch of sugar

FOR THE SPINACH SALAD

2 ears corn, husked

Olive oil, grapeseed, or canola spray

Roasted Poblano Dressing (page 260)

¼ small to medium jícama (5 ounces)

Juice of ½ lime

12 cups baby spinach leaves, washed and dried (about 12 ounces)

1 large red bell pepper, grill-roasted (page 74), peeled, seeded, and diced, or ½ cup diced store-bought, drained, roasted red peppers

1 medium avocado, cut in ½-inch dice

1 ounce queso fresco, crumbled (¼ cup)

Kosher salt (optional)

Fresh cilantro leaves, for serving

CONTINUED FROM PAGE 179

Lightly spray the corn all over with oil and place on the grill. Grill until nicely marked on all sides, turning with tongs as necessary, about 5 minutes total. Remove from the grill and let cool. When cool enough to handle, use a sharp knife to cut the kernels from the ears and set them aside. Discard the ears.

Prepare the roasted poblano dressing.

Remove the steak from the marinade and season on both sides with salt. Grill until the outside has nice grill marks and the center is pink, 2 to 3 minutes per side for medium-rare. Transfer to a cutting board and let rest for 5 minutes before slicing.

While the steak is resting, finish the spinach salad. Peel the jícama and cut it into ½-inch dice; you should have 1 cup. Toss with the lime juice and set aside. Put the spinach in a large bowl. Add the roasted peppers, the reserved corn, and the jícama. Add the avocado and queso fresco. Pour half of the roasted poblano dressing over the ingredients and toss to coat well. Taste and season with a pinch of salt if desired.

Thinly slice the steak against the grain.

Mound the salad in the center of a large serving platter. Fan the steak slices on top of the salad. Spoon the pickled onion with its juice on top and sprinkle with cilantro leaves. Serve.

Porcini-Crusted Bison New York Strip Steaks
with Baked Mushrooms and Worcestershire Jus

It's hard to go wrong with steak and mushrooms. Musky, earthy, dried porcini are ground to create a delicious crust for the bison, and an easy Worcestershire pan sauce gives the dish just the right amount of acidity to enhance all the flavors.

If you have never tried bison before, you are in for a real treat. Bison's flavor is clean, pure, and pleasantly meaty. This is due, in part, to the fact that bison are allowed to graze on grass; their diet tends to be far less manipulated than that of commercially raised beef. From a health perspective, bison has one-quarter the fat, almost 35 percent fewer calories, less cholesterol, and more iron than regular beef of the same cut. I recommend cooking bison just until rare or medium; it is not marbled with fat and will become dry if overcooked.

Serve with roasted asparagus and tomatoes; wilted spinach, chard, or kale; or simple cooked carrots or green beans (page 117), if desired. (Photograph on page 154.) **SERVES 4**

FOR THE MUSHROOMS

8 ounces portobello mushroom caps, gills scraped out with a spoon, cut into ½-inch cubes (3 cups)

8 ounces mixed mushrooms, such as chanterelles, hen of the woods, button, oyster, cremini, or stemmed shiitakes, halved or quartered if large (3 cups)

½ cup Chicken Stock (page 268) or store-bought low-sodium broth

¼ cup earthy red wine, such as a cabernet sauvignon, zinfandel, or syrah

2 tablespoons finely diced shallot

1 teaspoon minced garlic

2 sprigs fresh thyme or ½ teaspoon dried thyme

¼ teaspoon kosher salt

⅛ teaspoon freshly ground black pepper

Preheat the oven to 400°F.

Prepare the mushrooms. Combine the portobellos and other mushrooms in a 9 x 13-inch baking dish or ovenproof skillet just large enough so that the mushrooms are a bit crowded and touching each other. Add the stock, wine, shallot, garlic, thyme, salt, and pepper and stir to combine. Cover the pan with foil and bake for 30 minutes. If there is ½ cup or more liquid in the pan, pour it into a small saucepan. Simmer over medium heat until reduced by half, and add the reduced liquid back to the mushrooms. Discard the thyme sprigs, if using. Keep warm until serving.

While the mushrooms are roasting, prepare the bison. Put the dried porcinis in a spice or coffee grinder and grind to a coarse powder; you should have at least a bit more than 2 tablespoons. Reserve and set aside 1 teaspoon of the powder for the Worcestershire jus. Season all sides of the bison with salt and pepper. Liberally coat all sides with the remaining porcini powder.

½ ounce dried porcini mushrooms
   (½ cup)

1 pound (1½- to 2-inch-thick) bison New
   York strip steak, strip long, or filet,
   trimmed of all fat

½ teaspoon kosher salt

¼ teaspoon freshly ground black pepper

Grapeseed oil spray

FOR THE WORCESTERSHIRE JUS

2 tablespoons minced shallot

½ cup Chicken Stock (page 268) or
   store-bought low-sodium broth

1 tablespoon Worcestershire sauce

2 sprigs fresh thyme

Roasted Asparagus (page 118)

Roasted tomatoes (see Roasted
   Asparagus, page 118; optional)

Spray a small skillet with grapeseed oil and heat over medium heat until hot but not smoking. Put the bison in the pan; you should hear a sizzle. Cook until deep, crusty brown on both sides, about 4 minutes per side. Transfer the bison to a rimmed baking sheet (do not clean the skillet) and roast in the oven until an instant-read thermometer inserted into the thickest part of the steak reads 130° to 135°F for rare and 145°F for medium-rare, 7 to 10 minutes depending on the thickness. Let rest for 10 minutes before slicing.

While the bison is in the oven, make the Worcestershire jus. Place the skillet that the bison was seared in over medium heat. Add the shallot and cook, stirring occasionally, until softened and slightly brown, about 2 minutes. Add the stock, Worcestershire sauce, and thyme. Stir, scraping the bottom of the pan to loosen the cooked bits. Simmer until reduced by half, 3 to 4 minutes. Stir in the 1 teaspoon porcini powder and simmer for 1 minute. Discard the thyme sprigs. Set aside. Reheat gently if necessary just before serving.

While the bison is resting, prepare the roasted asparagus and the tomatoes, if desired. Pour any accumulated juices from the resting steak into the Worcestershire jus.

To serve, slice the steak against the grain ⅛ to ¼ inch thick. Place a bed of mushrooms on each of four plates. Fan a few slices of steak on top of the mushrooms. Drizzle some jus over the steak and around the plate. Serve with the roasted asparagus and tomatoes, if using.

tips from the golden door
your fitness toolbox

You know in principle that exercise is good for you, but it can be frustrating to hear this message repeatedly without concrete information on how and when to work out to receive the most benefit from your exertion. Trish Martin, fitness director at the Golden Door, recommends following the FITTE exercise guidelines.

F = FREQUENCY Perform cardiovascular exercise a minimum of three to four days per week to maintain your weight and receive health benefits and four to seven days per week for weight loss.

I = INTENSITY 80 percent of your total weekly workout hours should be used to perform cardiovascular exercise in your target heart rate zone, which means working at an intensity of 50 to 80 percent of your maximum heart rate. (The most effective way to track your heart rate is by using a heart-rate monitor.) The remaining 20 percent of your workout hours, or one to two days per week, should be high-intensity exercise, working at 85 to 95 percent of your maximum heart rate, or an all-out effort.

High-intensity training can be performed as a *steady state workout,* in which you hold your heart rate steady for the duration of the workout, or it can be achieved through *interval training,* which combines intervals of high-intensity training with lower intensity recovery. Interval durations can vary in length; research has shown that a high-intensity interval as short as 15 seconds can give positive results in weight loss, fat metabolization, and improvement in cardiovascular condition. As you increase your aerobic strength, the goal is to increase the duration of your intervals to, for instance, 2 minutes of high-intensity followed by 2 minutes of light-intensity or recovery.

T = TIME, OR DURATION For weight management, accumulate at least 30 minutes of exercise most days of the week. For weight loss, accumulate 60 to 90 minutes of cardiovascular exercise per day. This accumulated time can be achieved on some days in one long workout and on other days by combining two or three shorter sessions. Trish suggests that some days of the week you perform long-duration train-ing, or the full 60 to 90 minutes all at once, to improve your endurance.

T = TYPE OF EXERCISE Combine various types of exercise and equipment to keep your program fresh, prevent boredom, and reduce injuries. When you do not vary your exercise program and always perform the same exercises, use the same equipment, or work at the same intensity, you tend to adapt to that activity or level of activity; this is referred to as *exercise adaptation.* When this happens, you "plateau," or stop making physical improvements in overall fitness and body composition. In physical fitness, body composition is used to describe the percentages of fat, bone, and muscle in human bodies. The percentage of fat, commonly referred to as body fat percentage, is of most interest because it can be helpful in judging health in addition to body weight. Because muscular tissue takes up less space in our body than fat tissue, our body composition, as well as our weight, determines how lean we appear. Two people at the same height and same body weight may look completely

different from each other because they have a different body composition.

E = ENJOYMENT Always engage in activities you enjoy, so you'll stick with it!

Do resistance training to improve your resting metabolic rate (RMR). Muscle is a metabolically active tissue, which means the more muscle you have, the more calories you burn, even when you're inactive. Doing resistance training two to three times per week can help you burn as much as 50 extra calories per day while at rest. Measured cumulatively, this equals 350 additional calories burned over the course of a week. From the time we turn about 18 years old, we can experience a 2 to 3 percent reduction in RMR every decade due to a loss of muscle. Fortunately, resistance or strength training can help regain muscle mass and raise metabolism. Strength training can also slow the loss of bone that happens as we age, which is important for avoiding osteoporosis and lowering fracture risk.

Examples of exercises that improve strength include traditional weightlifting exercises using free weights, barbells, or commercial weight machines; exercises such as push-ups, which utilize your own body weight as resistance; and exercises that utilize elastic bands and tubing. In each case, the exercise causes the muscle to work against a resistance above normal levels achieved in every-day activities; this will lead to muscular adaptations and increases in strength. You should perform 8 to 10 exercises in some combination of upper body, lower body, and core (abdomen and back). The number of repetitions to complete with each exercise depends on your goals, but two to three sets of 8 to 12 repetitions is the standard recommendation. Generally, more weight with fewer repetitions will yield greater increases in strength and provide a greater increase in metabolism; less weight and more repetitions will develop muscular endurance. Research has shown that even people older than 90 can still develop muscular strength when they perform regular strength-training exercises.

Insert more movement into your everyday activities. In addition to the activities you may do often that automatically involve movement, such as gardening, vacuuming the house, or walking the dog, be mindful of moving more when you do those everyday activities that don't typically involve much motion. For instance, when you go shopping, park your car as far away as possible from the store so you have to walk farther to reach your destination; take the stairs instead of the elevator *every* time it's possible; walk in place while you brush your teeth, and stand instead of sit while talking on the telephone.

Take more steps every day and count them as you go. For health benefits and weight management take 10,000 steps per day. For weight loss, aim for 12,000 to 15,000 steps daily. Walk whenever possible; start by adding an easy 10-minute walk after at least one meal every day. Get a pedometer and track the number of steps you take each day. Pedometers work by measuring your hip movement. A pedometer that tracks your steps needs nothing more than to be attached and turned on. To track your mileage you will need to program your stride length into the device, which is easy to do; just follow the manufacturer's directions. (Claims by some makers that pedometers can provide calorie-burning information are generally inaccurate, since factors such as age, activity level, and metabolism play a huge role in burning calories but cannot be measured by the devices.)

Include weight-bearing exercise. To burn more calories and increase your bone mineral density, particularly in your hips, legs, and lower spine, include in your regimen weight-bearing exercises, which are exercises performed while standing on your feet. You don't need to carve out extra time for these because they can be worked into your cardiovascular and strength-training regimen. Weight-bearing cardiovascular exercise includes using an elliptical machine or a StairMaster (non- or low-impact) and walking, running, and aerobic dance (moderate- to high-impact). Swimming, cycling, and rowing, while also excellent forms of activity, are not weight-bearing.

Any strength-training exercise performed while standing on your feet is considered weight-bearing; examples include using free weights to perform squats or lunges for the lower body, or any upper body exercises done in a standing position.

Combine workouts to save time. If you are challenged for time, try combining your aerobic exercise with your strength-training workouts; this is referred to as circuit training. For example, do intervals of 2 minutes of cardio followed by 12 to 15 repetitions of resistance or strength training. For a 60-minute circuit, begin with a 7- to 10-minute progressive cardiovascular warm-up. Next, perform 12 to 15 repetitions of any strength-training exercise. Go back to the cardio segment for 2 minutes. Continue alternating strength and cardio segments for the duration of your workout. Finish with a 5- to 7-minute cool down.

desserts

Almond Pear Dots

Pear and almond, a classic combination, are a wonderful update to jam-dot cookies, an old favorite at the Golden Door. As an added bonus, these dots contain no animal products, so they are vegan, and no refined sugars. If you don't have time to make pear or apple butter, use no- or low-sugar store-bought. **MAKES ABOUT 32 COOKIES**

FOR THE PEAR OR APPLE BUTTER

3 ripe pears or apples, peeled and chopped small (about 3 cups)

⅓ cup pear juice or apple juice

¼ teaspoon ground cinnamon

Pinch of kosher salt

FOR THE COOKIES

Vegetable oil cooking spray

1 cup slivered almonds

1 cup old-fashioned oats

1 cup whole wheat flour

1 teaspoon ground cinnamon

½ cup maple syrup

⅓ cup fresh orange juice (from 1 to 2 oranges)

¼ cup grapeseed or canola oil

1 teaspoon pure vanilla extract

½ teaspoon pure almond extract

Prepare the pear butter. In a medium saucepan combine the pears, pear juice, cinnamon, and salt and bring to a boil over medium heat. Simmer briskly, stirring occasionally, until most of the liquid has evaporated and the bottom of the pot is slightly sticky and light golden, 15 to 20 minutes. Remove from the heat and let cool. Puree in a blender or food processor until smooth. Use immediately or store in a tightly covered container in the refrigerator for up to 4 days.

Make the cookies. Place an oven rack in the middle of the oven and preheat the oven to 375°F. Line a baking sheet with parchment paper and coat with cooking spray.

Put the slivered almonds in the work bowl of a food processor. Pulse five to six times until ground to a coarse meal. Transfer the ground almonds to a large bowl. Next pulse the oats five to six times in the food processor until ground to a coarse meal. Transfer to the bowl with the ground almonds. Add the flour and the cinnamon and whisk to blend the dry ingredients.

In a separate bowl, whisk together the maple syrup, orange juice, grapeseed oil, vanilla, and almond extract. Add to the dry ingredients and use a wooden spoon to mix until well blended.

Place 1 tablespoon of batter for each cookie 1 inch apart on the prepared baking sheet. Dip your thumb or the back of a spoon in water and make a well in the middle of each cookie. Fill the middle of each cookie with a scant 1 teaspoon pear butter.

Bake until golden brown, 15 to 20 minutes. Let stand on the baking sheets until firm, about 1 minute, and then transfer the cookies to a wire rack to cool completely. The cookies can be stored at room temperature in a tightly sealed container for up to 3 days.

Chocolate Chip Cookies

To me there is nothing worse than a "healthy" chocolate chip cookie; I've had so few that taste good or have a nice, chewy texture. With the help of Golden Door intern Emily Marciniak, I set out to create the best possible chocolate chip cookie: one that exudes classic chocolate chip cookie flavor but contains no animal products or refined sugars. What we came up with is crisp on the outside, slightly soft on the inside, and tastes sensational. **MAKES ABOUT 2 DOZEN COOKIES**

Vegetable oil cooking spray

½ cup old-fashioned rolled oats

1 cup whole wheat flour

⅓ cup chocolate chips

1 tablespoon ground flaxseed

½ teaspoon baking soda

¼ teaspoon kosher salt

¾ cup maple syrup

½ cup applesauce

3 tablespoons grapeseed oil

1 teaspoon pure vanilla extract

½ teaspoon fresh lemon juice

Preheat the oven to 350°F. Line a baking sheet with parchment paper and coat with cooking spray.

Put the oats in the work bowl of a food processor. Process until ground into a fine meal, about 10 seconds. Transfer to a large bowl. Add the flour, chocolate chips, ground flaxseed, baking soda, and salt. Whisk together the dry ingredients until well combined.

In a separate bowl, whisk together the maple syrup, applesauce, grapeseed oil, vanilla, and lemon juice. Pour into the dry ingredients and use a rubber spatula to fold the ingredients together until just incorporated. The batter will be very moist, like muffin batter.

Using a ¾-ounce scoop or rounded tablespoonfuls, spoon the batter 1½ inches apart on the prepared cookie sheet. Use the back of a wet spoon to slightly flatten each cookie.

Bake one sheet at a time until light golden brown, about 20 minutes turning the pan halfway through baking. Use a spatula to transfer the cookies to racks to cool completely. These are best eaten within 1 day of baking; store them at room temperature in a tightly sealed container.

Orange Almond Tuiles

Light, crisp tuiles, or "tiles" in French, are so called because they are usually formed into a slightly curved shape similar to ceramic roof tiles on old French houses. In fact, while still warm they can be molded into a variety of shapes, such as cups or cones. They are perfect for pairing with your favorite sorbet—I am especially fond of these with Pineapple, Crystallized Ginger, and Banana Sorbet (page 198)—ice cream, or fresh berries. If you have a silicone baking mat, this is the time to use it, for the baked tuiles are much easier to remove from these mats. If using parchment, work quickly to remove the tuiles from the parchment while they are still warm. **MAKES 18 TUILES**

Scant 1 cup sliced almonds

2 large egg whites

⅔ cup organic confectioners' sugar

2 teaspoons grated orange zest

1 teaspoon all-purpose flour

Preheat the oven to 375°F. Line a baking sheet with a baking mat or parchment paper.

Put the almonds in the work bowl of a food processor and process until they resemble very fine bread crumbs, about 30 seconds. Transfer the nuts to a bowl and add the egg whites, confectioners' sugar, orange zest, and flour. Use a rubber spatula to stir together just until combined.

Spread a heaping teaspoon of batter into a thin 3½-inch circle on the prepared cookie sheet. Continue to form tuiles, leaving 2 inches between them.

Bake until light golden brown, about 6 minutes. Use a palette knife, offset spatula, or thin-bladed knife to remove the cookies from the baking sheet and transfer them to the mold for shaping as indicated below. The cookies will harden quickly. If they become too hard before they are shaped, place them back in the oven for 30 seconds to soften them. They may also be served flat; transfer them directly to cooling racks to cool completely.

For a classic, curved tile shape, drape them over a rolling pin to cool completely.

For a cigarette shape, flip the warm tuile upside down on the work surface in front of you and lay a clean dowel or pencil across the bottom of the cookie. Quickly roll the cookie up around the dowel. Slide the dowel out and let the cookie cool completely.

For a cup shape, flip the cookie over into a small ramekin or other small dish and gently push the warm cookie into the dish, crimping as necessary to form a cup shape.

Stored in an airtight container at room temperature away from humidity, tuiles will stay crisp for 4 to 5 days.

Blueberry Lime Ice

Packed with antioxidants this tasty sweet-tart sorbet is especially healthy. The acidity of the lime and the sweetness of the apple make the flavor of the blueberries pop. Best of all, it is a snap to prepare. **SERVES 8**

3 pints fresh or frozen blueberries, plus more fresh blueberries for serving (optional)

½ cup fresh orange juice (from 2 oranges)

3 tablespoons thawed frozen apple juice concentrate

3 tablespoons fresh lime juice (from 2 limes)

6 to 12 orange slices, for serving (optional)

6 sprigs fresh mint, for serving (optional)

In a shallow, nonreactive dish, combine the blueberries, orange juice, thawed apple juice concentrate, and lime juice and stir well to combine. Cover and place in the freezer until frozen solid, 3 to 6 hours.

When the mixture is frozen, remove it from the freezer and let it stand at room temperature for 10 minutes. With a large metal spoon, break the frozen fruit up into smaller pieces. Transfer the mixture to the work bowl of a food processor. Process until smooth and creamy, 5 to 8 minutes, scraping down the sides of the work bowl and stirring the mixture occasionally. Serve immediately or place back into the freezer for up to 1 hour before serving. The sorbet will freeze solid again but it can simply be processed again until creamy just before serving.

To serve, place a scoop or two in each of eight martini glasses and garnish with fresh blueberries, orange slices, and mint, if desired. Serve.

White Peach Citrus Sorbet

This method for making sorbet can be used to make sorbet from many different types of ripe, seasonal fruit. Mango, peach, strawberries, and bananas are just a few of the fruits that I've used with great results. Best of all, you can make the fruit wait for you: any time you have a bunch of fruit that risks going to waste, simply peel or rinse and slice or dice it. For every 3 cups fruit, squeeze over the juice of 1 orange and 1 lemon. Freeze flat in a freezer bag. Then, whenever you need a quick dessert, process as directed below. These fresh fruit sorbets will curb your cravings for full-fat, sugary, frozen treats. Serve with Orange Almond Tuiles (page 193). If you cannot find a variety of white peach, any summer peach or nectarine will be just as delicious. Just make sure whatever you use is ripe and sweet. **SERVES 8**

2 pounds ripe white peaches, peeled (see below), pitted, and coarsely chopped

2 cups fresh orange juice (from 6 to 8 oranges)

¼ cup fresh lime juice (from 2 limes)

In a shallow nonreactive dish, stir together the chopped peaches, orange juice, and lime juice. Cover and place in the freezer until frozen solid, 3 to 6 hours.

Once the mixture is frozen, let it stand at room temperature for 10 minutes. With a large metal spoon, break up the frozen fruit into smaller pieces. Transfer the mixture to the work bowl of a food processor. Process until smooth and creamy, about 5 minutes, scraping down the sides of the work bowl occasionally.

Serve immediately or place back into the freezer for up to 1 hour before serving. The sorbet will freeze solid again, but it can simply be processed again until creamy just before serving.

Peeling Peaches

Bring a large saucepan of water to a boil; prepare a bowl full of ice water. Using a thin-bladed knife, cut a shallow X in the base of each peach. Plunge the peaches into the boiling water for 10 seconds. Use a slotted spoon to transfer them to the ice water. Starting at the X, use a paring knife to peel the skin from the peaches. If the skin is hard to remove, plunge the peach back into the boiling water for another 10 seconds, and then transfer it to the ice water and try again.

Pineapple, Crystallized Ginger, and Banana Sorbet

This sorbet is delicious, with the sweet, tropical flavors of pineapple and banana. The ginger actually aids in digestion and soothes the stomach. Serve with Orange Almond Tuiles (page 193). Or, if serving after a summer cookout, grill slices of fresh pineapple for a minute or two per side. Serve a scoop of the sorbet on top the grilled pineapple and garnish with strips of crystallized ginger, diced pineapple, and baby mint leaves. **SERVES 8**

Large knob of fresh ginger

**½ fresh pineapple, peeled and diced
(3 cups)**

2 bananas, thinly sliced

1 cup no-sugar-added pineapple juice

1 tablespoon minced crystallized ginger

Grate the ginger on the large-holed side of a box grater until you have about ⅓ cup. Collect the grated ginger in your hand and squeeze over a bowl to extract 1 tablespoon of the juice. Discard the grated ginger.

In a shallow nonreactive dish, stir together the ginger juice, pineapple, bananas, and pineapple juice. Cover and place in the freezer until frozen solid, 3 to 6 hours.

When the mixture is frozen, remove it from the freezer and let it stand at room temperature for 10 minutes. With a large metal spoon, break the frozen fruit up into smaller pieces. Transfer the mixture to the work bowl of a food processor. Process until smooth and creamy, about 5 minutes, scraping down the sides of the bowl occasionally. Stir in the crystallized ginger.

Serve immediately, or place back into the freezer for up to 1 hour before serving. The sorbet will freeze solid again but it can simply be processed again until creamy just before serving.

Meyer Lemon Yogurt *and Fresh Fruit Brûlée*

Draining yogurt overnight removes all of the excess liquid, creating a yogurt cheese with a creamy, luxurious texture but without fat and excess calories. When adding flavorings such as citrus zest, sweeteners, or vanilla to the yogurt, it is important to whisk in those flavorings before draining. Once the yogurt is drained and thick, you don't want to whisk or stir it or it will loosen and you'll lose the thick consistency. **SERVES 4**

1 quart nonfat plain yogurt

2 tablespoons honey

2 teaspoons grated Meyer lemon zest

2 kiwi fruit, peeled and sliced ¼ inch thick

¼ cup fresh blueberries

¼ cup fresh raspberries

¼ cup diced, peeled mango

2 tablespoons sugar

In a medium bowl, combine the yogurt, honey, and lemon zest. Whisk to combine. Place a strainer over a bowl and line it with three layers of cheesecloth. Pour the yogurt into the cheesecloth-lined strainer. Cover and refrigerate overnight to drain. When the yogurt is drained, spoon it into four 4-ounce crème brûlée dishes; do not stir the yogurt. Use the back of a spoon to level the yogurt in the dish.

Decoratively arrange the kiwi, blueberries, raspberries, and mango on top of each dish. Refrigerate until ready to serve, for up to 3 hours.

Right before serving, put the sugar and 1 tablespoon water in a small, heavy-bottomed saucepan. Place the pan over medium-high heat. When the sugar is melted, shake the pan over the heat, swirling the melted sugar constantly until the mixture reaches a deep golden brown, 2 to 3 minutes. Immediately drizzle a little of the syrup over each dish and serve.

Vanilla Crème Brûlée

Crème brûlée, among the world's greatest desserts, is not one you normally associate with spa cuisine. Although classic crème brûlée is a masterpiece of simple, wholesome ingredients, it does contain a fair amount of fat from heavy cream. This version satisfies the desire for a rich, creamy dessert without excess fat and calories. **SERVES 6**

1¼ cups whole milk

1 (12-ounce) can evaporated skim milk

⅓ cup raw sugar, plus 6 teaspoons for caramelizing the tops

1 tablespoon cornstarch

½ vanilla bean or 1 teaspoon pure vanilla extract

4 egg yolks

Preheat the oven to 350°F.

In a medium saucepan, combine the whole milk, evaporated skim milk, ⅓ cup sugar, and the cornstarch. Whisk until well blended. If using the vanilla bean, split it in half lengthwise with a sharp knife. Scrape out the seeds and add them and the pod to the milk mixture. Heat over medium heat, stirring occasionally, just until the mixture comes to a boil. Remove the pan from the heat. Remove and discard the vanilla bean pod halves, or, if using vanilla extract, stir it into the milk mixture.

Put the egg yolks in a large bowl and whisk lightly to break them up. Whisking constantly, slowly drizzle in 1 cup of the hot milk mixture. Once incorporated, add the rest of the milk, whisking constantly. Pour the mixture through a mesh strainer to get out any bits of cooked egg.

Place a folded kitchen towel in the bottom of a baking pan (to keep the dishes from sliding) and place six 4-ounce crème brûlée dishes on top. Divide the custard mixture among the dishes. Put the baking pan in the oven and pour hot water into the pan to halfway up the side of the dishes. Take care not to get any water into the dishes. Bake until the custard is just set, 40 to 50 minutes. The crème brûlées should not puff up; this is a good indication that they are overcooked.

Remove the baking pan from the oven and carefully remove the dishes from the water bath. Let cool for 15 minutes on the counter and then refrigerate until completely chilled, at least 3 hours.

When ready to serve, sprinkle a teaspoon of sugar on top of each crème brûlée. Use a butane torch to caramelize the sugar until light brown. Alternatively, place the custards on a sturdy baking sheet and position it about 5 inches below the broiler. Leave the oven door open and watch them carefully. You will likely need to turn them at least once to achieve even browning. Serve.

Lemongrass Crème Brûlée

To add lemony undertones to crème brûlée, follow the recipe above, infusing the milk with lemongrass instead of vanilla bean or vanilla extract.

Trim 4 stalks of lemongrass to the bulb end plus 3 inches of stalk. With the back of a chef's knife smash the bulbs. Combine the lemongrass, whole milk, and evaporated milk into a medium saucepan and bring almost to the boil, stirring occasionally. Remove the pan from the heat. Cover the pan and let stand for 20 minutes. Remove and discard the lemongrass. Stir in the cornstarch and sugar; omit the vanilla. Return the pan to medium heat and bring almost to a simmer.

Proceed with mixing the egg yolks into the milk and baking as directed above.

Fresh Strawberry Tartlets

Try making these tarts with all different fruits for a wonderful variety and colorful presentation. Blueberries, sliced blackberries, kiwi, diced mango, or pineapple are all great. Just follow this recipe, replacing the strawberries with other fruit, singly or in combination. Depending on how sweet the fruit is, you might be able to skip the sugar all together. **SERVES 12**

Grapeseed or canola oil or vegetable oil cooking spray, for preparing molds

2 cups raw almonds

1¾ cups pitted dates

2 pounds fresh strawberries, hulled and quartered

2 tablespoons fresh orange juice

1 tablespoon fresh lemon juice

1 tablespoon light brown sugar

1 teaspoon grated orange zest

1 teaspoon pure vanilla extract

Brush 12 tartlet molds (about 2⅜ inch x ⅜ inch is a good size) with grapeseed or canola oil or spray them with cooking spray. If tartlet molds are not available, you may shape the individual tarts by hand as directed below; line a baking sheet with parchment paper and lightly coat it with cooking spray.

Place the almonds in the work bowl of a food processor. Process until they resemble bread crumbs, about 30 seconds. Lightly oil a mixing bowl and transfer the ground almonds into it. Place the dates into the food processor with 1 teaspoon of water and pulse until they are well chopped (they will be a little clumpy). Add the dates to the almonds and stir with a wooden spoon until they hold together.

Distribute the mixture evenly among the prepared tartlet molds; there should be about 3 tablespoons per tartlet mold. Press the crumbs evenly onto the bottom and up the sides of the molds to form a crust. Alternatively, use a measuring cup or ramekin to scoop out about 3 tablespoons of the mixture. With lightly moistened hands, press the mixture together and then roll it into a tight ball. Press the ball into a 3-inch disk. Crimp up the edges to make a roughly ¼-inch rim, and place the shell on the prepared baking sheet. Repeat to make 12 tartlet shells. Refrigerate for 1 to 2 hours.

In a large bowl, combine the strawberries, orange juice, lemon juice, brown sugar, orange zest, and vanilla. Stir to mix well. Cover and refrigerate while you make the crust.

Carefully remove the crusts from the tartlet molds or use a metal spatula to remove the freeform tart shells from the cookie sheet. Place them on serving plates. Using a slotted spoon, pile berries into each crust and serve.

Blackberry Nectarine Crisp

Serve this simply as presented here, with a slice of nectarine and a pretty sprig of mint, or, for a more substantial dessert, serve with White Peach Citrus Sorbet (page 197) or store-bought lemon sorbet. **SERVES 12**

Vegetable oil cooking spray

3 cups fresh blackberries

3 large nectarines, pitted and sliced (3 cups), plus more for serving

¼ cup fresh orange juice (from 1 orange)

2 teaspoons pure vanilla extract

½ cup whole wheat flour

½ cup old-fashioned rolled oats

⅓ cup packed light brown sugar

3 tablespoons canola oil

2 tablespoons honey

1 teaspoon ground cinnamon

Pinch of freshly grated nutmeg

Fresh mint sprigs, for serving

Preheat the oven to 375°F. Coat a 9-inch baking dish or twelve 4-ounce ramekins with cooking spray.

In a large bowl, combine the blackberries, nectarines, orange juice, and vanilla. Stir gently until well combined. Set aside.

In a separate bowl, sift the flour. Add the oats, brown sugar, canola oil, honey, cinnamon, and nutmeg. Use your hands to mix the ingredients until well blended.

Spoon the fruit mixture into the prepared baking dish and scatter the crumb mixture evenly over the fruit. Bake until the fruit bubbles and the crumb topping is golden brown, 15 to 20 minutes for individual ramekins or 30 minutes for a single large dish. Place each ramekin on a small plate or spoon the crisp onto 12 small plates. Garnish each serving with 1 or 2 nectarine slices and a sprig of fresh mint. Serve hot.

Warm Flourless Chocolate Cake *with Orange Sauce*

Normally a flourless chocolate cake is made of lots of butter, chocolate, and eggs—undeniably delicious, but far too many calories and fat for a Golden Door dessert. This version is undeniably delicious, and also guilt-free! Good chocolate will have indicated on its packaging what percentage of cacao, or cocoa bean, solids it contains. Use good-quality chocolate with 60 percent to 70 percent cacao for this cake. Be sure not to let any water at all come into contact with the chocolate as it melts. Water or condensation will cause the chocolate to become grainy and unusable. When preparing this recipe, grate the orange zest for the cakes before juicing the oranges for the sauce. SERVES 8

Vegetable oil cooking spray

FOR THE SAUCE

1 cup fresh orange juice (from 3 oranges)

2 teaspoons cornstarch

1 tablespoon half-and-half

1 tablespoon Grand Marnier

FOR THE CAKES

**8 ounces good-quality dark chocolate
with 60% to 70% cacao, chopped**

1 large egg

2 very ripe bananas, sliced (1¼ cups)

**½ cup mashed yam (from 1 small baked,
peeled yam) or canned pumpkin**

¼ cup honey

1 tablespoon grated orange zest

1 teaspoon pure vanilla extract

3 large egg whites

Pinch of kosher salt

**1 orange, peeled and separated into
segments (see page 51), for serving**

Preheat the oven to 350°F. Spray eight 4-ounce ramekins with cooking spray until well coated and place them on a baking sheet.

Prepare the sauce. In a small saucepan, pour all but 1 tablespoon of the orange juice and place over low heat. In a small bowl, stir the cornstarch into the reserved 1 tablespoon orange juice until smooth. When the juice comes to a simmer, whisk in the cornstarch and juice slurry and continue to whisk for 30 seconds until thickened. Remove the pan from the heat and let cool for 15 minutes. Whisk in the half-and-half and the Grand Marnier. Set aside to keep warm or chill; the sauce can be served warm, at room temperature, or chilled.

Make the cakes. Place a bowl over a saucepan filled with a couple of inches of simmering water; the water should not touch the bowl. Place the chocolate in the bowl and let stand until the chocolate is shiny and soft to the touch, about 10 minutes. Stir with a rubber spatula until the chocolate is smooth. Remove from the heat.

Combine the egg, bananas, yam, honey, orange zest, and vanilla in a blender and process until very smooth. Add the banana mixture to the chocolate and stir together until just combined. Set aside.

CONTINUES ON PAGE 208

CONTINUED FROM PAGE 207

In another bowl, use an electric mixer to whip the egg whites and salt until they form soft peaks when the whip attachments are lifted up and out of the bowl, about 3 minutes. Carefully fold the egg whites into the chocolate mixture until just incorporated. Do not overmix; it is fine if streaks of white remain.

Spoon the mixture into the ramekins to about ¼ inch from the top. Bake until the tops are set when a ramekin is gently nudged and the centers are slightly puffed, 8 to 10 minutes. Transfer the ramekins to a cooling rack. When the ramekins are cool enough to handle, run a paring knife around the edges and turn over onto eight dessert plates. The center of the cake should be nice and soft.

Drizzle the sauce around each cake and garnish with orange segments. Serve.

Angel Food Cake *with Fresh Peach Coulis*

Airy angel food cake and fresh peaches are a perfect, light, summer dessert. There are a couple of things to remember when working with egg whites. First, eggs are easier to separate when cold, and they whip best when warmer, so separate them straight from the refrigerator and let the whites sit in the mixing bowl until they come to room temperature before whipping. Then, be sure not to over whip them—you want soft, fluffy peaks—and gently fold the flour into the egg whites to avoid deflating them. **SERVES 6**

FOR THE CAKE

6 large egg whites, at room temperature

¾ teaspoon cream of tartar

Pinch of kosher salt

¾ cup sugar

¾ teaspoon pure vanilla extract

½ cup unbleached all-purpose flour

FOR THE PEACH COULIS

3 ripe peaches, peeled (see page 197),
  pitted, and chopped

2 teaspoons fresh lemon juice

1 tablespoon sugar or honey (optional)

Thinly sliced fresh peaches, for serving

Place an oven rack in the center of the oven and preheat the oven to 350°F. Place six nonstick mini angel food cake pans or brioche molds on a baking sheet or have ready a nonstick jumbo muffin pan.

Prepare the cake. In the bowl of an electric mixer fitted with the whip attachment, whip the egg whites, cream of tartar, and salt on medium speed for a few seconds, gradually increasing the speed to medium-high, until the whites are foamy, about 45 seconds in all. Continue to beat until the whites have increased about four times in volume, 1 to 2 minutes. With the mixer running, add the sugar 1 tablespoon at a time, scraping down the bowl once or twice. Add the vanilla and continue to beat until the egg whites form soft peaks when the whip is lifted up and out of the bowl, 1 to 2 minutes after all the sugar has been added.

Sift the flour. Sprinkle about one-third of it over the egg whites. With a rubber spatula, gently fold the flour into the meringue. Be careful not to overmix and deflate the meringue. Gently fold in the remaining flour in two batches.

Spoon the batter into the pans and smooth the top. Rap the pans firmly on the work surface a few times to break up any bubbles. Place the baking sheet with the pans on the center rack and bake until the tops of the cakes are golden brown and the sides start to pull away from the pans, about 20 minutes.

Remove the pans from the oven and place them upside down on a wire rack until cool enough to handle. While still warm, run a thin knife around the edge of each pan. Let cool completely before unmolding.

CONTINUES ON PAGE 210

CONTINUED FROM PAGE 209

While the cakes are cooling, prepare the peach coulis. In a blender, combine the peaches and the lemon juice. Process until smooth. If necessary, stop the blender, push the ingredients down with a spoon, and blend again, repeating as necessary. Taste for sweetness. If you find that the peach coulis is not quite sweet enough, dissolve the sugar or honey in 2 tablespoons hot water and stir into the coulis a little at a time, until the desired sweetness is reached.

When the cakes are completely cool, unmold them. Place one cake on each of six plates. Pour a pool of the coulis around each cake. Garnish with thin slices of fresh peach.

tips from the golden door
keeping a food diary

Dr. Wendy Bazilian, the nutrition specialist at the Golden Door, jokes that for all the highly detailed and personalized information and advice she gives, she often receives the most credit for the weight loss and improved health the women and men she works with initially achieve when they simply keep a careful record of what they eat and drink. This is ironic not only because it's the clients themselves who do all the work but also because the first time she mentions the "dreaded" food diary to our guests she is invariably met with grimaces and groans of reluctance. However, those individuals who take her up on the challenge see remarkably consistent, positive results. In fact, research has shown that the simple process of writing down what you eat and drink can play a significant role in helping you achieve weight-loss goals and manage medical conditions such as blood pressure, cholesterol, blood sugar, and food allergies or sensitivities. Furthermore, keeping a consistent food diary is an important predictor of successful long-term weight management.

Even if weight loss or health conditions are not immediate concerns, Dr. Wendy has found that when kept regularly, a food diary can help people improve their eating habits; aid in advance meal planning; and empower individuals if they must seek medical advice—especially regarding health changes that occur gradually—by giving them a detailed record of their eating, exercise, and sleeping habits over time. In short, a food diary is an incredible source of information and a powerful motivator. Keeping one helps you look beyond "what" and "how much" you are eating to the pattern of your consumption and how it affects your energy, mood, and health over time. Here are Dr. Wendy's steps for keeping a successful food diary:

1. Pick a style. Keep it simple. You can use a notebook, staple some sheets of paper together, or use your PDA or computer. Make sure it's a format that will always be with you and is easy to use.

2. Write down every meal and snack you eat and every drink you consume during the day, from breakfast until you go to bed, and your levels of hunger and stress both before and after each meal. Make a simple chart with six simple headings and lots of space to fill in the following information (feel free to personalize it as necessary to help you meet your own goals):

- The meal and time you're eating: breakfast, lunch, dinner, or snack.
- The food or drink you consume.
- How the food or drink is prepared.
- How much you consumed.
- Your hunger before and after you eat or drink; use a scale from 0 to 10, where 0 is empty and ravenous and 10 is stuffed.
- Your level of stress before and after you eat or drink; use a scale from 0 to 10, where 0 is stress-free and 10 is severely stressed.

3. At the bottom of the chart include the following information to track your healthy behaviors:

- Sleep (wake-up time, number of hours of sleep, quality of sleep, how you feel)
- Water (approximate cups; goal 6+)
- Activity/exercise (time of day, type, duration)
- How I managed my stress today
- What I did well today (note at least two things)

4. Keep your diary every day for two weeks. If you skip a meal or forget, restart as soon as you remember. This is not about perfection, it's about practice. Remember that no one is judging how you keep your diary or what is in it and you shouldn't, either. You need time— two weeks at a minimum—to get into the habit.

5. After two weeks, keep your diary for three days a week for at least six weeks. Pick the same three days each week— two weekdays and one weekend day is best—and mark it on your calendar so you remember. If you're working toward a health goal such as weight loss or cholesterol reduction, continue to keep your diary three days a week until you meet your goal, and then for an additional six to eight weeks after you've met the goal to solidify your success. Many people so deeply appreciate the value of the food diary that they continue with it indefinitely.

6. For maintenance, track your food for three days every other week or once a month indefinitely (make it a recurring reminder in your electronic calendar and you'll never forget). Those additional 10 pounds don't just show up overnight, but when we don't have good systems and practices in place, it can be a shock at the end of the year when the scale reads 10 pounds heavier. When you monitor yourself with this simple practice, you're more likely to notice subtle changes in the quantity or quality of your food and drink consumption as well as your mood or sleep habits. Any of these can be indicators of weight changes or shifts in your health for better or worse to which you can respond, even if you never step on a scale or see your doctor infrequently.

7. Keeping a food diary over the long term can also be an important reinforcer and motivator of what you do well. Use a highlighter to mark the healthy, nutritious foods in your diet. Reinforcing the positive makes it more likely that you'll practice those behaviors again.

breakfast

Golden Door Oatmeal

Oats contain soluble fiber, which can help reduce LDL, the "bad" cholesterol, which is linked to lowering your risk of heart disease. Eating oats every day is a really easy—and delicious—way to improve the health of your heart. In this recipe, allowing the cinnamon stick to stand in the warm milk infuses the oatmeal with the wonderful flavor of this warm spice without it being overpowering. Delicately sweetened and topped with caramelized apples, toasted almonds, and raisins, ours is soul-satisfying oatmeal—perfect for crisp mornings. **SERVES 4**

¾ **cup skim milk**

1 (3-inch) cinnamon stick

1½ cups old-fashioned rolled oats

Grapeseed oil spray

**2 apples or pears, peeled and chopped
(about 2 cups)**

2 tablespoons light brown sugar

2 tablespoons raisins

1 tablespoon honey

**2 tablespoons sliced almonds, toasted
(page 135)**

Combine the milk and cinnamon stick in a small saucepan and bring just to the boil. Remove the pan from the heat, cover, and let stand for 10 minutes.

Meanwhile, in a medium saucepan, bring 3¾ cups water to a boil. Stir in the oats and reduce the heat to low. Simmer gently for 10 minutes. Remove the pan from the heat.

While the oatmeal is cooking, mist a medium saucepan with grapeseed oil and heat over high heat. Add the apples and brown sugar and cook, stirring, until the sugar melts and starts to brown, about 2 minutes. Stir in the raisins. Remove from the heat and set aside.

Strain the hot cinnamon-infused milk into the cooked oatmeal, add the honey, and stir to combine.

Divide the oatmeal among four warm bowls. Top each serving with the caramelized apples and raisins and sliced almonds. Serve hot.

Cinnamon Cranberry Granola

You can use any dried fruit you like in place of the cranberries; chopped dates or dried currants, tart cherries, and blueberries are some of my favorites. Enjoy this granola with fresh fruit, low-fat cottage cheese, or yogurt for a balanced, healthy, and delicious breakfast. It's also delicious as a cereal with milk or as part of the Yogurt Cream, Blueberry, and Cantaloupe Parfait (page 220). **MAKES 4 CUPS; SERVES 8**

2 cups old-fashioned rolled oats

⅓ cup raw sunflower seeds

⅓ cup sliced almonds

⅓ cup honey

⅓ cup dried cranberries, chopped dates, or dried currants

1 teaspoon ground cinnamon

Preheat the oven to 350°F.

On a rimmed baking sheet, spread the oats and sunflower seeds in a thin layer and toast in the oven for 10 to 12 minutes. Remove the pan from the oven and stir the oats and sunflower seeds, spreading them out evenly. Return to oven to bake until the mixture is light brown all over, about 10 minutes longer.

Add the sliced almonds to the oats and sunflower seeds and stir to combine. Return to the oven until the mixture is golden brown, about 5 minutes.

Remove the pan from the oven, and drizzle the honey over the oat mixture. Stir to combine. Bake for an additional 5 minutes.

Remove the pan from the oven and transfer the mixture to a large bowl. Stir in the dried cranberries and cinnamon. Allow the granola to cool to room temperature. Serve immediately or store at room temperature in a tightly sealed container for 4 to 5 days.

*Norberto's Muesli

Muesli was introduced around 1900 by a Swiss doctor, Maximilian Bircher-Benner, for patients in his hospital, where a diet rich in fresh fruit and vegetables was an essential part of therapy. Our Golden Door version is a guest favorite. Many say it is the best muesli they have ever had. It is lovingly prepared each week by Norberto Rojas, a cook who has been with the Golden Door for more than twenty years. Serve warm or cold with plain organic nonfat yogurt and fresh berries for a balanced, fiber-rich breakfast. SERVES 6

¼ cup diced dried figs

⅓ cup apple or pear juice, plus more for serving if needed

2 cups old-fashioned rolled oats

½ cup sliced or slivered almonds

¼ cup honey

1 medium Granny Smith apple, grated unpeeled (1 cup)

1 tablespoon grated orange zest

1 teaspoon ground cinnamon

3 cups nonfat plain yogurt, for serving

3 cups fresh fruit, such as fresh berries, sliced bananas, diced melon, or sliced peaches, for serving

Preheat the oven to 350°F.

Put the diced figs in a small bowl and pour in the apple juice. Let stand for 10 minutes. Drain the figs and set aside; reserve the apple juice if desired for moistening the muesli before serving.

On a rimmed baking sheet spread the oats in a thin layer and toast in the oven for 10 to 12 minutes. Remove the pan from oven and use a wooden spoon to stir the oats so they toast evenly. Return to the oven until lightly browned, 5 to 10 minutes.

Stir the sliced almonds into the oats on the baking sheet and return to the oven until lightly browned, about 5 minutes. Remove the pan from the oven. Drizzle the honey over the oats and almonds, and mix with a wooden spoon to blend. Bake for 5 minutes.

Remove the pan from the oven and transfer the oat mixture to a large bowl. Mix in the figs, apple, orange zest, and cinnamon. (You may serve the muesli immediately, while it is warm, or, once cool, store it in the refrigerator, tightly covered, for up to 5 days.)

To serve, divide the muesli among six bowls; if the muesli appears too dry, mix a few tablespoons of apple or pear juice into each serving. Spoon yogurt on top of each serving, and garnish with fresh fruit. Serve.

Yogurt Cream, Blueberry, and Cantaloupe Parfait

This beautiful, creamy parfait makes a well-balanced breakfast or a heavenly and healthful dessert. Calcium- and lean protein-packed yogurt, phylacteries-rich blueberries, potassium-packed cantaloupe, and a sprinkle of granola are a formidable nutritional combination. When they aren't in season, replace the blueberries and cantaloupe with any of your favorite, fresh, seasonal, local fruit. Make the yogurt cream ahead of time; it will easily keep in the refrigerator for a week or more. **SERVES 6**

1 quart plain, nonfat yogurt

3 tablespoons honey

¼ teaspoon pure vanilla extract

2 cups fresh blueberries

½ large cantaloupe, diced (2 cups)

¾ cup Cinnamon Cranberry Granola (page 217) or other granola

Fresh mint leaves, for serving (optional)

In a large bowl, combine the yogurt, honey, and vanilla and whisk together until well blended. Line a mesh strainer or colander with 3 layers of cheesecloth and place it over a bowl. Pour the yogurt mixture into the lined strainer. Cover and refrigerate for at least 3 hours or, preferably, overnight. Discard the liquid in the bowl. Once drained, the yogurt will be very thick and creamy.

Have ready six large, pretty, clear glasses, such as 15-ounce hurricane or parfait glasses. Put the yogurt cream in a piping bag fitted with a ½-inch or larger round tip or into a resealable plastic bag with one corner cut off. Pipe 2 to 3 tablespoons yogurt into each glass. Divide the blueberries among the glasses and then top with another 2 to 3 tablespoons yogurt. Divide the cantaloupe among the glasses.

If the yogurt was drained overnight, you can refrigerate the prepared parfaits for 2 to 3 hours. If not, serve immediately. Just before serving, top each parfait with 2 tablespoons of granola and garnish with mint leaves, if desired.

*Tecate Bread

This recipe originated at Rancho La Puerta in Tecate, Mexico, and was introduced to the Golden Door in the early 1970s by Ignacio Leon, who had been baking this wonderful bread at the Ranch for many years. It was an instant hit at the Door and has been a staple ever since, baked fresh daily in our kitchen. This hearty, nutty, crusty bread has a slightly chewy bite.

MAKES 2 LOAVES, 16 SLICES EACH

2 tablespoons active dry yeast

2 tablespoons honey

2½ cups tepid water

¼ cup canola oil

¼ cup dark molasses

1 cup wheat bran

1 tablespoon kosher salt

6 cups whole wheat flour, plus up to ½ cup flour for dusting

Vegetable oil cooking spray

In the bowl of an electric stand mixer fitted with the dough hook attachment, combine the yeast, honey, and water and stir to combine. Let stand until the yeast is dissolved and the mixture is foamy, about 5 minutes. (Note: if mixture is not bubbly and foamy it means the yeast is not active; throw the mixture away and start over with a newer yeast packet.)

Add the canola oil and molasses to the yeast mixture and mix on low speed to combine. With the mixer still running on low speed, add the wheat bran, salt, and flour. When all the ingredients have been incorporated, increase the mixer speed to medium and continue mixing until the dough is smooth and elastic, about 5 minutes. Transfer the dough to a bowl dusted with flour. Cover and set aside in a warm place to rise until the dough has about doubled in volume, 30 to 40 minutes.

Lightly spray two 8½ x 4½-inch loaf pans with cooking spray and set aside.

Dust a flat, smooth work surface with flour. Turn the dough onto the surface and punch down vigorously and knead until smooth and elastic, 2 to 3 minutes. Divide the dough in half and form each half into a loaf. Place the dough in the prepared pans. Cover the pans with a towel and let rise in a warm place for 20 to 30 minutes.

Preheat the oven to 350°F.

Bake the loaves for about 50 minutes, or until browned on the top and bottom and firm when pressed. Remove the bread from the pans and let them cool on a rack before slicing.

Tecate bread is best eaten within a day of being baked. For longer storage, slice the loaf and place in a tightly sealed, sturdy plastic bag and freeze for up to 1 month.

Cottage Griddle Cakes *with Blueberry-Peach Syrup*

These griddle cakes are elegant yet hearty. Whole wheat flour gives nutty flavor and earthy texture, while low-fat cottage cheese and buttermilk contribute tang and tenderness. The cane sugar and lemon zest provide sweet, citrus undertones. Topped with warm fruit poached in maple syrup, this dish makes a healthy breakfast feel decadent. **MAKES ABOUT 2 DOZEN (3-INCH) GRIDDLE CAKES; SERVES 8 TO 12**

FOR THE GRIDDLE CAKES

1 cup low-fat cottage cheese

¾ cup unbleached all-purpose flour

¾ cup whole wheat flour

¼ cup sugar

2 teaspoons baking powder

½ teaspoon baking soda

½ teaspoon kosher salt

1½ cups low-fat buttermilk

3 large egg whites

1 tablespoon unsalted butter, melted

1½ tablespoons grated lemon zest

Vegetable oil, for cooking

FOR THE SYRUP

1 cup fresh or thawed, frozen sliced peaches

1 cup fresh or thawed, frozen blueberries

⅓ cup maple syrup

Place a baking sheet in the oven and preheat the oven to 200°F.

Prepare the griddle cakes. Put the cottage cheese in a strainer placed over a bowl to drain off any excess liquid. In a medium bowl, whisk together the all-purpose flour, whole wheat flour, sugar, baking powder, baking soda, and salt. Transfer the drained cottage cheese to a large bowl. Add the buttermilk, egg whites, butter, and lemon zest. Whisk the liquid ingredients together until well blended. Use a wooden spoon to stir the dry ingredients into the wet ingredients just until blended; the batter will have lumps.

Pour a small amount of vegetable oil on a griddle or nonstick skillet and use a paper towel to coat the pan and soak up excess oil. Heat the pan over medium heat for a few minutes, until a few droplets of water dropped on the pan dance and sizzle. If the water stays in one place and boils slowly, the pan is too cold; if it steams away immediately, the pan is too hot.

Spoon 1 heaping tablespoon of batter onto the griddle for each griddle cake. Cook until the bottom is golden brown, about 2 minutes. Turn each griddle cake over and cook until golden brown on the other side, 1 to 2 minutes. Place the griddle cakes on the baking sheet in the preheated oven to keep warm until ready to serve.

Prepare the syrup. Combine the peaches, blueberries, and maple syrup in a small saucepan and bring to a simmer. Cook for about 3 minutes, until the peaches are slightly softened and the blueberries are just starting to pop.

Arrange 2 to 3 griddle cakes on each of 8 to 12 warmed plates. Spoon the syrup and fruit over and around the griddle cakes and serve.

Banana Almond Berry Muffins

This extremely versatile recipe yields sweet, tender fruit muffins, whether you make it just as written here or replace the berries and almonds with your favorite fruit or nut, such as diced pineapple or mango, dried fruits, walnuts, pecans, or macadamia nuts (in this case, omit the almond extract). The yield will vary slightly depending on what fruit you use.

Whole wheat pastry flour is lower in protein than regular whole wheat flour and therefore has less of the gluten that gives bread its strength and chewiness. Less protein in the flour means more tender baked goods. Whole wheat pastry flour can be found in the baking section of natural foods stores or the natural-food section of general supermarkets. Regular whole wheat flour can certainly be used in its place; the result will be a bit heavier but still absolutely delicious. **MAKES ABOUT 12 MUFFINS OR ABOUT 48 MINI MUFFINS**

Nonstick baking spray

½ cup sliced almonds

2½ cups whole wheat pastry flour or regular whole wheat flour

1½ teaspoons baking powder

½ teaspoon baking soda

1½ teaspoons ground cinnamon

⅛ teaspoon kosher salt

1 cup low-fat buttermilk

2 large eggs

⅔ cup packed light brown sugar

2 tablespoons canola oil

1 teaspoon pure vanilla extract

½ teaspoon almond extract

1 very ripe banana, sliced

2 cups fresh or frozen berries, such as blueberries, raspberries, blackberries, or chopped strawberries

Spray with nonstick baking spray a standard 12-cup muffin tin, or four 12-cup mini muffin tins. Preheat the oven to 400°F.

On a rimmed baking sheet, spread the almonds in a single layer. Toast in the oven, stirring the almonds or shaking the pan occasionally, until lightly browned and fragrant, 3 to 5 minutes. Remove from the oven and immediately transfer the almonds to a plate to cool completely. Set aside.

In large bowl, whisk together the flour, baking powder, baking soda, cinnamon, and salt.

In a blender, combine the buttermilk, eggs, brown sugar, canola oil, vanilla extract, almond extract, and banana. Blend until the mixture is smooth.

Make a well in the center of dry ingredients, and pour in the buttermilk mixture. Using a wooden spoon, stir gently just until combined. Stir in the berries and toasted almonds just until moistened. The batter will be lumpy with traces of flour; do not overmix. Spoon the batter into the muffin tins.

Bake until medium golden-brown, the muffins slightly pull away from the sides, and a toothpick inserted in the center of one comes out clean, 25 to 30 minutes for standard muffins or 15 to 20 minutes for mini muffins. Turn the pans halfway through baking for even browning. Serve warm or at room temperature.

The muffins are best eaten the day they are baked. For longer storage, place the muffins in an airtight container and refrigerate for 3 to 4 days. To freeze, place the muffins in a tightly sealed plastic freezer bag and freeze for up to 1 month.

*Tomato Cheese Toast

Our guests enjoy this Golden Door classic every Tuesday morning when it is served with fresh seasonal fruit and orange juice squeezed from oranges grown in our groves. If you don't have time to bake the Tecate Bread, any hearty whole wheat bread will work wonderfully. **SERVES 4**

4 slices Tecate Bread (page 221) or other whole wheat bread, toasted

2 medium ripe, red tomatoes, each cut into 8 slices

1½ teaspoons dried Italian seasoning

Pinch of freshly ground black pepper, or to taste

4 ounces Gruyère cheese, grated (2 cups)

Preheat the broiler. Line a baking sheet with foil.

Cut each slice of toasted bread in half diagonally and arrange the halves on the baking sheet. Top each half with 2 tomato slices, overlapping them. Sprinkle the tomatoes with the dried Italian seasoning and a little ground black pepper. Top with grated Gruyère cheese, covering the bread completely so it does not scorch.

Place the baking sheet about 5 inches from the heat and cook until the cheese is melted and lightly browned, 2 to 3 minutes. Serve immediately.

Eggs Florentine *with Smoked Turkey,*
Whole Wheat English Muffin, and Creamy Yellow Pepper Sauce

If you do not have time to roast your own peppers, look for them in jars or in the salad or olive bar area of your local market. Make sure the peppers are not marinated. **SERVES 4**

¼ cup plus 1 tablespoon 1% low-fat milk

2 large yellow bell peppers, roasted (see page 74), peeled, and chopped

1 tablespoon Neufchâtel cheese (light cream cheese)

2 teaspoons Dijon mustard

3 teaspoons fresh lemon juice (from 1 lemon)

Kosher salt

4 drops Tabasco sauce, plus more for serving

Olive oil spray

2 ounces fresh spinach (4 cups packed loose leaves)

Freshly ground black pepper

1 tablespoon vinegar

4 large eggs, preferably organic

4 ounces nitrate-free smoked turkey breast, thinly sliced (about 8 slices)

2 Whole Wheat English Muffins (page 229) or store-bought, halved and toasted

Heat the milk until steaming, about 30 seconds on high in the microwave. Pour it into a blender. Add the roasted peppers, Neufchâtel, mustard, 1 teaspoon of the lemon juice, ¼ teaspoon salt, and the Tabasco. Blend on low speed until smooth and creamy, about 30 seconds. Transfer the sauce to a microwave-safe bowl, cover, and set aside.

Mist a medium skillet with olive oil and heat on medium-high. Add the spinach—if it is not damp, add a tablespoon or two of water to the pan; the spinach should sizzle when it hits the pan. Add a pinch each of salt and pepper and the remaining 2 teaspoons of lemon juice. Cook, stirring, just until wilted, about 30 seconds. Remove the pan from the heat. Drain, using a spoon to press the spinach against one side of the pan to squeeze out excess moisture. Set aside.

In a large shallow pot, bring 1 quart of water and the vinegar to a boil. Reduce the heat so that the water is barely simmering. Crack one egg into a teacup at a time without breaking the yolk, and gently slide the egg into water. Poach until the whites are set and yolks are soft to the touch, 2½ to 3 minutes. Use a slotted spoon to transfer the eggs to a paper towel–lined plate.

Place the smoked turkey in a covered microwave-safe dish and heat on high until warmed through, about 15 seconds. Heat the sauce in the microwave until warm, about 40 seconds.

To serve, place one English muffin half on each of four plates. Spoon a little sauce on each muffin, followed by the wilted spinach. Place 2 slices of warm smoked turkey on top of the spinach. Place a poached egg on top of the turkey and spoon a little more sauce over and around the English muffin. Finish the dish with a few drops of Tabasco and ground black pepper. Serve.

WHOLE WHEAT ENGLISH MUFFINS

Commercially prepared whole wheat English muffins often have the texture and flavor of cardboard. Making your own is really fun, and the results are wonderful nutty flavor and nubby texture. **MAKES 18 MUFFINS**

1 package active dry yeast (2¼ teaspoons)

1 teaspoon sugar

⅓ cup warm water

1⅔ cups 2% low-fat milk, at room temperature

2 tablespoons olive oil

1 tablespoon distilled white vinegar

1 large egg, lightly beaten

1 teaspoon kosher salt

4 cups whole wheat flour

1 cup unbleached all-purpose flour

1 cup cornmeal, or as needed

Olive oil spray

In the bowl of an electric stand mixer fitted with the dough hook attachment, combine the yeast, sugar, and water. Stir to combine and let stand until the yeast has dissolved and is foamy, about 5 minutes. (Note: if mixture is not foamy it means the yeast is not active; throw it away and start over with a new yeast packet.)

Add the milk, olive oil, vinegar, and egg to the yeast mixture and mix on low speed until well blended. With the mixer running, add the salt along with 2½ cups of the whole wheat flour. Increase the speed to medium and mix for 4 minutes. Turn the mixer to low and add the remaining 1½ cups whole wheat flour and the all-purpose flour. Increase the speed to medium and mix until well blended, about 2 minutes. The mixture will be sticky. Cover and let stand in a warm area for 1 hour.

Preheat the oven to 350°F. Line two baking sheets with parchment paper.

Pour the cornmeal onto a small plate. With a ¼-cup measuring cup, scoop out ¼ cup of the dough. Using your hands, form the dough into a ball and flatten it into a 3-inch round. Press each side into the cornmeal and place it on the prepared baking sheet. Repeat with the remaining dough.

Heat a griddle or large cast-iron skillet over medium-low heat for 5 minutes. Spray the pan with olive oil. Place the muffins about ½ inch apart on the hot griddle or skillet. Cook until browned on the bottom, about 5 minutes. Turn the muffins over and brown on the other side, about 5 minutes. Repeat with all of the muffins; between batches wipe the griddle with a paper towel and spray again with oil

Return the muffins to the baking sheets and bake for 15 minutes. Transfer the muffins to a cooling rack to cool completely. To serve, use a fork to split a muffin in half through the middle to make two rounds, and toast. (English muffins can be stored in a resealable plastic bag at room temperature for 2 to 3 days. For longer storage, freeze for up to 2 months. When ready to use, thaw at room temperature, then split and toast as directed above.)

Crispy Potato Cakes *with Chive Scrambled Eggs and Smoked Salmon*

Warm crispy potato, fluffy eggs, and silky smoked salmon perfectly complement each other. Often potato pancakes depend on eggs to keep them bound together, but baking the potatoes for a short time before grating them brings out their natural starchiness, which provides all the glue needed to hold them together. The result is pure potato pancakes, with no unnecessary additions. **SERVES 4**

12 ounces russet or Yukon Gold potatoes (about 2 medium), scrubbed

1 tablespoon Neufchâtel cheese (light cream cheese), at room temperature

2 teaspoons very hot water

½ teaspoon fresh lemon juice

Freshly ground black pepper

Olive oil spray

¼ medium onion, diced (¼ cup)

¼ teaspoon onion powder

¼ teaspoon kosher salt, plus more for the eggs

2 large eggs

2 large egg whites

1 tablespoon minced fresh chives

4 ounces smoked salmon (4 slices)

4 fresh dill sprigs

Dill Oil (page 272), for serving

Preheat the oven to 400°F.

Bake the potatoes directly on a rack in the oven for 25 minutes. Remove them from the oven and let cool.

Meanwhile, in a small cup, combine the Neufchâtel cheese and hot water and use a fork or spoon to beat until smooth. Stir in the lemon juice and a pinch of pepper and stir until well blended. Set the lemon cream aside.

Spray a small sauté pan with olive oil, and heat over medium heat. Add the onion and cook, stirring frequently, until the onion is translucent and fragrant, 4 to 5 minutes. Remove from the heat and set aside.

When the potatoes are cool enough to handle, use a paring knife to peel the potatoes; the skin should come off easily. Grate them on the large-holed side of a box grater. Put the grated potato in a bowl. Add the onion to the potato along with the onion powder, ¼ teaspoon salt, and a pinch of pepper. Wet your hands with water, and use them to combine the mixture until well blended. With wet hands, form the potato mixture into four equal cakes, each about 3 inches across.

Spray a large nonstick skillet with olive oil and heat over medium heat. Put the potato cakes in the pan and cook until golden brown, about 4 minutes. Spray the uncooked side of the potato cakes with olive oil and turn them over. Cook until golden brown on the other side, about 4 minutes. Set aside and keep warm.

CONTINUES ON PAGE 232

CONTINUED FROM PAGE 230

Whisk together the eggs, egg whites, and a pinch each of salt and pepper. Spray a medium nonstick skillet with olive oil and heat over medium heat. Add the eggs to the pan and use a wooden spoon to gently stir them. When the eggs start to come together, after about 30 seconds, sprinkle in half the chives. Continue to cook, stirring, until eggs are set but still moist, 1 to 2 minutes. Immediately remove the pan from the heat.

Place a warm potato cake on each of four plates, spoon a couple of tablespoons of scrambled egg on top of each cake, and top with a folded slice of smoked salmon. Garnish with the remaining chives, the dill sprigs, the lemon cream cheese, and a few drops of dill oil. Serve.

Individual Sharp Cheddar Frittata
with Potato, Spinach, and Red Onion

Frittatas are great breakfast fare because of their versatility and ease. You can add just about anything to them: small amounts of diced meat such as smoked turkey or chicken; chopped vegetables such as cooked asparagus, zucchini, or roasted peppers; fresh herbs of any kind; and grated or crumbled cheese, for example. Once you've chosen your additions, there's no flipping or fussing involved; simply stir them into whisked eggs, transfer to baking dishes, and bake. **SERVES 4**

Vegetable oil cooking spray

2 teaspoons olive oil

¼ large red onion, diced (½ cup)

½ russet potato, diced (½ cup)

1 cup packed chopped fresh spinach

3 large eggs

4 large egg whites

1 ounce aged sharp Cheddar cheese, grated (½ cup)

¼ teaspoon kosher salt

⅛ teaspoon freshly ground black pepper

4 slices Tecate Bread (page 221) or other whole-grain bread, toasted

Preheat the oven to 425°F. Coat four 4-ounce ramekins or other small baking dishes with cooking spray and place on a baking sheet.

Heat the olive oil in a 10-inch skillet over medium heat. Add the onion and cook, stirring, until softened, 4 to 5 minutes. Add the potato and continue cooking, stirring occasionally, until the potato is fork-tender and the mixture is lightly browned, 5 to 6 minutes. Add the spinach and toss together until the spinach is just wilted, about 30 seconds. Remove the pan from the heat.

In a large bowl, whisk together the eggs and egg whites. Stir in the onion and potato mixture, Cheddar cheese, salt, and pepper.

Divide the egg mixture among the ramekins. Bake until the edges are set and the center has puffed up and is slightly loose when a ramekin is gently nudged, about 12 minutes. Serve hot with a slice of toast.

Egg White Omelet

with Fresh Herbs, Roasted Asparagus, and Baked Herbed Tomatoes

Baking tomatoes concentrates their sweet, tangy flavor. Here they take the place of fatty breakfast meats or greasy hash browns that might otherwise turn an innocent omelet into a calorie bomb. For an added treat, top each tomato with a little crumbled goat cheese or grated Parmesan, mozzarella, or Swiss cheese halfway through baking. Serve this dish with a slice of whole-grain toast. SERVES 4

FOR THE TOMATOES

2 ripe, red tomatoes, halved crosswise

2 teaspoons dried Italian seasoning

Pinch of kosher salt

Pinch of freshly ground black pepper

Olive oil spray

FOR THE OMELETS

16 asparagus spears, trimmed

2 teaspoons olive oil

Kosher salt and freshly ground white pepper

10 large egg whites

1 teaspoon minced fresh chervil leaves

1 teaspoon minced fresh thyme leaves

1 teaspoon minced fresh Italian parsley leaves

1 teaspoon minced fresh chives

Olive oil spray

1 ounce aged goat cheese (4 tablespoons)

Preheat the oven to 450°F.

Prepare the tomatoes. Arrange the tomato halves cut side up on a rimmed baking sheet. Sprinkle each tomato half with Italian seasoning, salt, and pepper. Spritz with olive oil. Bake for 30 minutes, until the tomatoes are lightly browned and dark and crusty on the edges. Remove from the oven and keep warm.

Prepare the omelets. Toss the asparagus with the olive oil and a pinch each of salt and pepper. Arrange the asparagus on a baking sheet in a single layer and roast in the oven until lightly browned, about 10 minutes. Remove from the oven and keep warm.

In a large bowl, whisk the egg whites until they are slightly fluffy, about 30 seconds. Whisk in the chervil, thyme, parsley, chives, ¼ teaspoon salt, and ⅛ teaspoon pepper.

Lower the oven temperature to 150°F.

To prepare an omelet, spray an 8-inch nonstick pan with oil and place the pan over medium heat to warm it slightly. Do not scorch the oil. Add ⅓ cup egg white mixture to pan. Use a rubber spatula to lightly stir the egg whites until they start to set. Cook until the bottom and sides of the omelet are set, but not at all brown, about 2 minutes. Flip the omelet over and cook through without browning, 1 to 2 minutes.

Place 4 roasted asparagus spears and 1 tablespoon goat cheese on one half of the omelet and fold the other half over. Slide it out of the pan and onto a plate. Place a tomato half alongside. Keep warm in the oven while you cook the remaining three omelets. Serve immediately.

tips from the golden door
making meditation a part of your life

A cookbook might seem an odd place to find a guide to meditation, a practice that many consider nearly impossible to master in the hustle and bustle of day-to-day life—and certainly in no way related to food. In fact, the teaching of meditation, a state of concentrated alertness, is an integral part of our program. Francine Hoffman, the inner focus coordinator at the Golden Door, considers the regular practice of meditation one of the most important steps on the path to overall mind-body renewal, as much a part of a healthy lifestyle as fresh food and regular exercise.

There are many known physiological benefits that come from regular meditation practice, including enhanced immune function and lowered blood pressure. Additionally, those who meditate have been shown to have fewer respiratory, heart, and digestive ailments. Mental benefits include improved concentration and focus. Meditation is also an extremely effective stress reducer. Recent studies on meditation indicate that regularly redirecting your focus to the present time reduces electrical activity in the area of the right brain associated with depression and anxiety and increases electrical activity in the area of

the left brain associated with feeling upbeat, enthusiastic, and energized. These positive feelings carry over to your daily life and can help you reshape your perceptions and behaviors, including those surrounding food and emotional eating. When the stress in our life seems insurmountable, we often choose fast, unhealthy food and unmindful eating. Food can be used as an emotional salve, and it's the wrong medicine for stress.

Francine believes that many people resist the idea of meditation at first because they think it is an exotic, esoteric practice that requires submitting to a particular set of beliefs foreign to most Westerners. In fact, in its purest sense, meditation is simply a time of relaxed concentration with focused attention; there is no special knowledge or experience necessary to begin. Nonetheless many people feel they can't meditate "correctly" and that whenever they try, they end up instead stuck with unwanted thoughts buzzing around their minds. In fact, you will reap the benefits of meditation whether or not the meditation is a good session or a dismal failure, regardless of whether your mind actually quiets down or stays very active. It's a common myth about medi-

tation that your goal must be to completely empty your mind. Achieving such a state is nearly impossible, even for the most seasoned practitioners. The goal of meditation is more like a weight-training workout: you are strengthening your ability to use your mind the way you want, by increasing your capacity to choose where and on what you put your attention during the course of the day. This strengthening effect accumulates over time and can help you end the destructive thinking that creates stress. Exercise and good nutrition build bodies for active, expressive lives; meditation builds minds for relaxed, happy, and peaceful lives.

There are many ways to focus your attention in a meditative practice. Some use a mantra, a word or sound that is repeated silently to maintain focus. Others use the physical sensation of the breath at their nostrils or the rising and falling of the abdomen with each breath. A technique that works for some is gazing, with the eyelids softly lowered but not closed, at a candle flame, flower, or other beautiful object. You can even meditate while walking slowly, as we do on our "meditation hike" or with a Zen approach that is very, very slow and deliberate, with careful attention to the way the foot is placed on the ground for each step. At the Golden Door, our Westernized approach to meditation is simple and accessible to beginners: we simply repeat a count from 1 to 4, synchronizing that count to each exhalation of breath.

Getting started on your own meditation practice is easy. Start with no more than 7 minutes daily for your first week or so of practice. Every week or two, add 1 to 2 minutes until you reach 15 to 20 minutes daily. If you can't manage a session that long, one or two 10-minute sessions a day is a good practice for busy people. Find something to time yourself, such as your watch, a timer, or a CD such as "Meditation End Chime" (see Resources, page 283), that has multiple tracks of timed silence, ranging from 10 to 70 minutes, followed by a gentle sound to bring you back.

Sit where you will be undisturbed, either in a straight-backed chair or cross-legged on a cushion on the floor with your back against a wall for support. An upright spine keeps you most alert. Close your eyes and take some moments to increase your breath volume by taking gradually deeper breaths while becoming aware of any body sensations. Gently push your bottom into the chair or cushion to help your spine stay elongated and purposely keep length between your breastbone and your navel. To relax your neck, lower your chin so it is slightly below the par-allel-to-the-floor point and do your best to soften the rest of your body. Turn your palms downward on your thighs as a symbolic gesture of releasing tension. When you feel more present, turn your palms upward. You are now ready to begin your meditation, or focusing practice. After a full exhale, inhale and silently bring to mind the word "and." On each exhale, silently count from 1 to 4; for example, [inhale] "and" [exhale] "1," [inhale] "and" [exhale] "2," and so on until you reach the number 4, then start again from 1. Continue in this way for the allotted time. When stray thoughts interrupt your focused counting, as they surely will, return again to [inhale] "and" [exhale] "1" as soon as you become aware of your loss of focus.

When it's time to end your practice, take a few moments to transition from the meditative state to your active life: lower your head, open your eyes slowly, and then lift your head to take in the space around you. Then, enjoy your day!

If you're having difficulty committing to this new practice, Francine has a few suggestions:

- If you regularly forget to take time for meditation, try to meditate early in the morning, before your day begins.
- If you find it particularly hard to sit still, try meditating after vigorous activity, when your body is ready to be still for several minutes.
- A successful strategy for regular practice is to link your meditation time to some discipline or habit you do every day, such as making coffee, driving to work, or exercising. For instance, after putting on the coffee to brew, sit down to meditate, making a fresh cup of coffee your reward when you're finished. If you drive frequently, get to your destination early enough to meditate 10 minutes before you get out of your car and you'll emerge calm and refreshed. Or try adding a 10-minute meditation practice before or after your treadmill workout.

Put into practice the strategy that works for you and the good habit of meditation will soon be a part of your daily routine.

To reinforce the link between relaxed alertness and eating, meditative practices can be incorporated directly into meal time. The One-Minute Rule, in which we appreciate the look and smell of the meal for one full minute before eating, is one of the tenets of mindful eating (see page 36), and is in itself a kind of meditation. From time to time at the Golden Door we carry the One-Minute Rule to its apotheosis and sit down together to a silent meal, during which we eat an entire meal in total silence. When your eyes and nose are pleased with the color, texture, and aroma of the food, your mind has time to anticipate the tastes to come and the digestive juices begin flowing, maximizing the enjoyment and health benefits of your meal.

*Cardamom Cinnamon
Mulled Apple Cider*

teas, juices, and other drinks

Hibiscus Sangria

This refreshing, fruit-sweetened sangria is perfect for a warm day or evening. The stimulating, tart flavor of dried hibiscus flowers is the source of the "zing" in many popular teas. They have some important health-promoting properties as well: dried hibiscus flowers are rich in flavonoids and antioxidants, and preliminary studies have shown that hibiscus flowers may play a role in regulating blood pressure and blood lipids like cholesterol. Dried hibiscus flowers can be found in the tea section of the market. **SERVES 8**

¼ cup dried hibiscus flowers

2 cups no-sugar-added pineapple juice, chilled

2 cups pomegranate or cranberry juice, chilled

1 cup no-sugar-added apple juice, chilled

½ large mango, peeled and cut into bite-size chunks (1 cup)

1 small ripe pear, cut into bite-size chunks (1 cup)

⅙ fresh pineapple, peeled and cut into bite-size chunks (1 cup)

1 orange, halved and sliced ¼ inch thick

½ cup green or red seedless grapes, halved

Ice cubes

In a medium saucepan, bring 4 cups of water to a boil and remove from the heat. Stir in the dried hibiscus flowers. Cover the pan and let stand for 20 minutes. The liquid will be very deep, vibrant red and very tart. Strain, discarding the hibiscus flowers. Refrigerate the hibiscus tea until cold, about 3 hours.

In a pitcher, pour the hibiscus tea along with the pineapple juice, pomegranate juice, apple juice, mango, pear, pineapple, orange slices, and grapes. Stir to combine. The sangria can be made to this point and stored in the refrigerator for 3 to 4 hours.

To serve, place ice into eight wineglasses and pour in the hibiscus sangria, making sure to get plenty of fruit in each glass. Serve.

Watermelon Cranberry Lime Slushy

Nothing is more refreshing on a hot day than an ice-cold slice of watermelon. This simple concoction is perfect for a summer cookout. At the Golden Door we serve this slushy in a martini glass garnished with a frozen watermelon spear, a slice of lime, and a sprig of mint for a stunning presentation. I'd venture a guess that a touch of vodka in this might be pretty good, too.

SERVES 6

¼ small seedless watermelon (about 3 pounds), rind removed

2 cups cranberry juice

2 tablespoons fresh lime juice (from 1 lime)

6 cups ice cubes

6 lime slices

6 fresh mint sprigs

Slice six 4-inch by ½-inch spears off the watermelon to use as a garnish. Arrange the spears on a baking sheet lined with plastic wrap or waxed paper. Place in the freezer until frozen solid, 45 minutes to 1 hour.

Cut the remaining watermelon into dice; you should have about 3½ cups. In a blender, combine the diced watermelon, cranberry juice, and lime juice and blend on medium speed until well combined, about 20 seconds.

Return the juice to the blender and add the ice. Blend on high speed until the ice is finely crushed.

Pour into six glasses and garnish each with a frozen watermelon spear, lime slice, and mint sprig. Serve immediately.

Agave Lime Soda

Who would have thought that soda pop would have a place at a spa? One reason we can serve this sweet treat is because it's made with agave syrup, also known as agave nectar and is made in Mexico from the agave plant, which also gives us tequila. Agave syrup is sweeter and thinner than honey with a much milder taste and a lower glycemic index and glycemic load than either honey or sugar. Use it to sweeten cold drinks such as iced tea because, unlike honey or sugar, it dissolves easily in cold liquids. Look for pure agave syrup or nectar in your local natural-food store.

Add fresh chopped mint to this drink for a delicious virgin mojito. Or substitute your own favorite citrus for the lime juice. Fresh lemon, blood orange, or grapefruit juice all make very refreshing fruit-flavored soda. **SERVES 4**

¼ **cup fresh lime juice (from 2 limes)**

¼ **cup agave syrup**

16 ounces sparkling water, chilled

Ice cubes

4 slices lime

In a large pitcher, stir together the lime juice and agave syrup until the agave syrup is completely incorporated, about 1 minute. Add the sparkling water and stir lightly to combine.

Fill four 6-ounce glasses with ice. Pour the soda into each glass, and garnish with a lime slice. Serve.

*Potassium Broth

Potassium Broth is always a part of the midmorning juice break at the Golden Door, during which guests in need of a little pick-me-up gather near the pool for a cup of this hot tomato-based broth and a tray of crudités (see page 16). This Golden Door classic is essentially homemade V-8 juice. It is a great way to clear out the crisper drawer of your refrigerator, instead of throwing away those limp vegetables that are no longer good for salad. Keep the broth in the refrigerator all week and heat a single serving in a microwave-safe mug whenever you need your own pick-me-up. At the Door, our regular condiment tray is always stocked with crushed red pepper flakes, ground flaxseed, and oat bran. Add a little of each to your cup of broth to not only add more zip but texture and nutrients. SERVES 12

5 cups low-sodium tomato juice

3 cups vegetable trimmings, such as celery, tomato, carrot, mushroom, onion, scallion, lettuce, parsley stems, basil stems, bell pepper

Pour the tomato juice and 2 cups of water into a large saucepan. Stir in the vegetable trimmings. Bring just to a boil over medium heat. Reduce the heat and simmer for 40 minutes. Strain, discarding the vegetable trimmings. Serve hot. (Once cool, extra broth can be stored in a tightly covered container in the refrigerator for up to 1 week. Heat the broth before serving.)

Fresh Lavender and Orange Chamomile Tea *with Honey*

This tea is completely inspired by the grounds here at the Golden Door. The Golden Door is practically surrounded by orange groves and our garden is home to a wide variety of herbs, including a huge patch of lavender. Just as I have been inspired by our landscape countless times, so you too can be by your own. You may not have an orange tree, but many fresh herbs are extremely easy to grow, and I can't stress enough what a huge difference they'll make in your cooking. Lavender, a member of the mint family, is especially easy to grow. Try planting some in your garden or start a container herb garden in whatever out-door space you have: a small backyard, a patio, or a window sill. Lavender does have a large, spreading root system, but it likes growing in a tight spot so the pot does not need to be too large. It does well with lots of sun and can be moved indoors in the winter if you live in a cold climate. SERVES 6

1 orange, sliced ¼ inch thick

¼ cup loose dried chamomile flowers or 6 chamomile tea bags

4 sprigs fresh lavender, about 3 inches long

¼ cup honey

Bring 6½ cups of water to a boil and remove from heat. Stir in the orange slices, chamomile, and lavender. Cover the pan and let stand for 6 minutes.

Strain the tea and stir in the honey. Warm to just below a simmer if necessary. Serve immediately.

Cardamom Cinnamon Mulled Apple Cider

Many cider recipes call for added sugar, but I find apple cider is plenty sweet without it. This warm cider is perfect for chilly days. (Photograph on page 238.) **SERVES 6**

1 orange

1½ quarts organic apple cider

3 cardamom pods

2 whole cloves

2 whole star anise

1 (3-inch) cinnamon stick, plus 6 more
    for serving

6 orange slices, for serving

Using a vegetable peeler, remove the zest from the orange in strips; avoiding as much of the white pith as possible. Put them in a medium saucepan. Juice the orange and add the juice to the saucepan with the zest. Pour in the apple cider and add the cardamom pods, cloves, star anise, and cinnamon stick.

Over medium-low heat, bring the mixture to a low simmer. Cook so that it is just lightly bubbling around the edges for 25 minutes. Strain the cider into six mugs. Add an orange slice and a cinnamon stick to each mug and serve hot.

Hot Cocoa

On a cold winter day, few things compare to a hot, creamy cup of chocolaty cocoa. This version is low in fat but full of rich chocolate taste. While cocoa made with skim milk can be a bit thin, whisking in nonfat dry milk makes the cocoa nice and creamy while still keeping it light. **SERVES 6**

3 cups 1% low-fat milk

¼ cup unsweetened Dutch-processed
    cocoa powder

¼ cup nonfat or low-fat dry milk

¼ cup raw sugar

2 tablespoons dark chocolate chips

¼ teaspoon ground cinnamon

Put the milk into a medium saucepan and heat over medium-low heat to just below a simmer. Remove from the heat. Add the cocoa powder, dry milk, sugar, chocolate chips, and cinnamon and whisk until the dry milk is dissolved and the chocolate is melted, about 30 seconds.

Serve immediately or return to low heat to keep warm. Whisk again before dividing among six espresso cups. Serve.

From left to right:
Creamy Miso Dressing,
Cranberry Vinaigrette,
Roasted Red Pepper Remoulade,
and Herb Oil

vinaigrettes and dressings

Lemon-Caper Vinaigrette

This vinaigrette is particularly good with fish and shellfish salads. **MAKES 1½ CUPS**

½ cup fresh lemon juice (from 3 to 4 lemons)

¼ cup chopped fresh Italian parsley leaves

4½ teaspoons drained, chopped capers

1 tablespoon Dijon mustard

1 garlic clove, minced

⅛ teaspoon freshly ground black pepper

2 tablespoons extra-virgin olive oil

Place a medium mixing bowl on a folded kitchen towel. Place in the bowl the lemon juice, parsley, capers, Dijon mustard, garlic, pepper, and ½ cup water. Whisk to combine. Whisking constantly, slowly pour in the olive oil and continue whisking until well blended. Store in a tightly covered container in the refrigerator for 2 to 3 days. Shake well before using.

Avocado-Citrus Vinaigrette

The tart acidity of citrus brings out the nutty flavor and creaminess of avocado, which stands in for oil in this dressing. This pairs well with the Beer-Steamed Shrimp (page 19) as well as with grilled chicken, seafood, or vegetables, or in a bean salad. (Photograph on page 264.) **MAKES 1½ CUPS**

½ medium avocado, peeled, pitted, and chopped

½ cup fresh orange juice (from 2 oranges)

3 tablespoons fresh lime juice (from 2 limes)

½ teaspoon minced garlic

¼ serrano chile, seeded and chopped (¾ teaspoon)

¼ cup packed fresh cilantro leaves

Pinch of kosher salt, or to taste

Pinch of freshly ground black pepper, or to taste

In a blender, combine the avocado, orange juice, lime juice, garlic, chile, and ⅓ cup water and process until smooth. Add the cilantro and pulse until it is chopped but not pureed. Season with salt and pepper. Store in a tightly covered container in the refrigerator until ready to use; this is best used the day it is made.

Asparagus Vinaigrette

Simple recipes like this one exemplify why fresh, high-quality ingredients are so important. Here the asparagus is the star, enhanced by lemon, a touch of garlic, and extra-virgin olive oil to round out the flavor. This vinaigrette is rich and luxurious but contains very little oil. Brightly colored, the vinaigrette is served with Wild Salmon with Quick-Preserved Lemon Mashed Potatoes (page 132), and is also excellent drizzled over grilled or pan-fried chicken breast or fish. **MAKES 1 CUP**

6 ounces asparagus

¼ cup plus 1 tablespoon ice water

1 tablespoon fresh lemon juice

1 tablespoon extra-virgin olive oil

½ teaspoon chopped garlic

¼ teaspoon kosher salt

⅛ teaspoon freshly ground white pepper

To trim asparagus, with two hands hold a stalk of asparagus by both ends and bend in half. The woody end will snap right off; discard. Slice the trimmed asparagus crosswise ¼ inch thick; you should have 1 cup.

Bring a medium pot of water to a rapid boil. Prepare a medium bowl of ice water. Add the chopped asparagus to the boiling water and cook just until crisp-tender, 1 minute. Drain the asparagus and immediately transfer it to the ice-water bath for 2 minutes to cool. Drain well and transfer the asparagus to a blender.

Add to the blender the ice water, lemon juice, olive oil, garlic, salt, and pepper. Blend on high until creamy, about 30 seconds. Store in a tightly covered container in the refrigerator for 1 to 2 days. (The dressing may separate while sitting; stir or shake to blend before using.)

Gazpacho Vinaigrette

This fresh dressing is a fun twist on gazpacho, itself sometimes referred to as a "salad in a bowl." It is excellent with Pan-Roasted Halibut with Crab Mashed Potatoes (page 136). If English cucumbers are not available, use another type, but peel it if the skin is waxed. (Photograph on page 264.) **MAKES 2¾ CUPS**

1 medium ripe, red tomato, diced (1 cup)

½ small English cucumber, seeded and diced (1 cup)

1 medium red bell pepper, seeded and diced (1 cup)

¼ small red onion, diced (¼ cup)

1 garlic clove, sliced

¾ cup low-sodium tomato juice

2 tablespoons sherry vinegar

2 tablespoons extra-virgin olive oil

2 teaspoons tomato paste

¼ teaspoon kosher salt, or to taste

¼ teaspoon freshly ground black pepper, or to taste

Combine the tomato, cucumber, bell pepper, red onion, garlic, tomato juice, vinegar, olive oil, tomato paste, salt, and pepper in a shallow dish or bowl and toss to combine; the tomato paste does not need to be thoroughly mixed in. Cover and chill for 1 to 3 hours to meld the flavors.

Transfer the mixture to a blender and puree until smooth but bits of vegetables remain, 10 to 15 seconds. Store in a tightly covered container in the refrigerator until ready to use; this dressing is best used the day it is made.

Whole-Grain Mustard and Honey Vinaigrette

This vinaigrette is creamy yet has a nice tanginess. Serve with Grilled Dijon Chicken Breast Salad with Pears and Candied Walnuts (page 156) or any grilled or pan-fried poultry dish. It is also good with roasted salmon. **MAKES ⅔ CUP**

2 tablespoons whole-grain Dijon mustard

2 tablespoons smooth Dijon mustard

1 tablespoon honey

2 tablespoons apple cider vinegar

1 tablespoon extra-virgin olive oil

Pinch of freshly ground black pepper

¼ cup chopped fresh Italian parsley
leaves

In a blender, combine both mustards, the honey, vinegar, ¼ cup water, the olive oil, and pepper. Blend for approximately 10 seconds until combined. Add the parsley and pulse six times to roughly chop the parsley but not puree it. Store in a tightly covered container in the refrigerator for 1 to 2 days.

Cranberry Vinaigrette

This simple vinaigrette adds the perfect sweet-and-sour note to the Walnut-Crusted Turkey Scallopini with Smashed Yams (page 170). It is also delicious drizzled over a fall salad of mixed greens, sliced pears or apples, toasted nuts, and a little goat or blue cheese. (Photograph on page 250.) **MAKES SCANT ⅔ CUP**

Olive oil spray

1 tablespoon thinly sliced shallot

½ cup fresh or frozen cranberries

1 tablespoon light brown sugar

2 tablespoons fresh orange juice

½ teaspoon honey

Pinch of kosher salt

Pinch of freshly ground black pepper

Spray a small saucepan lightly with olive oil and heat it over medium heat. Add the shallot and cook, stirring, until translucent, about 2 minutes. Add the cranberries, brown sugar, and ½ cup water. Bring to a simmer and cook until the cranberries have popped and the liquid is a vibrant red color, about 6 minutes.

Transfer the mixture to a blender and add the orange juice, honey, salt, and pepper. Blend on high until smooth, about 20 seconds. Store in a tightly covered container in the refrigerator for 4 or 5 days.

Lemon-Tahini Dressing

Serve this tangy, nutty dressing with any grilled, broiled, or roasted seafood, poultry, or vegetables. **MAKES 1 CUP**

¼ cup tahini

2 tablespoons fresh lemon juice (from 1 lemon)

1 tablespoon white balsamic vinegar

1 tablespoon mirin

1 teaspoon sriracha or Vietnamese chile-garlic sauce

2 tablespoons fresh Italian parsley leaves

In a blender, combine the tahini, lemon juice, vinegar, mirin, sriracha, and ½ cup water. Blend until smooth, about 10 seconds. Add the parsley and pulse 5 times; the parsley should be chopped and evenly distributed throughout the dressing. Store in a tightly covered container in the refrigerator for 4 to 5 days.

Roasted Poblano Dressing

Mildly spicy poblano chiles are roasted to soften them and add delicious, smoky flavor. When blended with the other ingredients the peppers become a creamy, emulsified dressing. Serve this with Adobo-Marinated Grass-Fed Flank Steak with Spinach Salad (page 179) or whenever you want to add or highlight southwestern flavors—on grilled poultry or meat or on a simple salad of corn, tomatoes, avocado, and jícama, for example. (Photograph on page 264.) **MAKES 1 CUP**

2 whole poblano chiles, roasted (page 74), peeled, and seeded

4 teaspoons sherry vinegar

1 tablespoon agave syrup or honey

1 garlic clove

¼ teaspoon kosher salt

⅓ cup fresh cilantro leaves

In a blender, combine the poblano chiles, vinegar, agave syrup, garlic, salt, and ¾ cup water. Blend until well combined but not completely smooth, about 20 seconds. Add the cilantro and pulse a few times until it is chopped. Store in a tightly covered container in the refrigerator for up to 2 days.

Creamy Ranch Dressing

Creamy ranch dressing, like the creamy Caesar dressing on page 263, is typically made with copious amounts of mayonnaise and cream or sour cream. This version, however, is based on a creamy foundation that is much lower in calories and fat: blended low-fat cottage cheese, which becomes very creamy, and buttermilk. This creamy base can be flavored many ways to create delicious low-fat creamy dressings that don't taste or feel like a compromise. **MAKES 1½ CUPS**

¾ cup low-fat buttermilk

½ cup low-fat cottage cheese

1 tablespoon apple cider vinegar

2 teaspoons Dijon mustard

½ teaspoon minced garlic

¼ cup chopped fresh Italian parsley
   leaves

2 tablespoons chopped fresh basil leaves

1 tablespoon chopped fresh dill leaves

Pinch of kosher salt, or to taste

Pinch of freshly ground black pepper, or
   to taste

In a blender, combine the buttermilk, cottage cheese, vinegar, mustard, and garlic. Process until smooth, about 30 seconds. Add the parsley, basil, and dill. Process for 5 seconds, until just blended; the dressing should clearly have bits of herbs throughout. Season with salt and pepper. Store in a tightly covered container in the refrigerator for 3 to 4 days.

Creamy Miso Dressing

Once blended, silken tofu has the consistency of mayonnaise. With salty, savory miso paste, lime, and ginger, this excellent dressing is reminiscent of the miso dressing served in your favorite sushi restaurant. Serve with the Sesame-Crusted Wild Salmon Salad (page 130). (Photograph on page 250.) **MAKES 2 CUPS**

Large knob of fresh ginger

6 ounces silken soft tofu

2 tablespoons light yellow miso paste

1 tablespoon Dijon mustard

2 tablespoons unseasoned rice vinegar

2 tablespoons mirin

2 tablespoons fresh lime juice (from 1 lime)

¼ cup fresh cilantro leaves

Grate the ginger on the large-holed side of a box grater until you have about 2 tablespoons. Collect the grated ginger in your hand and squeeze over a bowl to extract the juice. You should have about 1 teaspoon of juice; if you don't, grate more ginger and squeeze out the juice until you do. Discard the grated ginger.

Put the ginger juice in a blender along with the tofu, miso paste, mustard, rice vinegar, mirin, lime juice, and ½ cup water. Blend until smooth, about 30 seconds. Add the cilantro and pulse until chopped, about 5 seconds. Store in a tightly covered container in the refrigerator for up to 1 week.

Creamy Caesar Dressing

Starting from the same creamy base as is used to make the creamy ranch dressing on page 261, here anchovy and capers are added to make a creamy Caesar that is just as good as its full-fat counterpart. **MAKES 1½ CUPS**

¾ cup low-fat buttermilk

½ cup low-fat cottage cheese

1 tablespoon fresh lime juice

2 teaspoons Dijon mustard

½ teaspoon minced garlic

2 whole anchovy fillets

¼ cup coarsely chopped fresh Italian
    parsley leaves

2 teaspoons drained capers

6 dashes Tabasco sauce

Pinch of kosher salt, or to taste

Pinch of freshly ground black pepper,
    or to taste

In a blender, combine the buttermilk, cottage cheese, lime juice, mustard, garlic, and anchovy fillets. Process until smooth, about 30 seconds. Add the parsley, capers, and Tabasco. Process for 5 seconds, until just blended; the dressing should clearly have bits of herbs throughout. Season with salt and pepper. Store in a tightly covered container in the refrigerator for 3 to 4 days.

Clockwise from bottom left:
Gazpacho Vinaigrette,
Roasted Poblano Dressing,
Avocado-Citrus Vinaigrette

Roasted Red Pepper Remoulade

Here, as in the creamy miso dressing on page 262, blended silken tofu takes the role traditionally played by mayonnaise in classic remoulade. Serve with Maryland Crab Cakes with Caramelized Pineapple (page 144). (Photograph on page 250.)

MAKES 2 CUPS

1 large or 2 small red bell peppers, roasted (page 74), peeled, and seeded

6 ounces silken soft tofu

2 tablespoons apple cider vinegar

1 tablespoon Dijon mustard

2 tablespoons chopped cornichons or dill pickle

2 tablespoons coarsely chopped flat-leaf parsley

1 tablespoon capers

1 teaspoon freshly ground black pepper

Chop and set aside 1 cup of roasted pepper. Save any leftover roasted pepper for another use.

In a blender, combine the tofu, vinegar, mustard, and ¼ cup water. Blend until smooth, about 30 seconds. Add the 1 cup chopped peppers, the cornichons, parsley, capers, and pepper. Pulse until the ingredients are incorporated but still slightly chunky. Store in a tightly covered container in the refrigerator for up to 2 days.

basics

Chicken Stock

Chicken stock is the backbone of so many Golden Door recipes, especially soups, that it is very important to me that it taste good. Making your own stock means you can choose which fresh vegetables and subtle herbs will flavor it and ensure that there is no added salt in it, unlike even the highest quality low-sodium chicken stock. Chicken backs and parts can be extremely fatty and need a lot of trimming. I've had to toss out as much as a third of the total weight, so count on buying more than is called for below. This recipe uses 3 pounds trimmed *chicken parts.* **MAKES 5½ QUARTS**

About 4½ pounds chicken parts (backs, bones, necks, and wings) trimmed of skin and excess fat (3 pounds)

2 large carrots, peeled and cut in several large pieces

2 large celery stalks, cut into several large pieces

1 large onion, peeled and cut into 8 wedges

3 sprigs fresh thyme or 1½ teaspoons dried thyme

1 teaspoon black peppercorns

1 bay leaf

Rinse the chicken parts in cold water and transfer to a large stockpot. Add 6 quarts cold water and bring to a boil over medium-high heat, using a ladle to skim away any scum and solids from the surface as the water heats.

Reduce the heat and add the carrots, celery, onion, thyme, peppercorns, and bay leaf. Return the water to a very slow simmer, and simmer, uncovered, for 3 hours, occasionally skimming the surface of excess fat.

Strain the stock through a mesh strainer into a large pot or bowl. Place the pot in a larger pot or bowl filled with ice water to cool. Skim away any excess fat that collects at the top. When completely cool, store the stock in a tightly sealed container in the refrigerator for 3 to 4 days, or divide among several smaller containers and freeze for up to 6 months.

Vegetable Stock

Stock from fresh vegetables is easily made and much tastier and less salty than store-bought. Here is a basic vegetable stock, but you can always use other vegetables from your own garden or kitchen leftovers such as parsnips, leeks, or scallions; all make flavorful stock. I prefer to avoid using cabbage, beets, eggplants, bell peppers, or broccoli in vegetable stock, for these flavors can become overwhelming. **MAKES 6 CUPS**

2 large carrots, peeled and coarsely chopped

2 celery stalks, coarsely chopped

1 large onion, peeled and coarsely chopped

1 fennel bulb, trimmed and coarsely chopped

8 ounces button mushrooms, trimmed and sliced

3 plum tomatoes, quartered

1 garlic clove, peeled and halved

4 sprigs fresh thyme, or 1 teaspoon dried thyme

2 bay leaves

In a stockpot, combine the carrots, celery, onion, fennel, mushrooms, tomatoes, garlic, and 2 quarts cold water. Partially cover the pot and over medium-high heat bring the water to a boil. Reduce the heat and skim the foam from the surface. Stir in the thyme and bay leaves. Simmer gently, partially covered, for 1 hour.

Strain the stock; do not press on the vegetables because it will make the stock cloudy. Once cool, store in a tightly sealed container in the refrigerator for 3 to 4 days or in the freezer for up to 6 months.

Balsamic Reduction

Gently cooking balsamic vinegar until it is quite reduced concentrates the sugars, taking a lot of the acidic tang out of the vinegar and leaving behind a sweet, tangy syrup with a faintly winey note. This balsamic reduction adds delicious flavor to grilled vegetables, pizza, grilled meats and poultry, and even fruit, especially strawberries and melon. Once made, it can be refrigerated for several months. If the reduction becomes too firm in the refrigerator, simply warm it in a hot water bath until loosened. **MAKES ¼ CUP**

1 cup balsamic vinegar

1 small shallot, sliced

1 garlic clove, halved

2 sprigs fresh thyme

6 black peppercorns

1 teaspoon light brown sugar

In a small nonreactive saucepan, combine the balsamic vinegar, shallot, garlic, thyme, peppercorns, and brown sugar. Bring to a boil and then reduce the heat. Simmer until the liquid is reduced to ¼ cup and resembles a shiny, slightly thick glaze, about 30 minutes. Be careful not to reduce it too much, for the sauce will thicken more as it cools.

Strain and discard the solids. Once cool, store in a tightly covered container in the refrigerator for up to 6 months.

Herb Oil

Herb oils add striking color and delicious herbal essence to many dishes. The method of blanching the herbs, shocking them in ice water, and squeezing out all excess moisture ensures that the oil is very vibrant and flavorful. (Photograph on page 250.)

MAKES ⅓ CUP

1½ cups packed fresh herbs such as basil or Italian parsley leaves, dill sprigs, or chives

½ cup grapeseed oil

Pinch of kosher salt

Bring a large saucepan of water to a boil; prepare a bowl full of ice water.

Plunge the herb leaves or sprigs into the boiling water for 10 seconds and then immediately transfer them to the ice water bath for 2 minutes to stop the cooking. Remove the herbs from the ice water and place them in a clean kitchen towel. Use your hands to squeeze out as much moisture from the herbs as possible.

Coarsely chop the herbs and place them in a blender. Add the oil and salt and blend on high for 1 minute. Place a strainer lined with a double layer of cheesecloth or a fine-mesh strainer over a bowl. Strain the oil, pressing lightly to extract more from the herbs; let it stand until all the oil has passed through the strainer. Discard the solids.

The herb oil can be refrigerated for up to 4 days. Do not heat the oil, as this will destroy its delicate flavor and bright green color.

Caramelized Onions

You'll see one of my favorite ingredients, caramelized onions, used throughout this book. Even if you are not a big fan of onions, give caramelized onions a try; they add a fantastic, savory-sweet note to many dishes. The secret to truly caramelizing the onions—as opposed to simply browning, or even burning them—is patience. Cook them down very slowly to concentrate the natural sugars in the onions. **MAKES 1½ CUPS**

Olive oil spray

2 large onions, halved and thinly sliced
(4 cups)

½ cup Chicken Stock, Vegetable Stock
(pages 268 and 269), store-bought
low-sodium broth, or water

2 tablespoons balsamic vinegar

Pinch of kosher salt, or to taste

Pinch of freshly ground black pepper,
or to taste

Spray a skillet with olive oil and heat over medium heat. Add the onions, and cook, stirring occasionally, for 30 minutes until brown, stirring in 2 tablespoons of the stock whenever the bottom of the skillet starts to get dry and browned. You may not need all of the stock.

Add the balsamic vinegar, increase the heat to medium-high, and cook for about 4 minutes longer, stirring occasionally; the onions should be deep golden brown and very soft. Transfer the caramelized onions to a bowl and season with salt and pepper.

Once cool, store the caramelized onions in a tightly sealed container in the refrigerator for up to 5 days.

Semolina Dough for Pizzettas

This dough is very versatile; it can be shaped and baked into burger buns and baguette-style loaves as well as pizza crusts and calzones. To freeze pizza crusts so that you'll always have some available for quick pizzas, roll the dough out and bake it until lightly golden as indicated in Individual Vegetable Pizzetta (page 90). Let the crust cool completely, wrap it tightly, and freeze. To use, simply remove the crust from the freezer and unwrap it. Add toppings and bake in a preheated 400°F oven until hot and bubbly, about 15 minutes. **MAKES ABOUT 12 OUNCES; ENOUGH DOUGH FOR 6 (6-INCH) OR 2 (12-INCH) PIZZA PIES**

¾ **teaspoon active dry yeast**

¾ **teaspoon honey**

⅔ **cup warm water**

2 **teaspoons olive oil, plus more for oiling the bowl and sheet pan**

¾ **cup unbleached all-purpose flour, plus more for kneading**

¾ **cup semolina flour**

¾ **teaspoon kosher salt**

In the bowl of an electric stand mixer fitted with the dough hook, combine the yeast, honey, and water. Stir gently and let stand for 5 to 10 minutes; the mixture will be foamy (Note: if mixture is not bubbly and foamy it means the yeast is not active; throw the mixture away and start over with a newer yeast packet.) Stir in the olive oil.

Add the all-purpose and semolina flours and the salt and mix on low speed until the dough comes together and pulls away from the sides of the mixer, about 1 minute. Increase the speed to medium-low and mix until the dough is only slightly sticky, 6 to 7 minutes longer. Turn the dough out on a lightly floured surface and knead it by hand until smooth and elastic, about 2 minutes.

Transfer the dough to a lightly oiled bowl and turn it over once. Cover the bowl with a clean dish towel. Place the bowl in a warm place until the dough is doubled in size, about 30 minutes.

Remove the dough from the bowl, and cut it into 6 equal pieces. Form each section into a ball. Lightly oil a sheet pan and place the dough balls on the pan. Cover with plastic wrap and refrigerate until ready to use, up to 2 days. (For longer storage, wrap each dough ball individually in plastic wrap and freeze for up to 2 months. To use the dough, unwrap it and place it in a lightly oiled bowl. Cover the bowl and let stand at room temperature until the dough is defrosted.)

SEMOLINA DOUGH FOR BURGER BUNS

Here are alternate ingredient quantities for when you want to make a larger batch. **MAKES ABOUT 18 OUNCES; ENOUGH DOUGH FOR 6 (2½-INCH) BURGER BUNS**

1 teaspoon active dry yeast

1 teaspoon honey

¾ cup warm water

2½ teaspoons olive oil, plus more for oiling the bowl and sheet pan

1 cup unbleached all-purpose flour

1 cup semolina flour

1 teaspoon kosher salt

Follow instructions for semolina dough for pizzettas.

Nutritional Information *The nutritional information provided here is per serving.*

APPETIZERS

CRUDITÉ PLATTER (page 16)

120 calories 13 g carb
5 g fat 4 g fiber
0.9 g sat fat 3 mg cholesterol
8 g protein 280 mg sodium

HUMMUS (page 18)
Per 2½-tablespoon serving

65 calories 6 g carb
4 g fat 1 g fiber
0.5 g sat fat 0 mg cholesterol
2 g protein 119 mg sodium

BEER-STEAMED SHRIMP WITH AVOCADO-CITRUS VINAIGRETTE AND MIXED GREENS (page 19)

152 calories 9 g carb
5 g fat 2 g fiber
0.8 g sat fat 129 mg cholesterol
19 g protein 265 mg sodium

BEER-STEAMED SHRIMP COCKTAIL (page 21)

127 calories 10 g carb
2 g fat 0 g fiber
0.3 g sat fat 132 mg cholesterol
17 g protein 564 mg sodium

MARYLAND-STYLE COCKTAIL SAUCE (page 21)
Per 2-tablespoon serving

29 calories 7 g carb
0 g fat 0 g fiber
0 g sat fat 2 mg cholesterol
0 g protein 351 mg sodium

SPINY LOBSTER AND MANGO GAZPACHO SHOOTERS (page 22)

52 calories 7 g carb
2 g fat 0.7 g fiber
0.2 g sat fat 7 mg cholesterol
3 g protein 77 mg sodium

BAKED ARTICHOKE SPINACH DIP WITH CORN CRISPS (page 24)

162 calories 27 g carb
2 g fat 10 g fiber
1 g sat fat 6 mg cholesterol
13 g protein 597 mg sodium

CORIANDER-CRUSTED TUNA ON WONTON CRISPS WITH SESAME SLAW AND WASABI CREAM (page 26)

258 calories 15 g carb
7 g fat 2 g fiber
1.5 g sat fat 44 mg cholesterol
31 g protein 690 mg sodium

CORN AND SCALLION PANCAKES WITH OVEN-ROASTED CHIPOTLE SALSA (page 29)

109 calories 15 g carb
6 g fat 2 g fiber
4 g sat fat 32 mg cholesterol
1 g protein 218 mg sodium

CHICKEN AND SCALLION POTSTICKERS WITH CHILE LIME SAUCE (page 32)

175 calories 19 g carb
6 g fat 0.7 g fiber
1.3 g sat fat 35 mg cholesterol
12 g protein 706 mg sodium

MANGO-AVOCADO SUMMER ROLLS WITH SWEET AND SOUR DIPPING SAUCE (page 34)

173 calories 31 g carb
5 g fat 5 g fiber
0.8 g sat fat 0 mg cholesterol
3 g protein 464 mg sodium

SALADS

AVOCADO, ORANGE, AND JÍCAMA WITH CORIANDER DRESSING (page 40)

190 calories 25 g carb
11 g fat 8 g fiber
1.6 g sat fat 0 mg cholesterol
3 g protein 76 mg sodium

SUGAR SNAP AND SNOW PEA SALAD WITH ORANGE SESAME VINAIGRETTE (page 43)

92 calories 14 g carb
2 g fat 3 g fiber
0.3 g sat fat 0 mg cholesterol
4 g protein 75 mg sodium

WATERCRESS, STRAWBERRY, AND GOAT CHEESE SALAD (page 44)

125 calories 7 g carb
10 g fat 2 g fiber
2.7 g sat fat 7 mg cholesterol
3 g protein 119 mg sodium

HEIRLOOM TOMATO SALAD (page 47)

73 calories 6 g carb
5 g fat 1 g fiber
0.7 g sat fat 0 mg cholesterol
1 g protein 87 mg sodium

CHOPPED VEGETABLE SALAD WITH WHITE BALSAMIC DIJON VINAIGRETTE (page 48)

81 calories 11 g carb
4 g fat 3 g fiber
0.6 g sat fat 0 mg cholesterol
2 g protein 189 mg sodium

SHAVED FENNEL WITH PARMESAN SHAVINGS AND LEMON (page 50)

127 calories 10 g carb
9 g fat 4 g fiber
2 g sat fat 7 mg cholesterol
3 g protein 193 mg sodium

CITRUS SALAD WITH EXTRA-VIRGIN OLIVE OIL AND CRACKED BLACK PEPPER (page 51)

165 calories 26 g carb
7 g fat 5 g fiber
1 g sat fat 0 mg cholesterol
2 g protein 48 mg sodium

PERSIMMON, POMEGRANATE, AND TANGERINE SALAD WITH ROASTED SHALLOT BALSAMIC DRESSING (page 52)

124 calories	28 g carb
2 g fat	4 g fiber
0.2 g sat fat	0 mg cholesterol
2 g protein	79 mg sodium

FOREST MUSHROOMS AND FRISÉE WITH TRUFFLE-BEET VINAIGRETTE (page 54)

153 calories	23 g carb
5 g fat	11 g fiber
0.7 g sat fat	0 mg cholesterol
7 g protein	183 mg sodium

BROCCOLI ALMOND SALAD IN RADICCHIO CUPS (page 55)

77 calories	12 g carb
3 g fat	3 g fiber
0.6 g sat fat	2 mg cholesterol
5 g protein	126 mg sodium

CELERY ROOT AND FUJI APPLE SLAW WITH CIDER DRESSING (page 57)

138 calories	26 g carb
4 g fat	5 g fiber
0.4 g sat fat	0 mg cholesterol
3 g protein	267 mg sodium

SOUPS

MISO SOUP (page 60)

38 calories	6 g carb
0.2 g fat	3 g fiber
0 g sat fat	14 mg cholesterol
4 g protein	494 mg sodium

WONTON SOUP (page 61)

145 calories	20 g carb
2 g fat	1 g fiber
0.2 g sat fat	22 mg cholesterol
13 g protein	522 mg sodium

TRUFFLED MUSHROOM SOUP WITH POPPED WILD RICE (page 63)

125 calories	13 g carb
4 g fat	2 g fiber
0.5 g sat fat	6 mg cholesterol
7 g protein	387 mg sodium

THAI COCONUT VEGETABLE SOUP (page 66)

81 calories	13 g carb
4 g fat	2 g fiber
3.2 g sat fat	0 mg cholesterol
2 g protein	207 mg sodium

LEMONGRASS-GINGER BROTH WITH SHRIMP AND SNOW PEAS (page 68)

54 calories	3 g carb
0.5 g fat	0.7 g fiber
0 g sat fat	51 mg cholesterol
9 g protein	399 mg sodium

*BROCCOLI BASIL SOUP (page 69)

35 calories	7 g carb
0.4 g fat	3 g fiber
0 g sat fat	0 mg cholesterol
3 g protein	200 mg sodium

CREAMY CAULIFLOWER SOUP WITH CARAMELIZED CAULIFLOWER (page 71)

101 calories	12 g carb
3 g fat	4 g fiber
1.4 g sat fat	11 mg cholesterol
9 g protein	113 mg sodium

GARDEN VEGETABLE SOUP WITH PISTOU (page 72)

120 calories	19 g carb
1 g fat	6 g fiber
0.5 g sat fat	10 mg cholesterol
10 g protein	308 mg sodium

WHITE BEAN, ROASTED TOMATO, AND ROSEMARY SOUP (page 73)

309 calories	48 g carb
5 g fat	12 g fiber
0.7 g sat fat	8 mg cholesterol
18 g protein	545 mg sodium

ROASTED POBLANO, CORN, AND POTATO SOUP (page 75)

150 calories	25 g carb
3 g fat	4 g fiber
1.1 g sat fat	13 mg cholesterol
8 g protein	280 mg sodium

ITALIAN CHICKEN SAUSAGE, OVEN-DRIED TOMATO, AND ORZO SOUP (page 76)

194 calories	25 g carb
5 g fat	3 g fiber
0.2 g sat fat	30 mg cholesterol
14 g protein	827 mg sodium

SPICY CHICKEN AND HOMINY SOUP WITH CRISP TORTILLA STRIPS (page 79)

200 calories	21 g carb
7 g fat	5 g fiber
2.2 g sat fat	32 mg cholesterol
16 g protein	645 mg sodium

SWEET CORN SOUP WITH BLUE CRAB AND AVOCADO RELISH (page 80)

215 calories	22 g carb
9 g fat	5 g fiber
0.9 g sat fat	44 mg cholesterol
14 g protein	488 mg sodium

VEGETARIAN MAIN DISHES

CARROT-WALNUT PÂTÉ AND WHOLE WHEAT CHAPATI WRAP (page 86)

278 calories	34 g carb
15 g fat	7 g fiber
1.2 g sat fat	0 mg cholesterol
7 g protein	768 mg sodium

WHOLE WHEAT CHAPATI (page 87)

55 calories	7 g carb
3 g fat	1 g fiber
0.2 g sat fat	0 mg cholesterol
1 g protein	41 mg sodium

QUINOA TABBOULEH WITH SPINACH AND FETA HUMMUS AND WHOLE WHEAT CHAPATI (page 88)

366 calories	43 g carb
17 g fat	6 g fiber
2.7 g sat fat	6 mg cholesterol
12 g protein	387 mg sodium

INDIVIDUAL VEGETABLE PIZZETTA (page 90)

199 calories	31 g carb
3.7 g fat	3 g fiber
1.3 g sat fat	6 mg cholesterol
12 g protein	532 mg sodium

GOLDEN DOOR PIZZA SAUCE (page 92)

Per 2-tablespoon serving

24 calories	3 g carb
1 g fat	0 g fiber
0.1 g sat fat	0 mg cholesterol
1 g protein	131 mg sodium

MARINATED VEGETABLE FOCACCIA SANDWICH WITH WHITE BEAN, RADICCHIO, AND CARAMELIZED ONION SALAD (page 93)

466 calories	63 g carb
21 g fat	10 g fiber
2.5 g sat fat	0.4 mg cholesterol
12 g protein	867 mg sodium

BAKED FALAFEL WITH GRILLED EGGPLANT PUREE AND CUCUMBER, TOMATO, AND YOGURT SALAD (page 96)

268 calories	35 g carb
11 g fat	10 g fiber
1.4 g sat fat	0.6 mg cholesterol
10 g protein	366 mg sodium

RED LENTIL VEGGIE BURGERS WITH GARLICKY YAM FRIES AND SPICY MANGO KETCHUP (page 98)

295 calories	58 g carb
3 g fat	10 g fiber
0.3 g sat fat	0 mg cholesterol
12 g protein	245 mg sodium

VEGETABLE STIR-FRY WITH CARAMELIZED TOFU AND FORBIDDEN RICE (page 101)

363 calories	49 g carb
14 g fat	7 g fiber
2.4 g sat fat	0 mg cholesterol
18 g protein	949 mg sodium

SOFT ROSEMARY-LEMON POLENTA WITH SWEET CORN, OYSTER MUSHROOMS, AND RAINBOW CHARD (page 104)

267 calories	44 g carb
8 g fat	9 g fiber
1.4 g sat fat	3 mg cholesterol
8 g protein	502 mg sodium

ROASTED TOMATO SAUCE (page 106)

Per ¼-cup serving

23 calories	5 g carb
0 g fat	1 g fiber
0 g sat fat	0 mg cholesterol
1 g protein	127 mg sodium

PINTO BEAN AND VEGETABLE CHILI TOSTADA WITH SALSA FRESCA AND AVOCADO-CILANTRO CREAM (page 107)

260 calories	47 g carb
5 g fat	11 g fiber
1 g sat fat	3 mg cholesterol
11 g protein	402 mg sodium

VEGETABLE PAVÉ WITH ROASTED GARLIC LENTILS AND DRESSED FIELD GREENS (page 110)

238 calories	30 g carb
10 g fat	7 g fiber
2 g sat fat	5 mg cholesterol
11 g protein	467 mg sodium

WHOLE WHEAT AND FLAX FETTUCCINE WITH ASPARAGUS AND PORCINI-SHIITAKE CREAM (page 112)

397 calories	56 g carb
11 g fat	13 g fiber
3.2 g sat fat	81 mg cholesterol
23 g protein	392 mg sodium

SAUTÉED GREENS WITH GARLIC AND LEMON (page 118)

78 calories	10 g carb
3 g fat	6 g fiber
0.4 g sat fat	0 mg cholesterol
6 g protein	176 mg sodium

ROASTED ASPARAGUS (page 118)

13 calories	2 g carb
0 g fat	1 g fiber
0 g sat fat	0 mg cholesterol
1 g protein	61 mg sodium

ROASTED CAULIFLOWER, CARROTS, AND ONION (page 119)

59 calories	13 g carb
1 g fat	4 g fiber
0 g sat fat	0 mg cholesterol
3 g protein	107 mg sodium

SEAFOOD

TERIYAKI BLACK COD WITH STICKY RICE CAKES AND SEARED BABY BOK CHOY (page 122)

264 calories	32 g carb
2 g fat	3 g fiber
0.2 g sat fat	42 mg cholesterol
26 g protein	895 mg sodium

MISO-GLAZED MERO WITH SHIITAKE MUSHROOM QUINOA AND GRILLED PINEAPPLE AND MANGO SALSA (page 125)

292 calories	33 g carb
5 g fat	3 g fiber
0.4 g sat fat	36 mg cholesterol
30 g protein	242 mg sodium

TUNA NIÇOISE WITH LEMON-CAPER VINAIGRETTE (page 128)

373 calories	25 g carb
14 g fat	6 g fiber
3.2 g sat fat	157 mg cholesterol
36 g protein	742 mg sodium

SESAME-CRUSTED WILD SALMON SALAD WITH CREAMY MISO DRESSING (page 130)

375 calories   26 g carb
12 g fat   6 g fiber
1.7 g sat fat   52 mg cholesterol
35 g protein   457 mg sodium

WILD SALMON WITH QUICK-PRESERVED LEMON MASHED POTATOES AND ASPARAGUS VINAIGRETTE (page 132)

278 calories   16 g carb
10 g fat   2 g fiber
2.3 g sat fat   54 mg cholesterol
29 g protein   232 mg sodium

BARRAMUNDI WITH BUTTERNUT SQUASH RISOTTO AND CITRUS-ALMOND SALSA (page 134)

324 calories   28 g carb
9 g fat   4 g fiber
1.3 g sat fat   47 mg cholesterol
28 g protein   210 mg sodium

PAN-ROASTED HALIBUT WITH CRAB MASHED POTATOES, SPINACH, AND GAZPACHO VINAIGRETTE (page 136)

310 calories   25 g carb
9 g fat   4.4 g fiber
1.6 g sat fat   60 mg cholesterol
34 g protein   539 mg sodium

PAN-ROASTED LOBSTER WITH BASIL POTATO PUREE AND WARM TOMATO-CORN SALAD (page 139)

307 calories   27 g carb
12 g fat   4 g fiber
2 g sat fat   66 mg cholesterol
24 g protein   885 mg sodium

DUNGENESS CRAB, QUINOA, AND MANGO STACK WITH LEMON-TAHINI DRESSING (page 142)

288 calories   20 g carb
14 g fat   4 g fiber
1.8 g sat fat   61 mg cholesterol
22 g protein   387 mg sodium

MARYLAND CRAB CAKES WITH CARAMELIZED PINEAPPLE AND ROASTED RED PEPPER REMOULADE (page 144)

279 calories   22 g carb
14 g fat   5 g fiber
1.8 g sat fat   79 mg cholesterol
20 g protein   441 mg sodium

SESAME-SCALLION CRAB SALAD MAKI (page 148)

173 calories   24 g carb
2 g fat   1 g fiber
0.1 g sat fat   44 mg cholesterol
12 g protein   338 mg sodium

UDON NOODLE VEGETABLE SALAD (page 150)

158 calories   30 g carb
1.3 g fat   3 g fiber
0 g sat fat   0 mg cholesterol
7 g protein   279 mg sodium

AHI TUNA WITH SESAME SEEDS (page 151)

93 calories   0 g carb
2 g fat   0.2 g fiber
0.2 g sat fat   34 mg cholesterol
18 g protein   351 mg sodium

PICKLED CUCUMBER, DAIKON, AND GINGER SALAD (page 152)

48 calories   6 g carb
1 g fat   1 g fiber
0 g sat fat   0 mg cholesterol
1 g protein   35 mg sodium

GINGER-SOY SHIITAKE MUSHROOMS (page 153)

7 calories   1 g carb
0 g fat   0.1 g fiber
0 g sat fat   0 mg cholesterol
0.5 g protein   101 mg sodium

FRESH FRUIT (page 153)

60 calories   16 g carb
0.4 g fat   3 g fiber
0 g sat fat   0 mg cholesterol
1 g protein   2 mg sodium

POULTRY AND LEAN MEATS

GRILLED DIJON CHICKEN BREAST SALAD WITH PEARS AND CANDIED WALNUTS (page 156)

395 calories   28 g carb
19 g fat   5 g fiber
2.3 g sat fat   66 mg cholesterol
32 g protein   743 mg sodium

CANDIED WALNUTS (page 158)

111 calories   5 g carb
10 g fat   1 g fiber
0.9 g sat fat   0 mg cholesterol
2 g protein   31 mg sodium

PAN-ROASTED LEMON CHICKEN AND MARINATED GREEK VEGETABLE SALAD (page 159)

311 calories   16 g carb
14 g fat   3 g fiber
3.2 g sat fat   74 mg cholesterol
30 g protein   555 mg sodium

PARMESAN CHICKEN SCHNITZEL WITH WARM POTATO AND GARDEN BEAN SALAD AND CREAMY MUSTARD SAUCE (page 162)

383 calories   34 g carb
10 g fat   4 g fiber
3.9 g sat fat   85 mg cholesterol
40 g protein   934 mg sodium

CRISPY DUCK BREAST WITH CRACKED WHEAT, CARAMELIZED SHALLOTS, AND BLACKBERRY GASTRIQUE (page 165)

301 calories   40 g carb
7 g fat   5 g fiber
1.8 g sat fat   82 mg cholesterol
20 g protein   391 mg sodium

SMOKED PAPRIKA ROASTED GAME HEN WITH SPICY CHICKEN SAUSAGE AND VEGETABLE PILAF (page 168)

573 calories   36 g carb
29 g fat   4.1 g fiber
9.2 g sat fat   199 mg cholesterol
42 g protein   404 mg sodium

WALNUT-CRUSTED TURKEY SCALLOPINI WITH SMASHED YAMS AND CRANBERRY VINAIGRETTE (page 170)

338 calories	30 g carb
11 g fat	5 g fiber
1 g sat fat	45 mg cholesterol
32 g protein	308 mg sodium

TURKEY BURGERS WITH SHARP CHEDDAR CHEESE, CARAMELIZED ONIONS, AND *GOLDEN DOOR KETCHUP (page 172)

383 calories	50 g carb
9 g fat	3 g fiber
2.7 g sat fat	51 mg cholesterol
27 g protein	855 mg sodium

***GOLDEN DOOR KETCHUP** (page 173)

62 calories	15 g carb
0 g fat	1 g fiber
0 g sat fat	0 mg cholesterol
1 g protein	26 mg sodium

GRILLED LAMB CHOPS WITH ROSEMARY ROASTED NEW POTATOES AND APPLE-MINT SALAD (page 174)

310 calories	21 g carb
17 g fat	2.7 g fiber
3.5 g sat fat	45 mg cholesterol
16 g protein	407 mg sodium

MOROCCAN SPICE-RUBBED LAMB LOIN WITH CHICKPEAS, FETA, AND OLIVES (page 176)

287 calories	29 g carb
10 g fat	5 g fiber
2.5 g sat fat	49 mg cholesterol
21 g protein	553 mg sodium

ADOBO-MARINATED GRASS-FED FLANK STEAK WITH SPINACH SALAD AND ROASTED POBLANO DRESSING (page 179)

402 calories	40 g carb
15 g fat	11 g fiber
4.2 g sat fat	42 mg cholesterol
33 g protein	613 mg sodium

PORCINI-CRUSTED BISON NEW YORK STRIP STEAKS WITH BAKED MUSHROOMS AND WORCESTERSHIRE JUS (page 182)

215 calories	12 g carb
4 g fat	3 g fiber
1.1 g sat fat	83 mg cholesterol
31 g protein	539 mg sodium

DESSERTS

ALMOND PEAR DOTS (page 190)

89 calories	12 g carb
4 g fat	2 g fiber
0.4 g sat fat	0 mg cholesterol
2 g protein	9 mg sodium

CHOCOLATE CHIP COOKIES (page 191)

88 calories	15 g carb
3 g fat	1 g fiber
0.8 g sat fat	0 mg cholesterol
1 g protein	48 mg sodium

ORANGE ALMOND TUILES (page 193)

51 calories	6 g carb
3 g fat	1 g fiber
0.2 g sat fat	0 mg cholesterol
2 g protein	6 mg sodium

BLUEBERRY LIME ICE (page 194)

64 calories	8 g carb
1 g fat	5 g fiber
0 g sat fat	0 mg cholesterol
1 g protein	2 mg sodium

WHITE PEACH CITRUS SORBET (page 197)

68 calories	17 g carb
0 g fat	2 g fiber
0 g sat fat	0 mg cholesterol
1 g protein	1 mg sodium

PINEAPPLE, CRYSTALLIZED GINGER, AND BANANA SORBET (page 198)

72 calories	18 g carb
0 g fat	2 g fiber
0 g sat fat	0 mg cholesterol
1 g protein	2 mg sodium

MEYER LEMON YOGURT AND FRESH FRUIT BRÛLÉE (page 199)

189 calories	43 g carb
0 g fat	2 g fiber
0 g sat fat	5 mg cholesterol
11 g protein	137 mg sodium

VANILLA CRÈME BRÛLÉE (page 200)

173 calories	25 g carb
5 g fat	0 g fiber
2 g sat fat	142 mg cholesterol
7 g protein	103 mg sodium

LEMONGRASS CRÈME BRÛLÉE (page 201)

173 calories	25 g carb
5 g fat	0 g fiber
2 g sat fat	142 mg cholesterol
7 g protein	103 mg sodium

FRESH STRAWBERRY TARTLETS (page 203)

237 calories	30 g carb
12 g fat	6 g fiber
1 g sat fat	0 mg cholesterol
6 g protein	1 mg sodium

BLACKBERRY NECTARINE CRISP (page 204)

134 calories	23 g carb
4 g fat	4 g fiber
0 g sat fat	0 mg cholesterol
2 g protein	3 mg sodium

WARM FLOURLESS CHOCOLATE CAKE WITH ORANGE SAUCE (page 207)

274 calories	42 g carb
10 g fat	4 g fiber
6 g sat fat	25 mg cholesterol
5 g protein	67 mg sodium

ANGEL FOOD CAKE WITH FRESH PEACH COULIS (page 209)

133 calories	31 g carb
0 g fat	1 g fiber
0 g sat fat	0 mg cholesterol
5 g protein	96 mg sodium

BREAKFAST

GOLDEN DOOR OATMEAL (page 216)

265 calories / 51 g carb
4 g fat / 5 g fiber
0.6 g sat fat / 1 mg cholesterol
7 g protein / 24 mg sodium

CINNAMON CRANBERRY GRANOLA (page 217)

206 calories / 34 g carb
6 g fat / 4 g fiber
0.7 g sat fat / 0 mg cholesterol
5 g protein / 1 mg sodium

*NORBERTO'S MUESLI (page 219)

257 calories / 46 g carb
6 g fat / 6 g fiber
0.7 g sat fat / 0 mg cholesterol
6 g protein / 3 mg sodium

YOGURT CREAM, BLUEBERRY, AND CANTALOUPE PARFAIT (page 220)

189 calories / 40 g carb
2 g fat / 3.5 g fiber
0.2 g sat fat / 3.3 mg cholesterol
9 g protein / 99 mg sodium

*TECATE BREAD (page 221)

116 calories / 22 g carb
2 g fat / 4 g fiber
0.2 g sat fat / 0 mg cholesterol
4 g protein / 185 mg sodium

COTTAGE GRIDDLE CAKES WITH BLUEBERRY-PEACH SYRUP (page 222)

224 calories / 38 g carb
5 g fat / 3 g fiber
1.9 g sat fat / 9 mg cholesterol
10 g protein / 513 mg sodium

BANANA ALMOND BERRY MUFFINS (page 224)

206 calories / 34 g carb
6 g fat / 4 g fiber
0.8 g sat fat / 32 mg cholesterol
6 g protein / 175 mg sodium

*TOMATO CHEESE TOAST (page 226)

254 calories / 26 g carb
12 g fat / 4 g fiber
5.6 g sat fat / 31 mg cholesterol
13 g protein / 305 mg sodium

EGGS FLORENTINE WITH SMOKED TURKEY, WHOLE WHEAT ENGLISH MUFFIN, AND CREAMY YELLOW PEPPER SAUCE (page 227)

246 calories / 31 g carb
8 g fat / 7 g fiber
2.9 g sat fat / 239 mg cholesterol
18 g protein / 751 mg sodium

WHOLE WHEAT ENGLISH MUFFINS (page 229)

147 calories / 27 g carb
2 g fat / 4 g fiber
0.4 g sat fat / 11 mg cholesterol
6 g protein / 122 mg sodium

CRISPY POTATO CAKES WITH CHIVE SCRAMBLED EGGS AND SMOKED SALMON (page 230)

159 calories / 17 g carb
4 g fat / 1 g fiber
1.6 g sat fat / 117 mg cholesterol
12 g protein / 422 mg sodium

INDIVIDUAL SHARP CHEDDAR FRITTATA WITH POTATO, SPINACH, AND RED ONION (page 233)

264 calories / 30 g carb
10 g fat / 5 g fiber
2.9 g sat fat / 142 mg cholesterol
15 g protein / 468 mg sodium

EGG WHITE OMELET WITH FRESH HERBS, ROASTED ASPARAGUS, AND BAKED HERBED TOMATOES (page 235)

136 calories / 8 g carb
6 g fat / 3 g fiber
2 g sat fat / 7 mg cholesterol
14 g protein / 288 mg sodium

TEAS, JUICES, AND OTHER DRINKS

HIBISCUS SANGRIA (page 240)

129 calories / 33 g carb
0 g fat / 2 g fiber
0 g sat fat / 0 mg cholesterol
1 g protein / 11 mg sodium

WATERMELON CRANBERRY LIME SLUSHY (page 243)

56 calories / 14 g carb
0 g fat / 0 g fiber
0 g sat fat / 0 mg cholesterol
0 g protein / 6 mg sodium

AGAVE LIME SODA (page 244)

64 calories / 16 g carb
0 g fat / 0 g fiber
0 g sat fat / 0 mg cholesterol
0 g protein / 0 mg sodium

*POTASSIUM BROTH (page 245)

24 calories / 5 g carb
0 g fat / 1 g fiber
0 g sat fat / 0 mg cholesterol
1 g protein / 74 mg sodium

FRESH LAVENDER AND ORANGE CHAMOMILE TEA WITH HONEY (page 247)

57 calories / 15 g carb
0 g fat / 0 g fiber
0 g sat fat / 0 mg cholesterol
0 g protein / 3 mg sodium

CARDAMOM CINNAMON MULLED APPLE CIDER (page 248)

132 calories / 33 g carb
0 g fat / 0 g fiber
0 g sat fat / 0 mg cholesterol
0 g protein / 25 mg sodium

HOT COCOA (page 249)

133 calories / 21 g carb
3 g fat / 1 g fiber
1.6 g sat fat / 8 mg cholesterol
7 g protein / 84 mg sodium

VINAIGRETTES AND DRESSINGS

LEMON-CAPER VINAIGRETTE (page 252)
Per 2-tablespoon serving

25 calories	1 g carb
2 g fat	0 g fiber
0.3 g sat fat	0 mg cholesterol
0 g protein	49 mg sodium

AVOCADO-CITRUS VINAIGRETTE (page 253)
Per 3-tablespoon serving

27 calories	3 g carb
2 g fat	1 g fiber
0.2 g sat fat	0 mg cholesterol
0 g protein	30 mg sodium

ASPARAGUS VINAIGRETTE (page 255)
Per 2-tablespoon serving

20 calories	1 g carb
2 g fat	0.4 g fiber
0.3 g sat fat	0 mg cholesterol
0 g protein	60 mg sodium

GAZPACHO VINAIGRETTE (page 256)
Per ¼-cup serving

41 calories	3 g carb
3 g fat	0.8 g fiber
0.4 g sat fat	0 mg cholesterol
1 g protein	61 mg sodium

WHOLE-GRAIN MUSTARD AND HONEY VINAIGRETTE (page 257)
Per 2-tablespoon serving

50 calories	5 g carb
3 g fat	0.3 g fiber
0.4 g sat fat	0 mg cholesterol
0 g protein	203 mg sodium

CRANBERRY VINAIGRETTE (page 258)
Per 2-tablespoon serving

20 calories	5 g carb
0 g fat	0.5 g fiber
0 g sat fat	0 mg cholesterol
0 g protein	49 mg sodium

LEMON-TAHINI DRESSING (page 259)
Per 2-tablespoon serving

50 calories	3 g carb
4 g fat	0.4 g fiber
0.6 g sat fat	0 mg cholesterol
1 g protein	3 mg sodium

ROASTED POBLANO DRESSING (page 260)
Per 2-tablespoon serving

14 calories	3 g carb
0 g fat	0.4 g fiber
0 g sat fat	0 mg cholesterol
0 g protein	61 mg sodium

CREAMY RANCH DRESSING (page 261)
Per 2-tablespoon serving

15 calories	1 g carb
0.3 g fat	0 g fiber
0.2 g sat fat	1 mg cholesterol
2 g protein	50 mg sodium

CREAMY MISO DRESSING (page 262)
Per 2-tablespoon serving

13 calories	1 g carb
0.4 g fat	0 g fiber
0 g sat fat	0 mg cholesterol
1 g protein	199 mg sodium

CREAMY CAESAR DRESSING (page 263)
Per 2-tablespoon serving

16 calories	1 g carb
0.3 g fat	0 g fiber
0.2 g sat fat	2 mg cholesterol
2 g protein	89 mg sodium

ROASTED RED PEPPER REMOULADE (page 265)
Per 2-tablespoon serving

10 calories	1 g carb
0.3 g fat	0.3 g fiber
0 g sat fat	0 mg cholesterol
1 g protein	43 mg sodium

BASICS

CHICKEN STOCK (page 269) Per 1-cup serving

23 calories	1.2 g carb
0.2 g fat	0 g fiber
0 g sat fat	9.3 mg cholesterol
4 g protein	19 mg sodium

VEGETABLE STOCK (page 269) Per 1-cup serving

8.6 calories	1.9 g carb
0.1 g fat	.7 g fiber
0 g sat fat	0 mg cholesterol
0.4 g protein	19 mg sodium

BALSAMIC REDUCTION (page 270)
Per 1-teaspoon serving

9 calories	3 g carb
0 g fat	0 g fiber
0 g sat fat	0 mg cholesterol
0 g protein	7 mg sodium

HERB OIL (page 272) Per 1-teaspoon serving

40 calories	0 g carb
5 g fat	0 g fiber
0.3 g sat fat	0 mg cholesterol
0 g protein	10 mg sodium

CARAMELIZED ONIONS (page 273)
Per 2-tablespoon serving

19 calories	4 g carb
0 g fat	0.6 g fiber
0 g sat fat	0.4 mg cholesterol
1 g protein	23 mg sodium

SEMOLINA DOUGH FOR PIZZETTAS (page 274)

143 calories	27 g carb
2 g fat	1 g fiber
0.3 g sat fat	0 mg cholesterol
4 g protein	240 mg sodium

SEMOLINA DOUGH FOR BURGER BUNS (page 275)

190 calories	36 g carb
2 g fat	2 g fiber
0.3 g sat fat	0 mg cholesterol
6 g protein	321 mg sodium

Resources

ORGANIZATIONS

Monterey Bay Aquarium and Seafood Watch (page 125)
886 Cannery Row
Monterey, CA 93940
831-648-4888
www.seafoodwatch.org
The Seafood Watch program, run by the Monterey Bay Aquarium, recommends which fish and shellfish to buy and which to avoid, based on whether or not they are raised and/or fished under sustainable conditions.

EatWild (page 179)
9609 SW 288th Street
Vashon, WA 98070
866-453-8489
www.eatwild.com
For a directory of pasture-raised beef available close to your home.

LocalHarvest (page 115)
220 21st Avenue
Santa Cruz, CA 95062
831-475-8150
www.localharvest.org
To find a farmer's market or CSA in your area.

SHOPPING

Potsticker Press (page 32)
www.houserice.com/potpres.html
This simple tool makes quick work of forming and sealing potstickers.

Redmond Real Salt (page 13)
www.realsalt.com
Natural, unrefined sea salt that has not been processed and comes in several grinds.

Meditation CD (page 237)
Meditation End Chime: Selectable silence up to 70 minutes followed by three bowl strikes
www.dharmacrafts.com
A CD with multiple tracks of timed silence, ranging from 10 to 70 minutes, followed by a gentle sound to bring you back from meditation.

Penzeys Spices (page 173)
800-741-7787
www.penzeys.com and many stores located throughout the U.S.
An excellent source for high-quality spices including adobo spice, smoked paprika, and juniper berries.

FOR MORE INFORMATION

The SuperFoodsRx Diet: Lose Weight with the Power of SuperNutrients by Wendy Bazilian, PhD, MA, RD, Steven Pratt, MD, and Kathy Matthews

SuperFoodsRx: Fourteen Foods That Will Save Your Life by Steven Pratt, MD, and Kathy Matthews, with menus designed and written by Wendy Bazilian, featuring recipes from the Golden Door

Acknowledgments

A lot goes into writing a cookbook, and this was certainly not a task that I could have completed on my own. I would like to thank those who helped make this book a reality and who helped make me who I am today.

Carrie, Samuel, Pearle, and Ruby, for believing in me and always being there for me.

My late father, Lloyd Rucker, and my mom, Sandra Rucker, for their love and support.

My big sister, Donna Hoffman, my number one fan, for her unwavering loyalty.

Uncle Den, Aunt Linda, Ricky, and Scotty, for some of the best memories of my life. The entire Rucker, Dunmyer, and Hayes family: we don't see one another enough, but that does not change the bonds we share.

The Zagarella family, for their love and support.

My awesome staff, who manned the ship while I worked on this book: Chris Bennett, Kayla Roche, Norberto Rojas, Justin Kunkler, Rodolpho Hernandez, Karen Perry, Modie Moore, and Sara Hauman. I owe you all a round—or five!

The Golden Door garden staff, for their care and dedication in supplying the kitchen with the highest quality produce possible.

Rachel Caldwell, our fearless leader. This book would not have happened without her, and her dedication is an inspiration to us all.

Deborah Szekely, founder of the Golden Door and my best critic, who continues to awe me with her energy and vision.

My mentor, Chef Michel Stroot, for training me in the ways of "spa cuisine" and for paving the path for me to follow.

Dr. Wendy Bazilian, for her contributions to this book and for listening and caring. Her enthusiasm for food and life is truly inspiring.

Marah Stets, for showing me how to write a cookbook and for putting up with me along the way. There is no way this book could have come together without her. I am eternally grateful!

Tom Siekmann, CJ Grenadier, Alisa Dunn, Martha Shissler, Sue Annetts, Anne Hersley, and Tom Posey, for all their hard work and support for this project.

Rica Allannic, Jane Treuhaft, and all the folks at Clarkson Potter. What a pleasure to work with such a group of talented professionals.

Cyd McDowell, Mimi Freund, Quentin Bacon, Lauren Volo, Maeve Sheridan, and Chelsea Zimmer, for an incredible photo shoot.

Michael Boschert, my "partner in crime" and the Boschert family, for getting me started on this path.

Scott Braglio, for being a mentor and great friend.

Michael Messina, for his nonstop encouragement.

Andy Harris and Barry Kellman, for their support.

Damian Charron, for always being like a brother to me, no matter how much time passes.

Last but not least, a huge thank-you to all of our Golden Door guests. As a chef, there is no greater gift than seeing the smile on someone's face as they enjoy a dish I have created. For that you have my undying gratitude.

Index